Tatuajes de Calaveras

Johnny Karp

Tatuajes de calaveras
Johnny Karp

ISBN 978-1-926917-14-6

Impreso en EE.UU

Copyright © 2010 Psylon Press

Todos los derechos reservados. Excepto para uso en análisis. No se puede reproducir ninguna parte de este libro sin el claro permiso de su autor. Para solicitar informaciones de permisos, escribir a admin@psylonpress.com

Tanto el autor como el editor no asumen la responsabilidad del uso o el mal uso de la información contenida en este libro.

Otros libros con el mismo autor

- Tatuajes de cruz
- Tatuajes de ángeles
- Tatuajes de mariposas
- Tatuajes de hadas
- Tatuajes de zodiaco
- Tatuajes de escorpiones
- Tatuajes de colibrí
- Tatuajes de dragones
- Tatuajes de delfines
- Tatuajes de querubín

Más libros, en desarrollo.

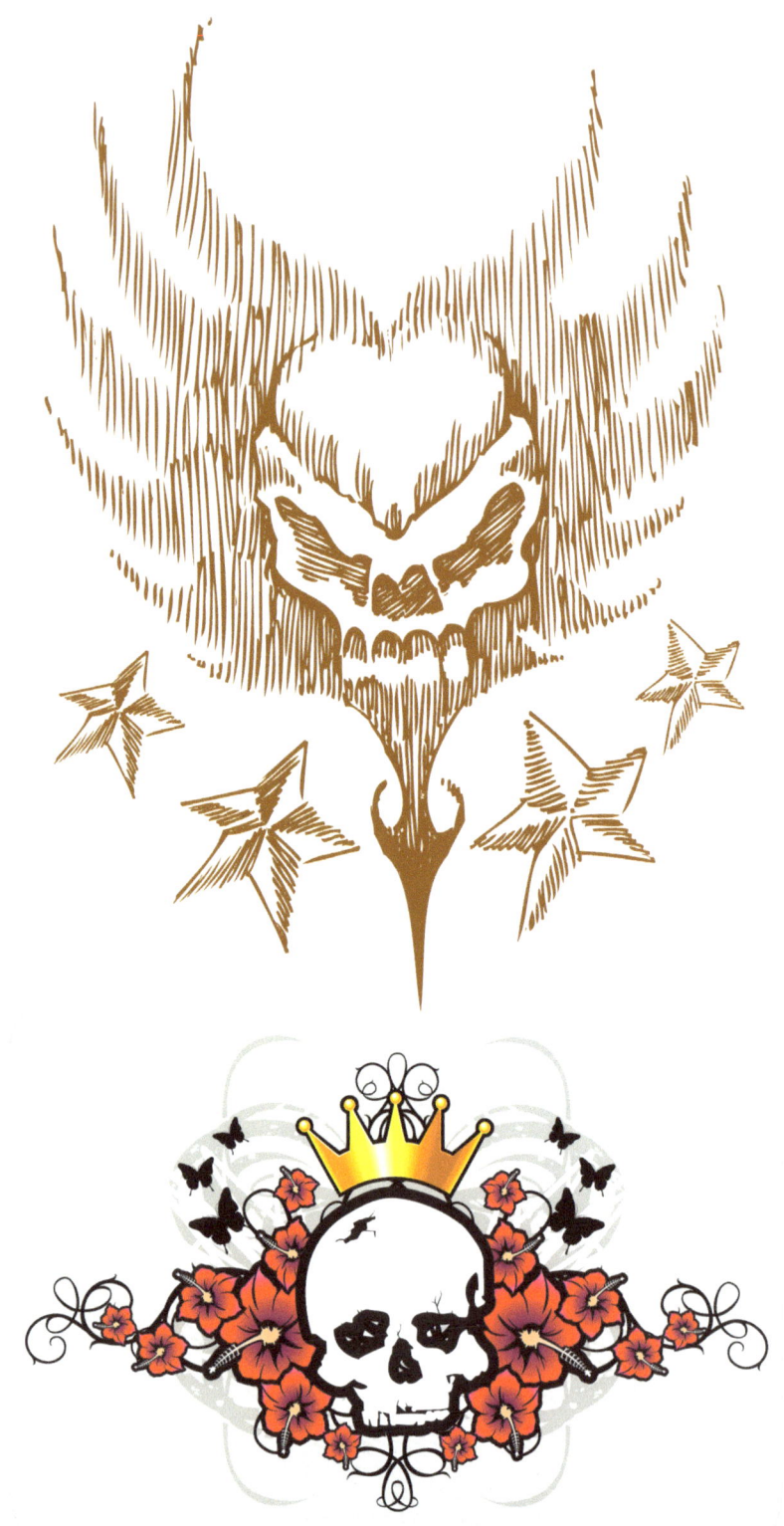

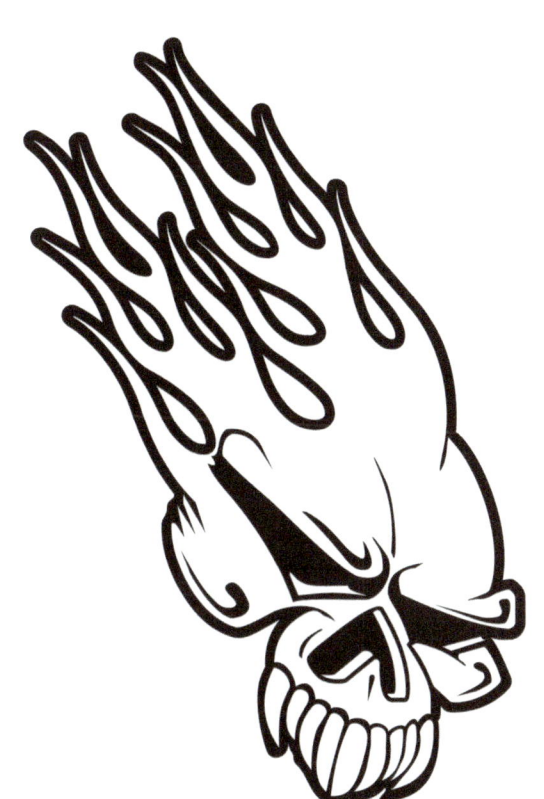

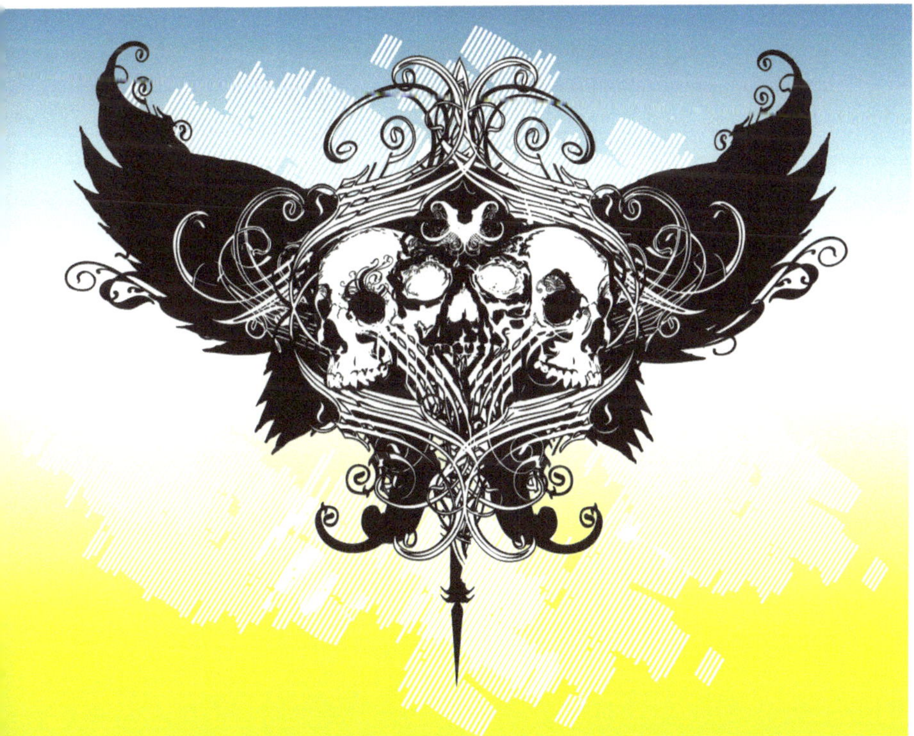

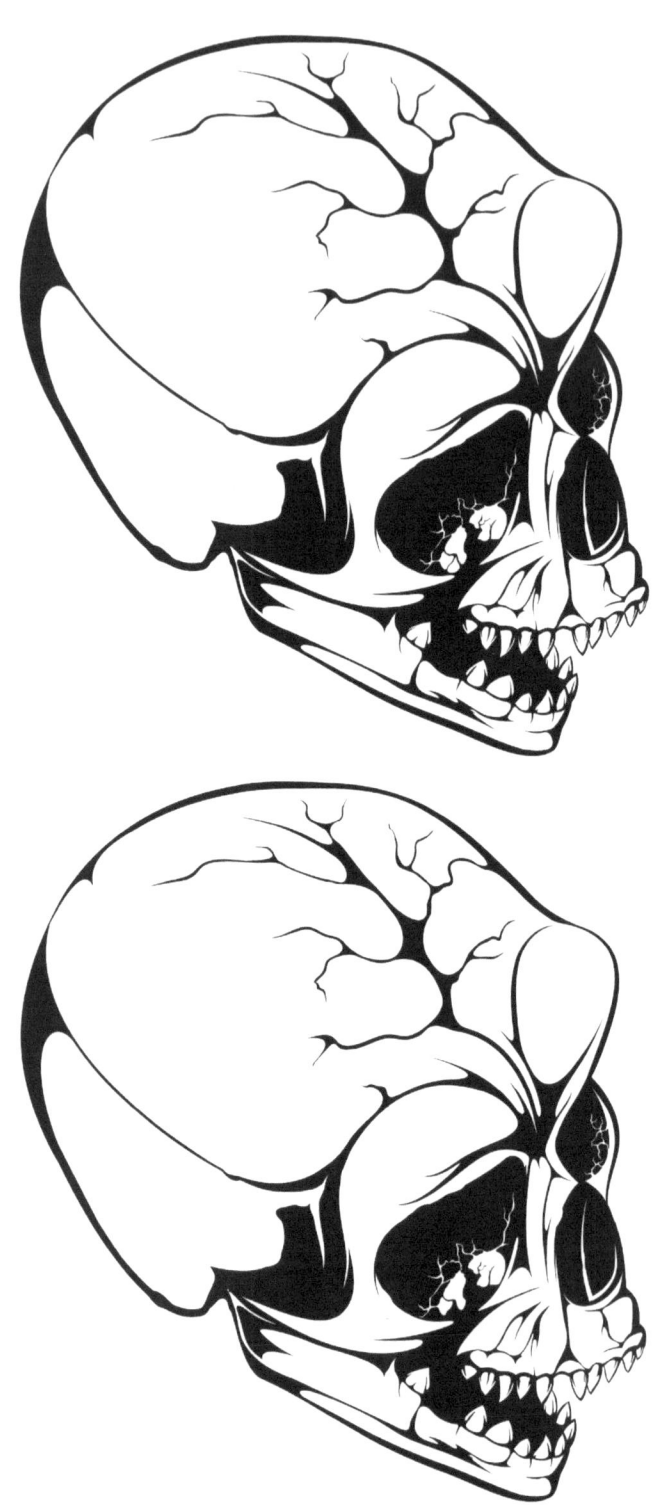

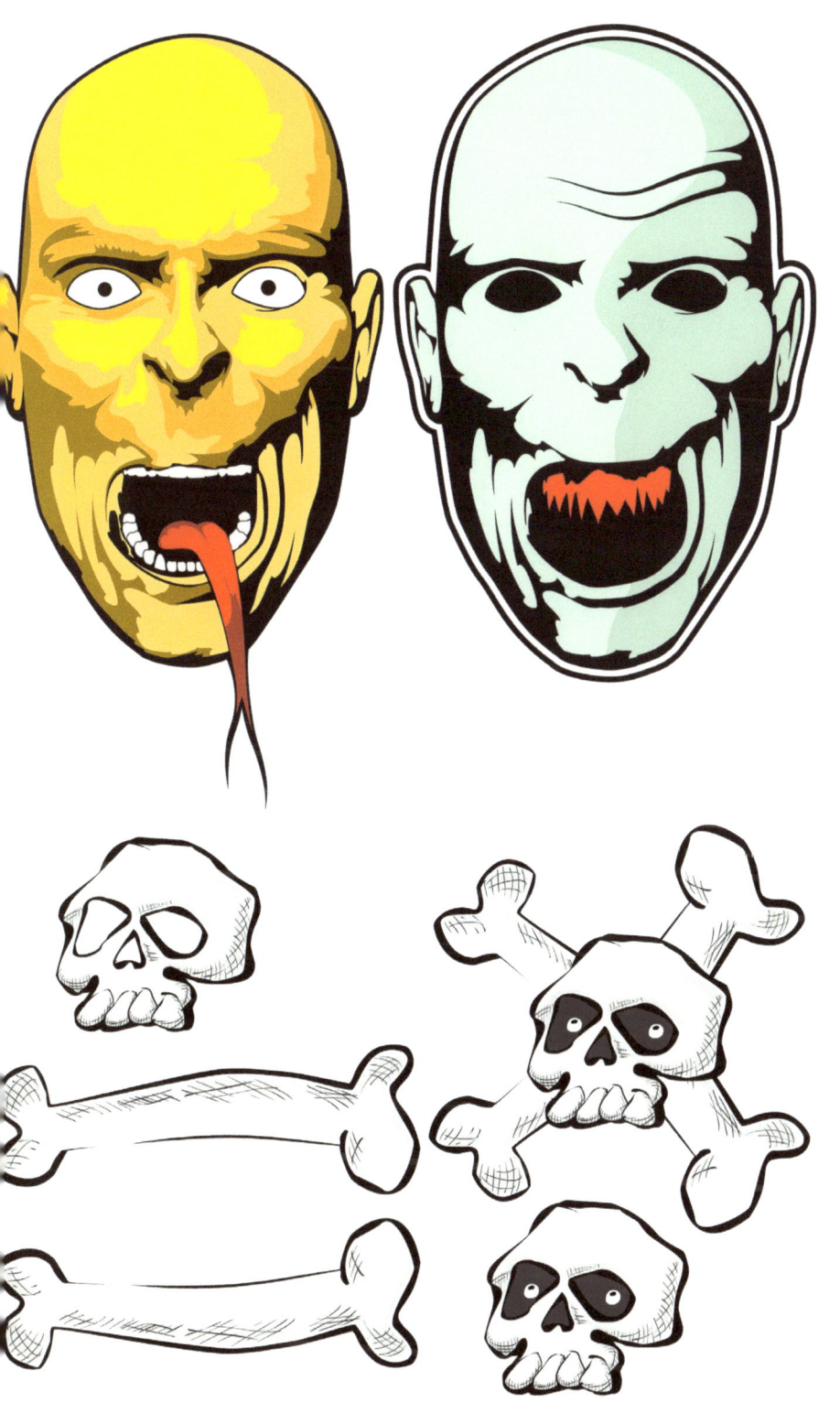

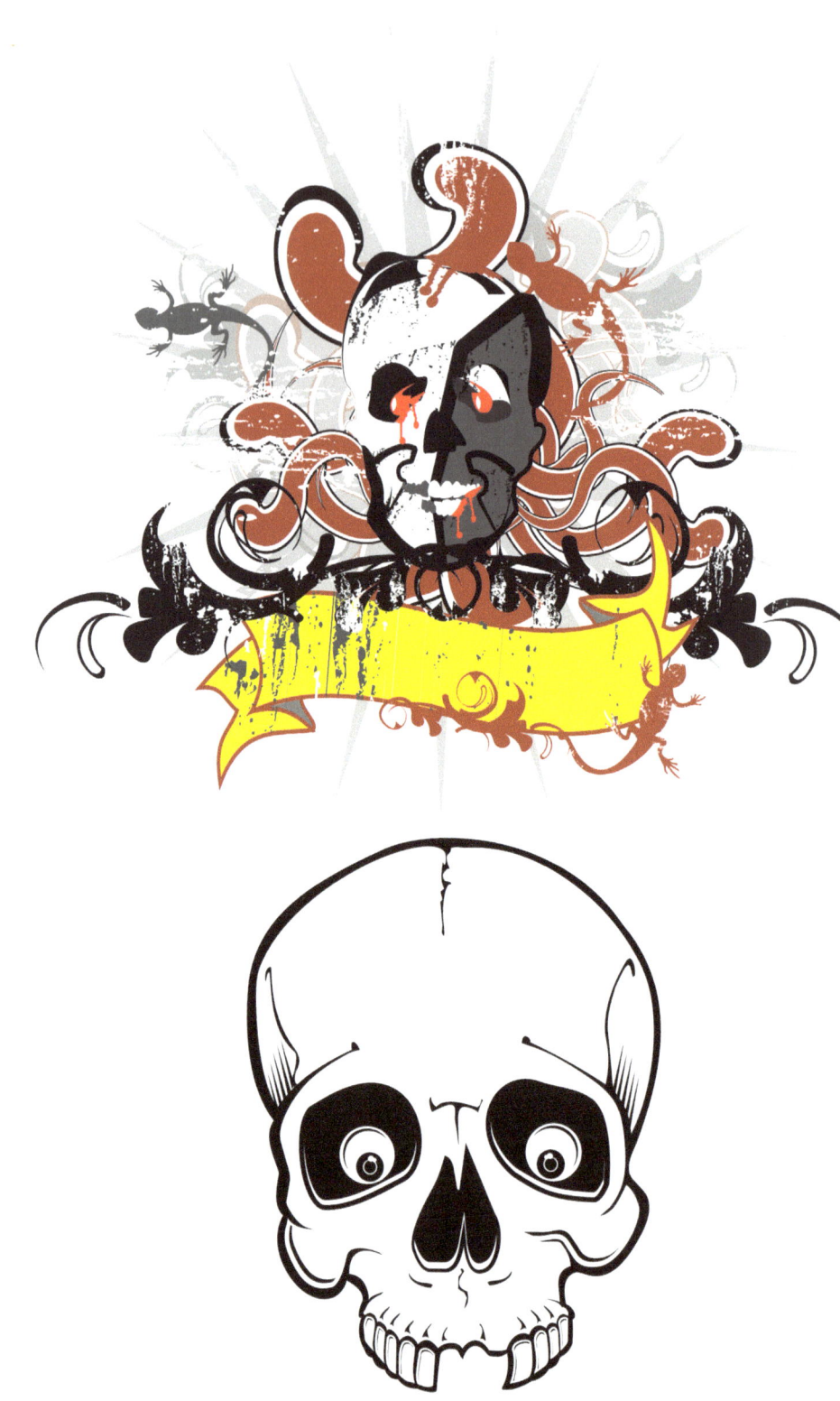

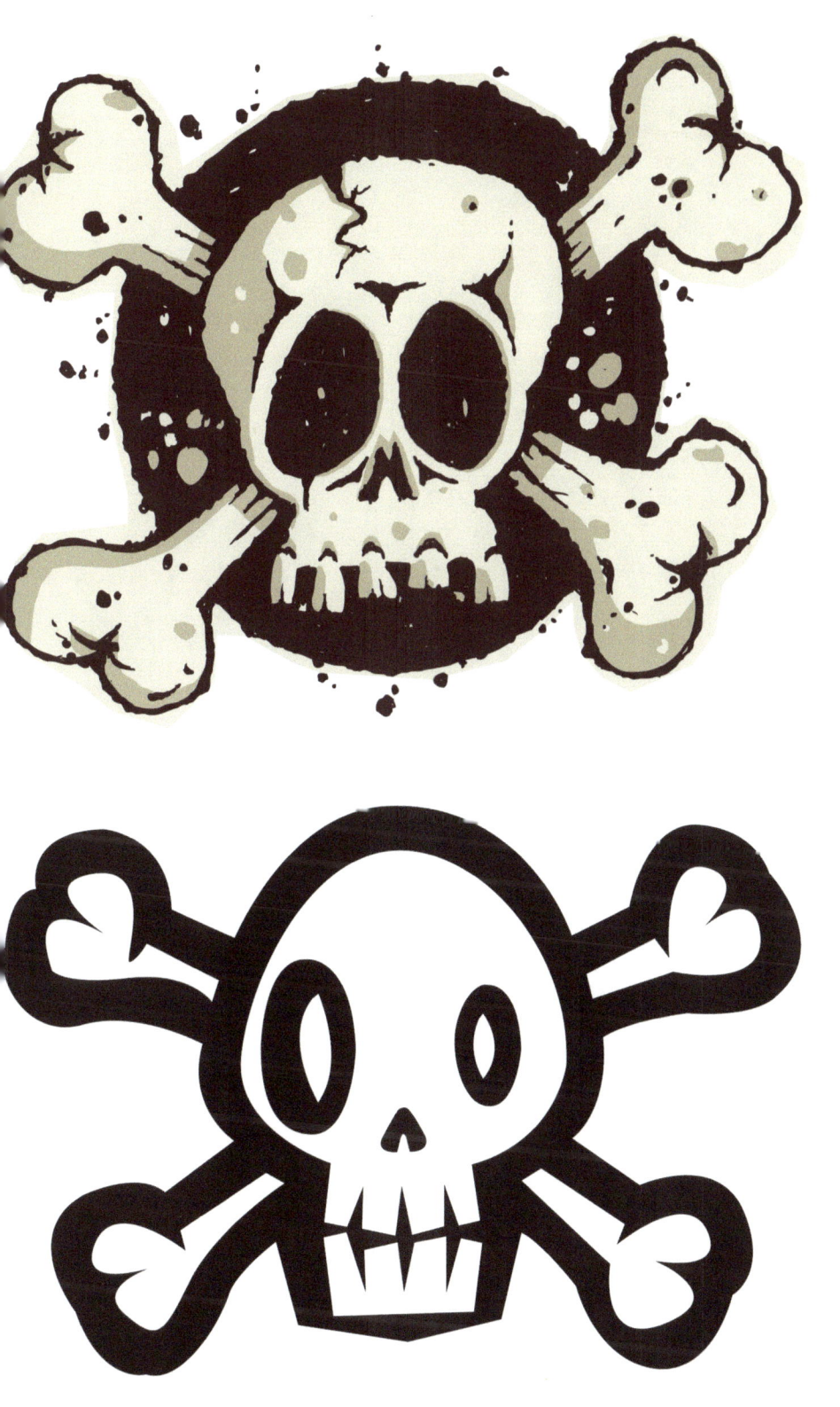

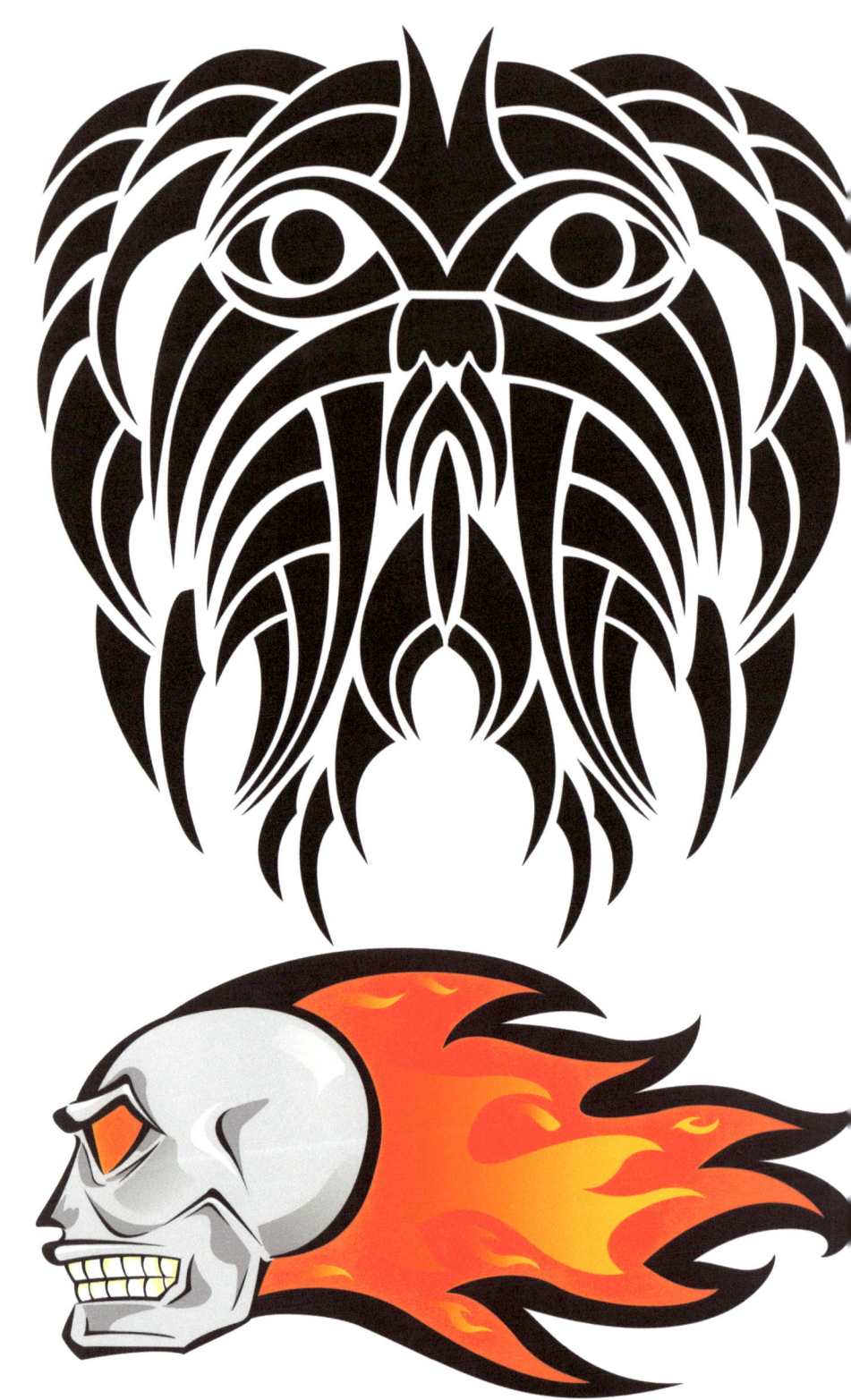

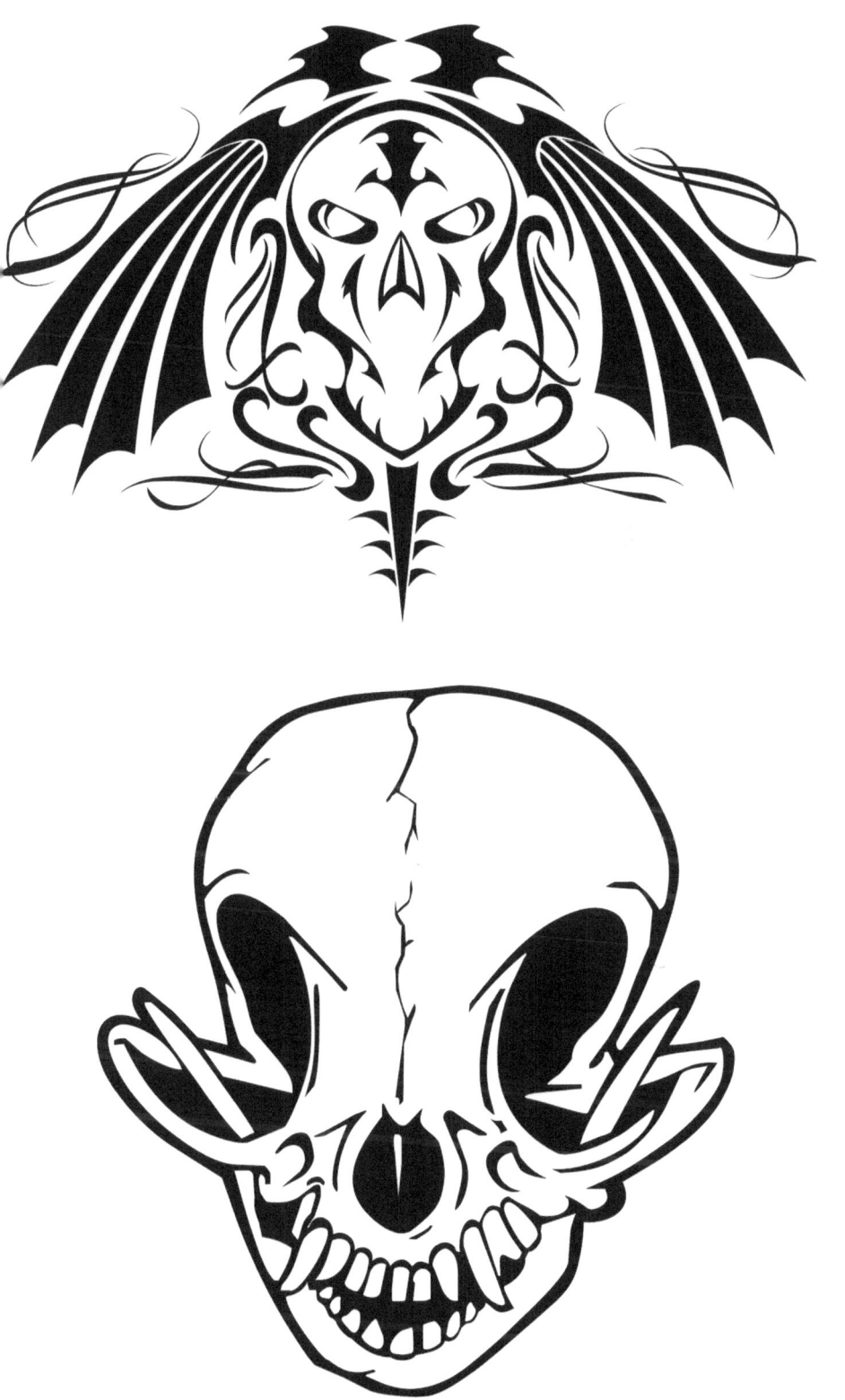

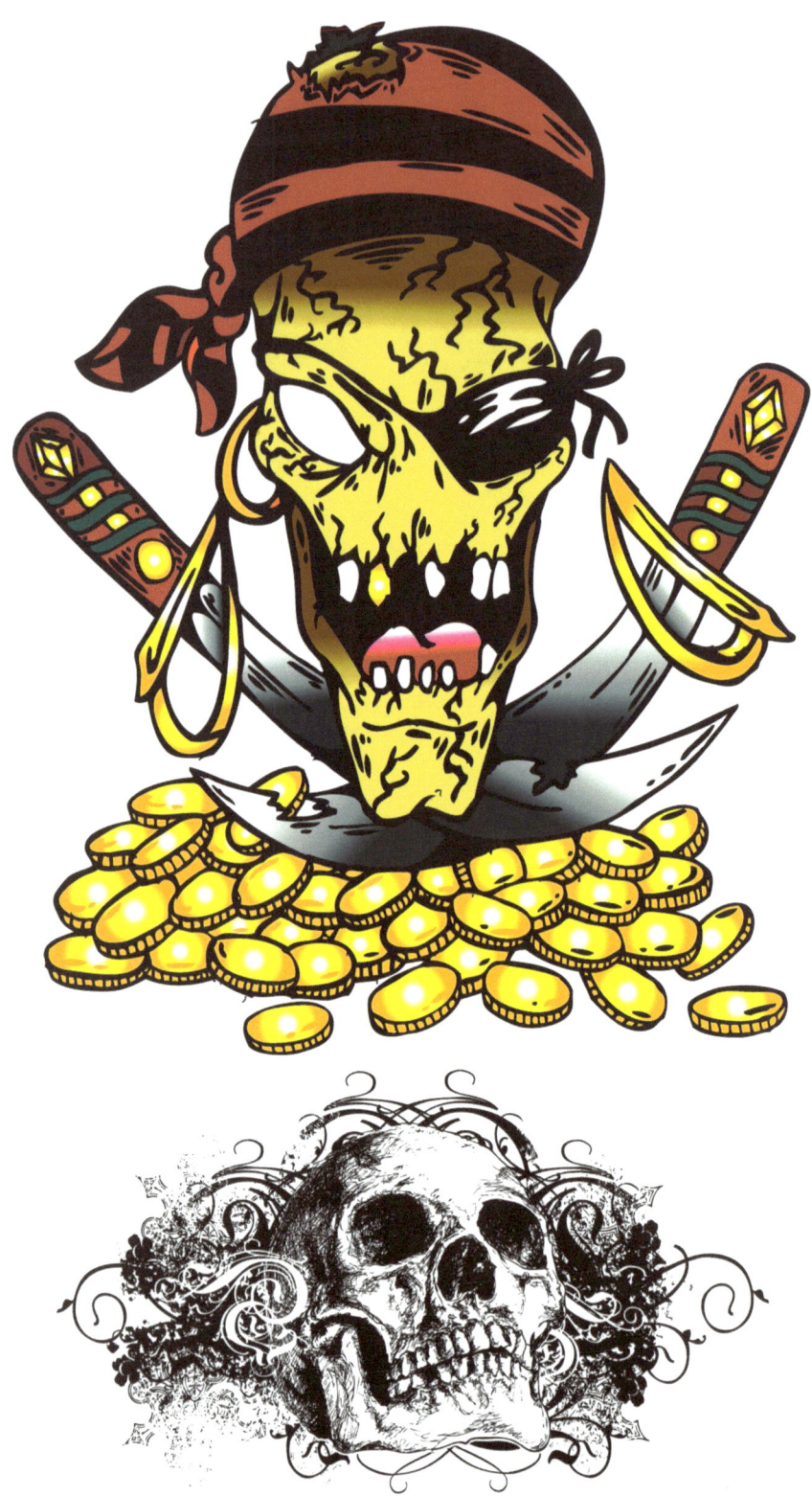

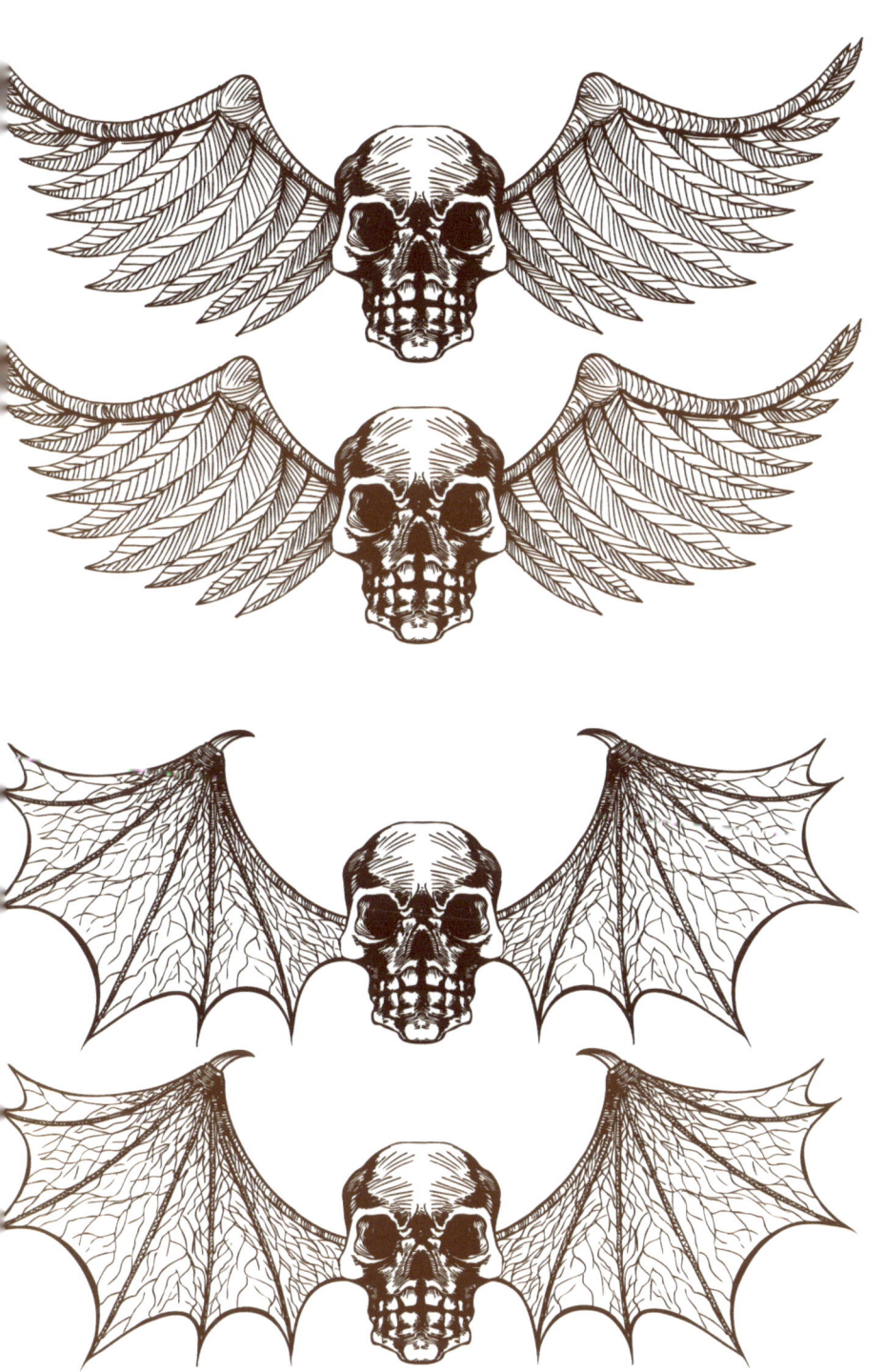

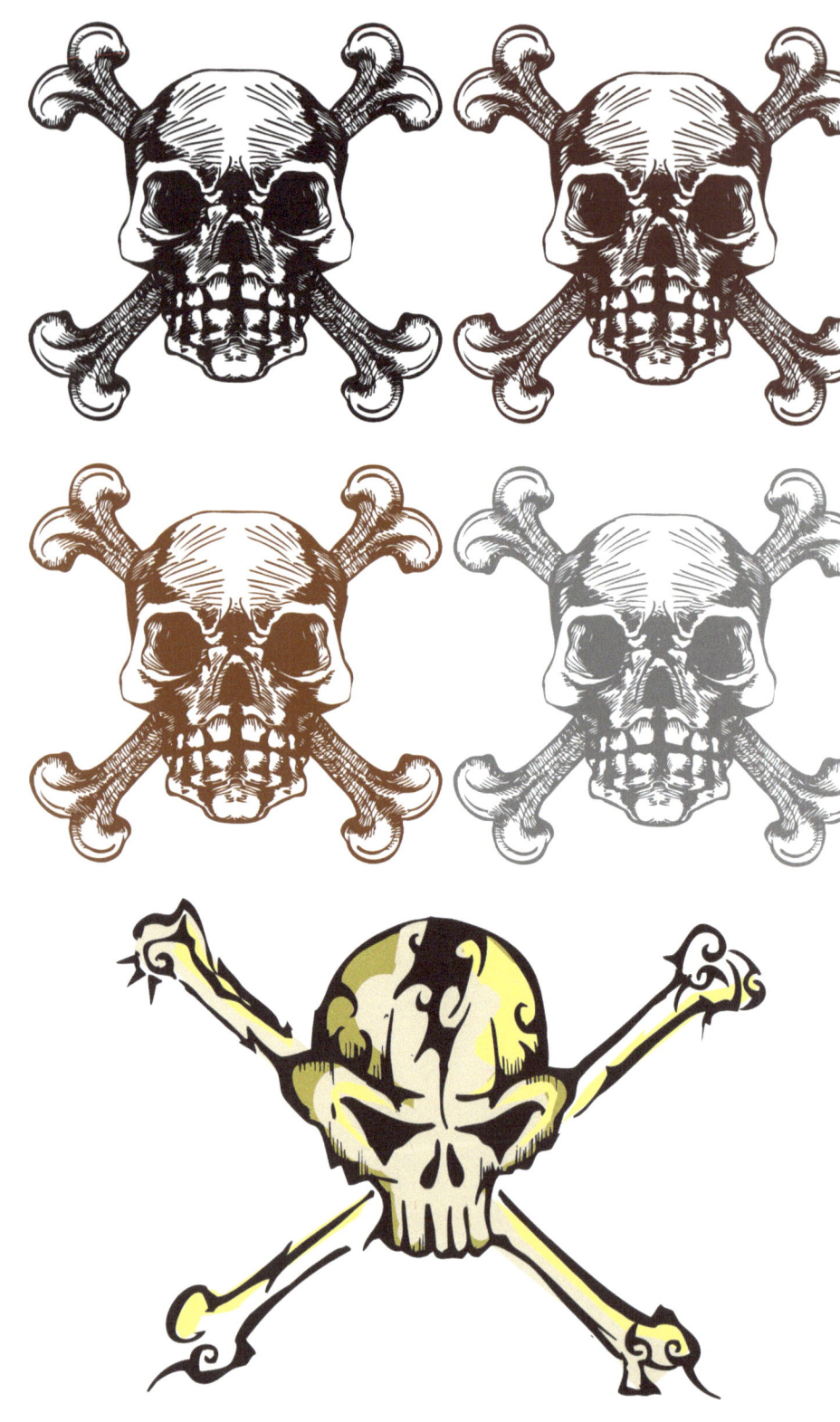

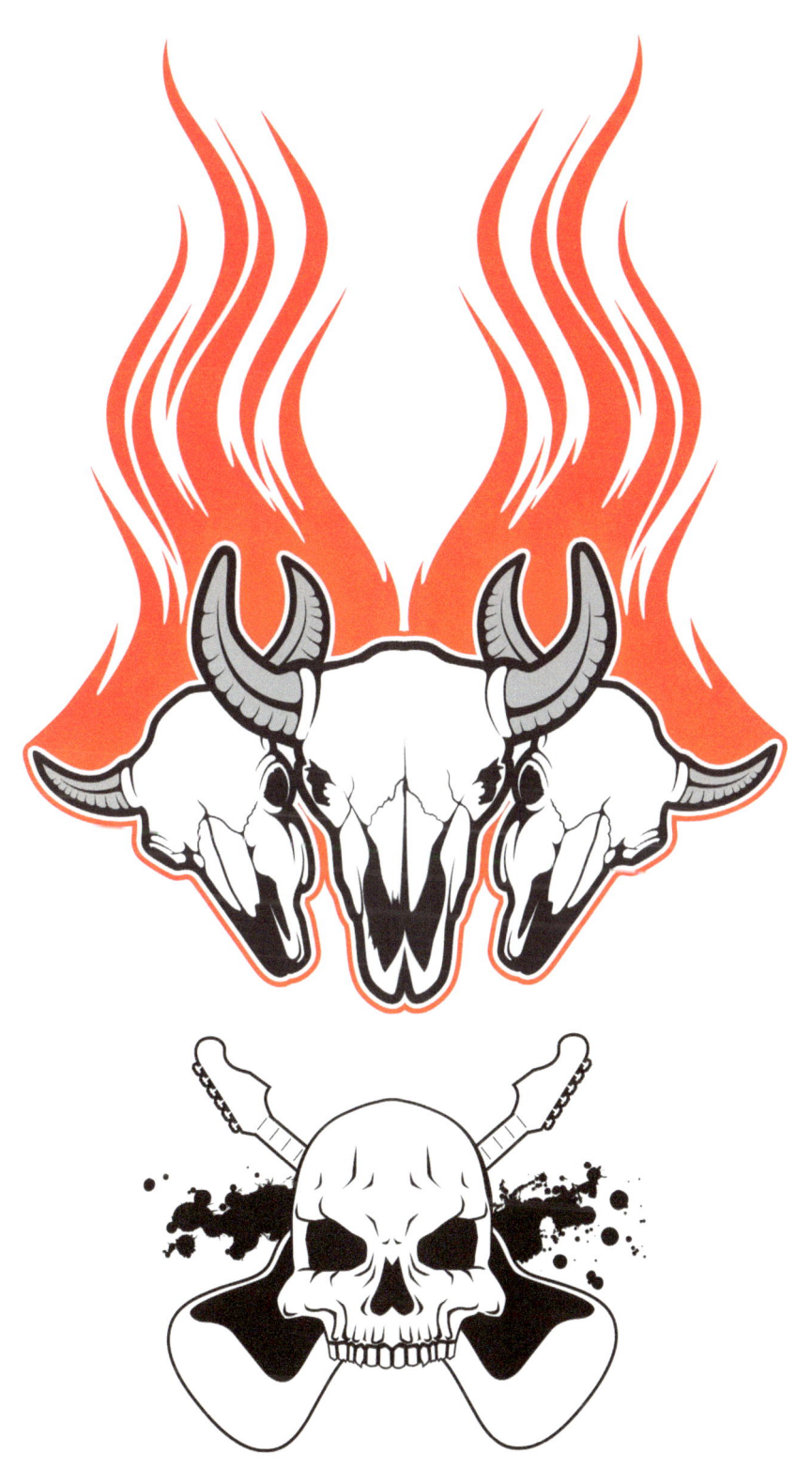

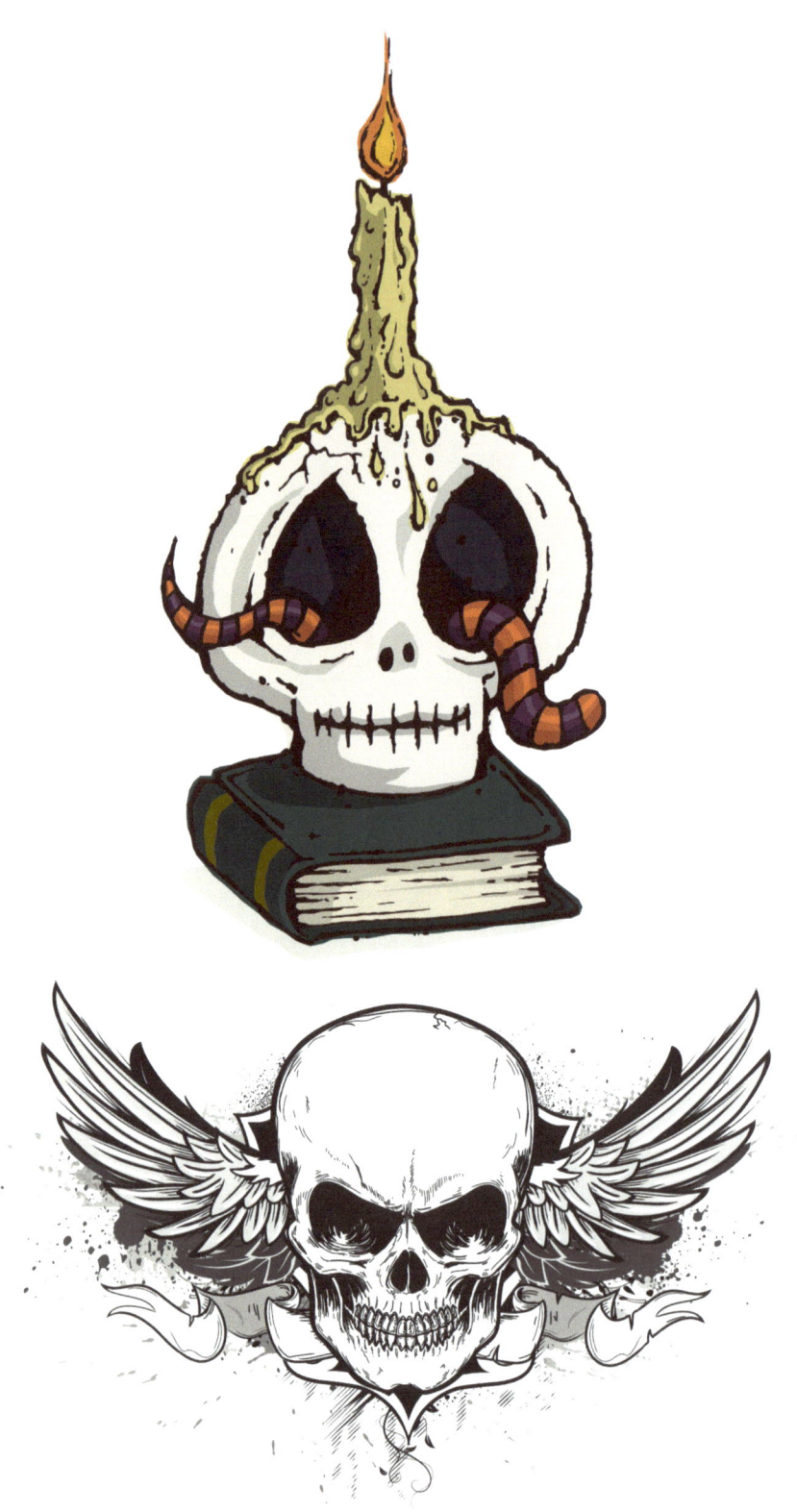

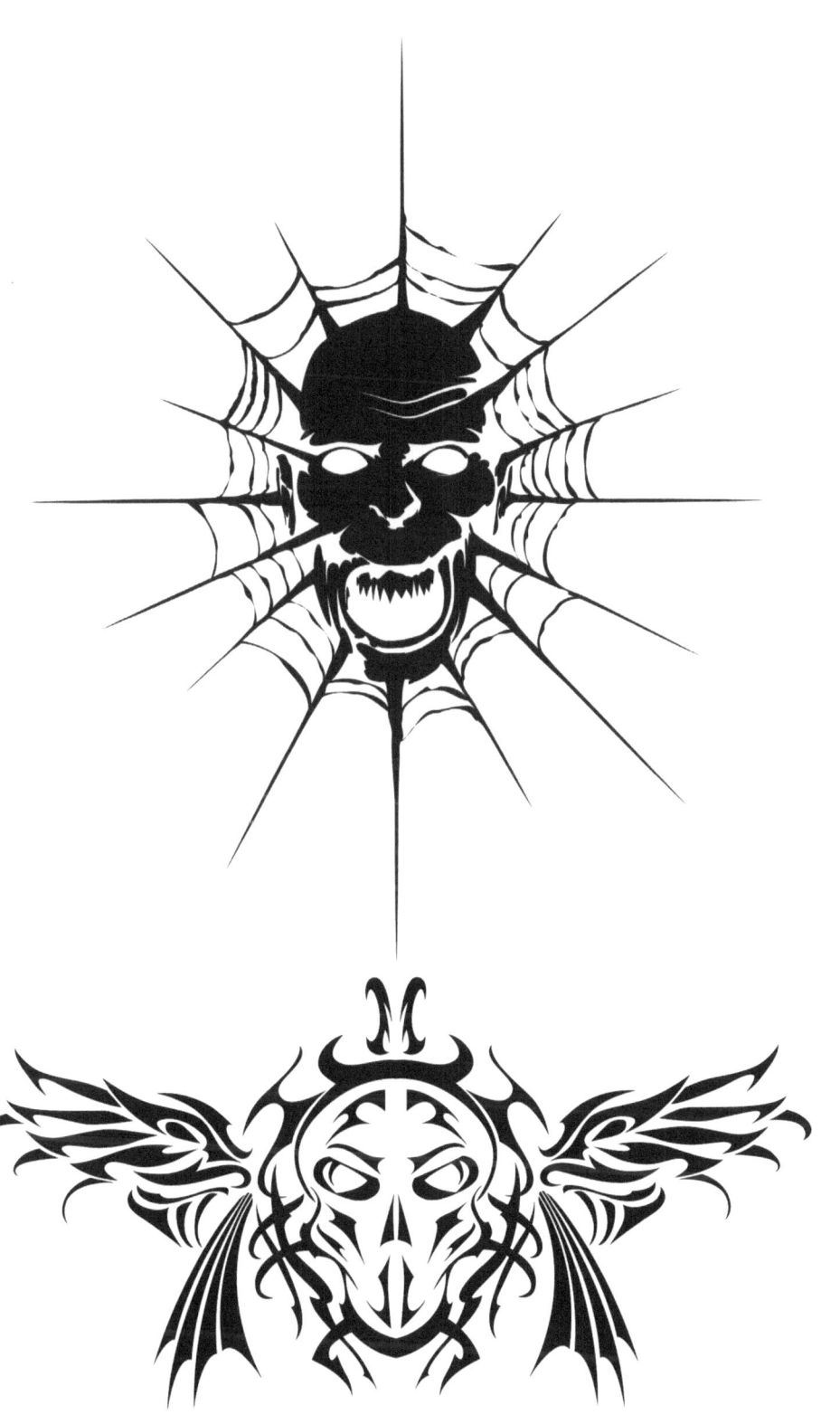

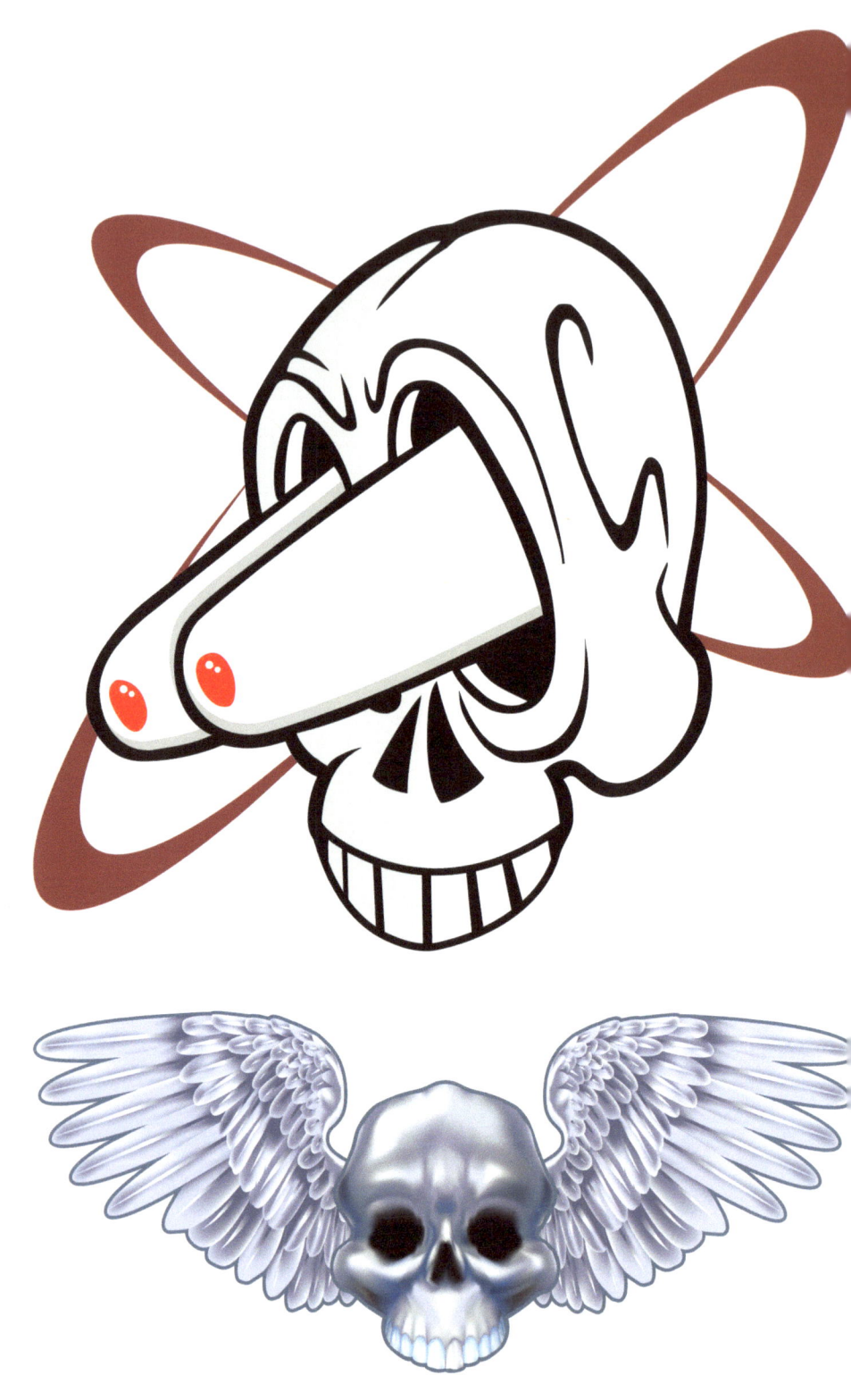

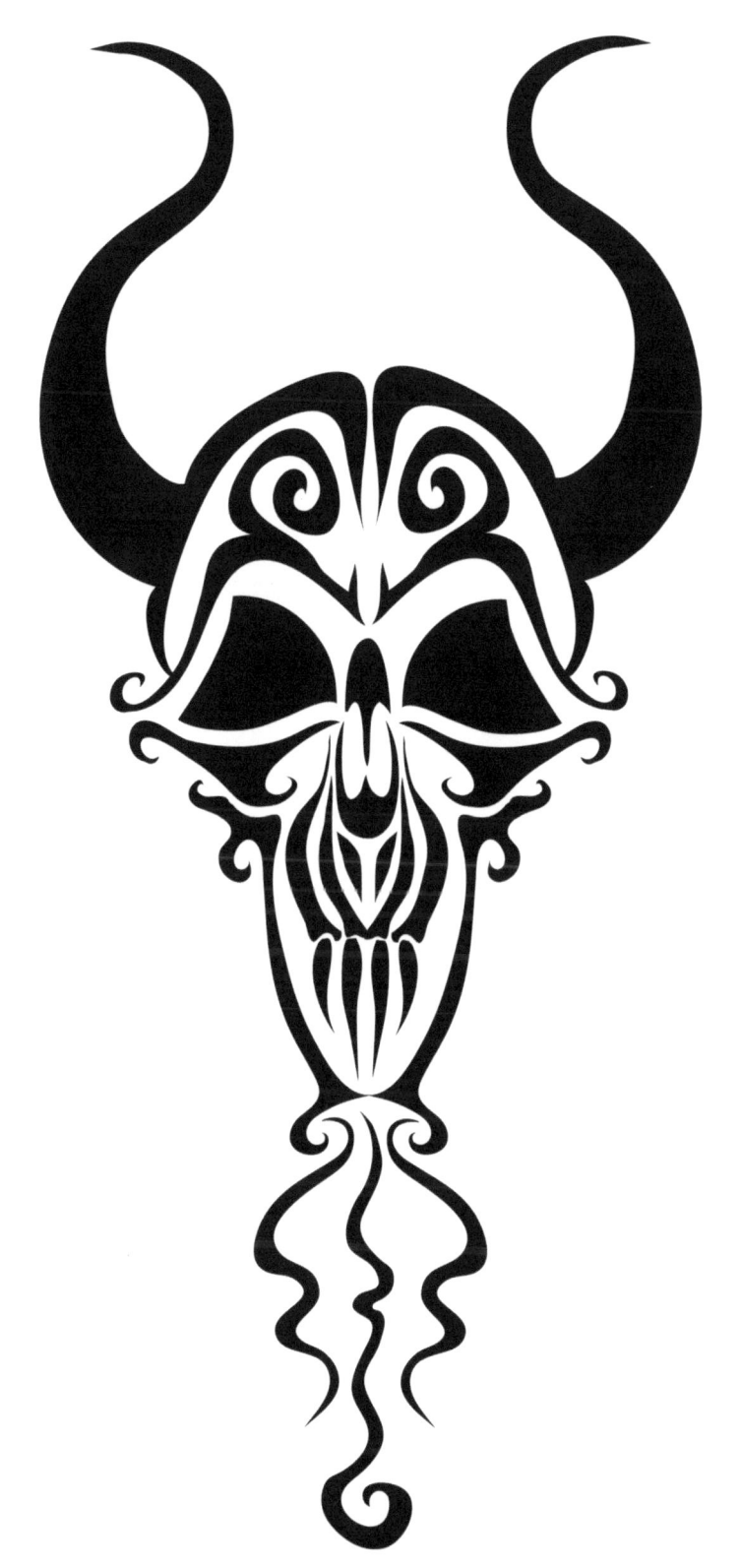

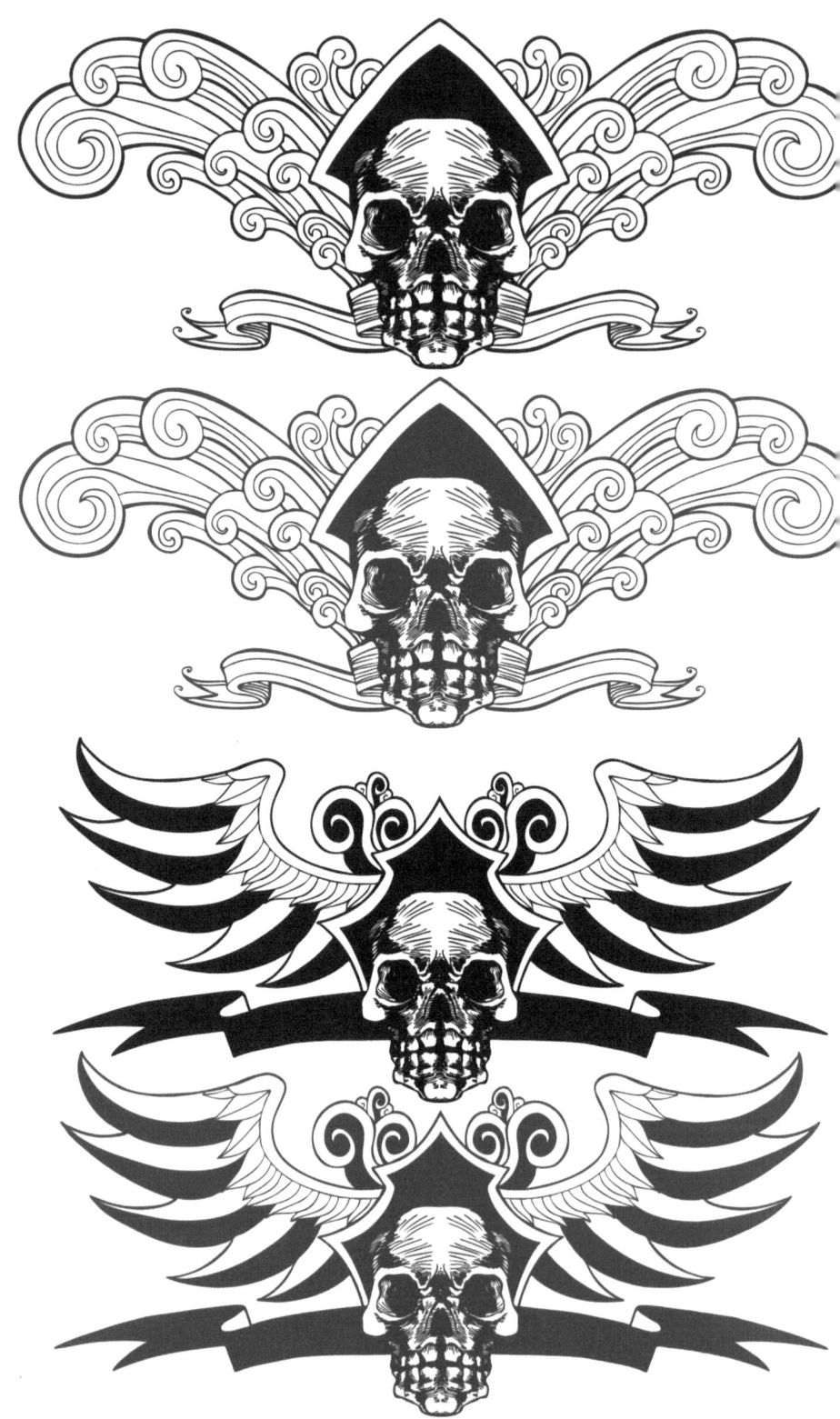

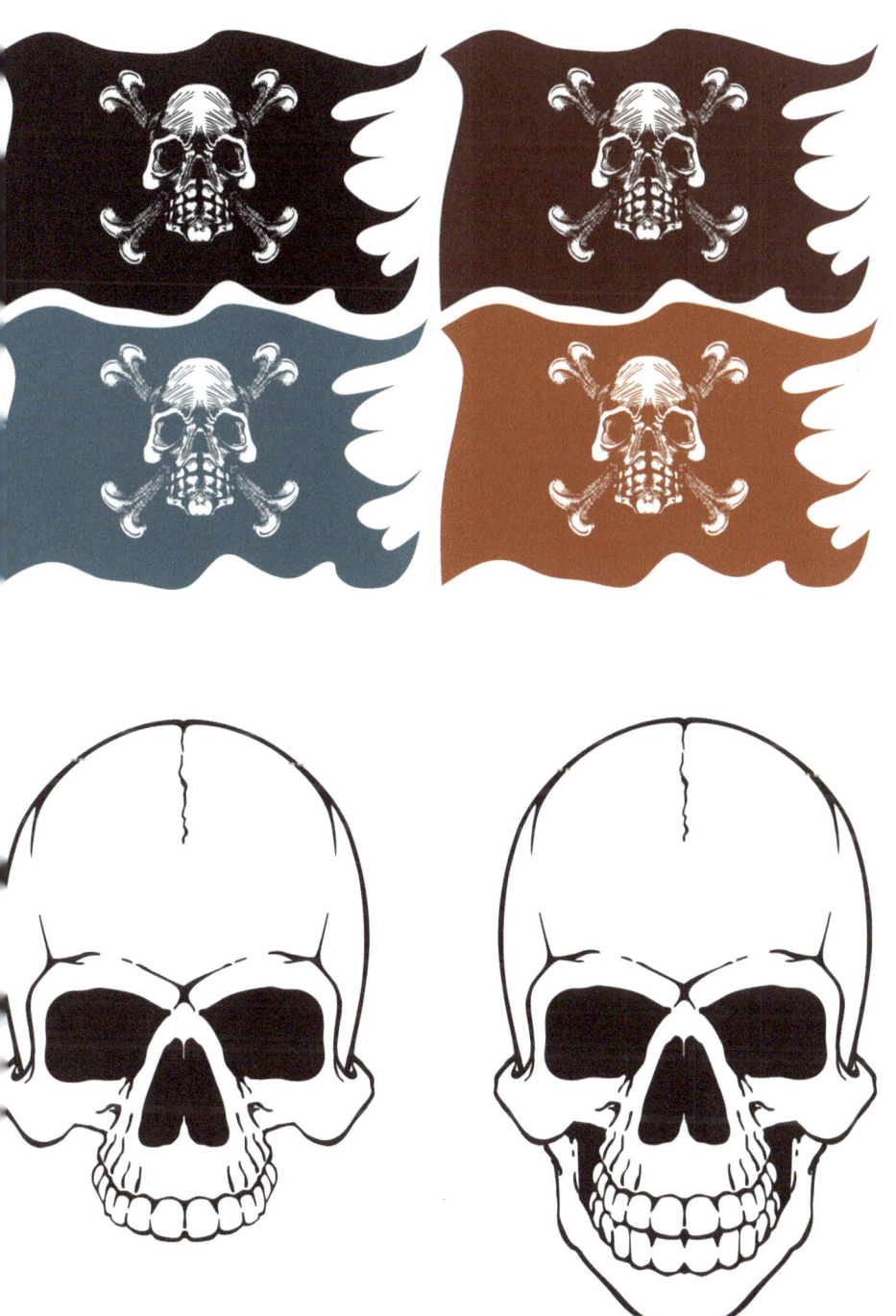

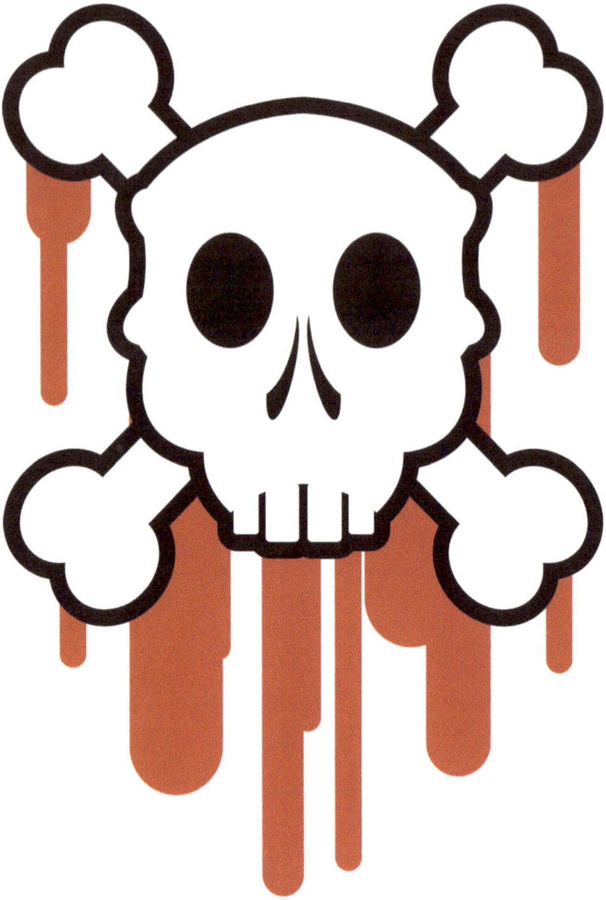

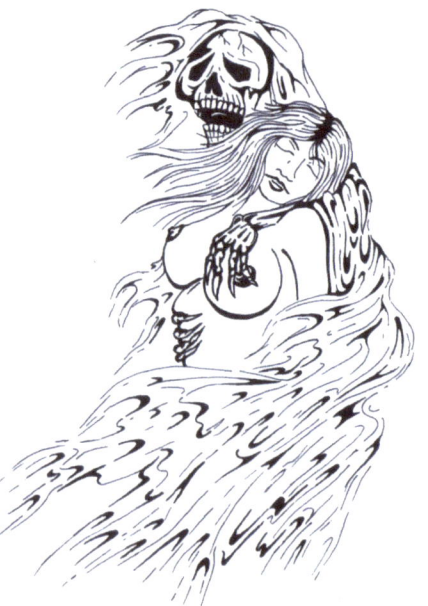
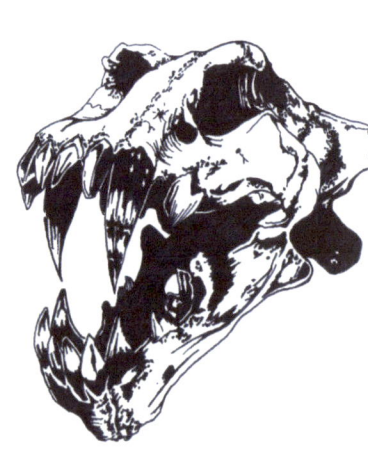

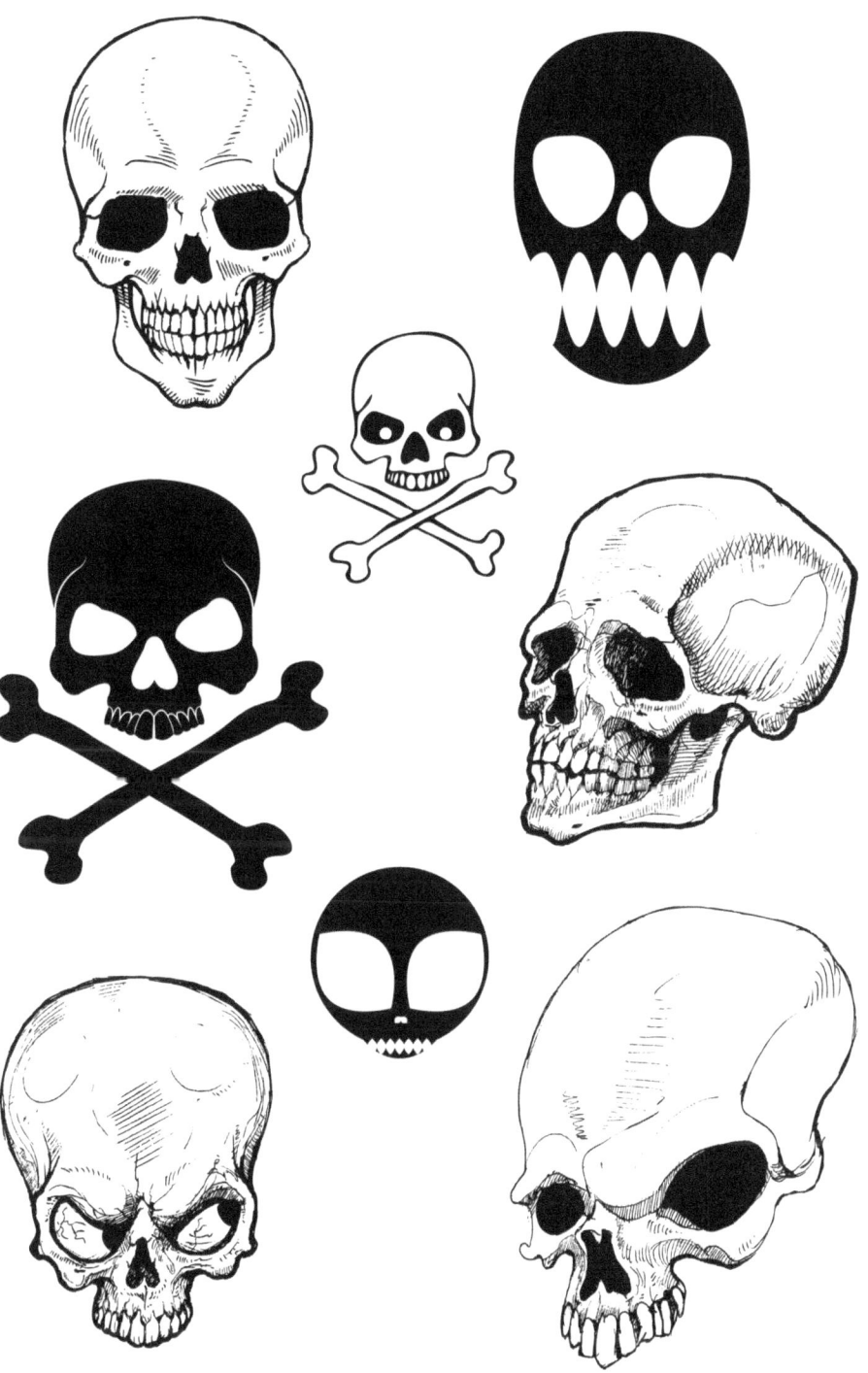

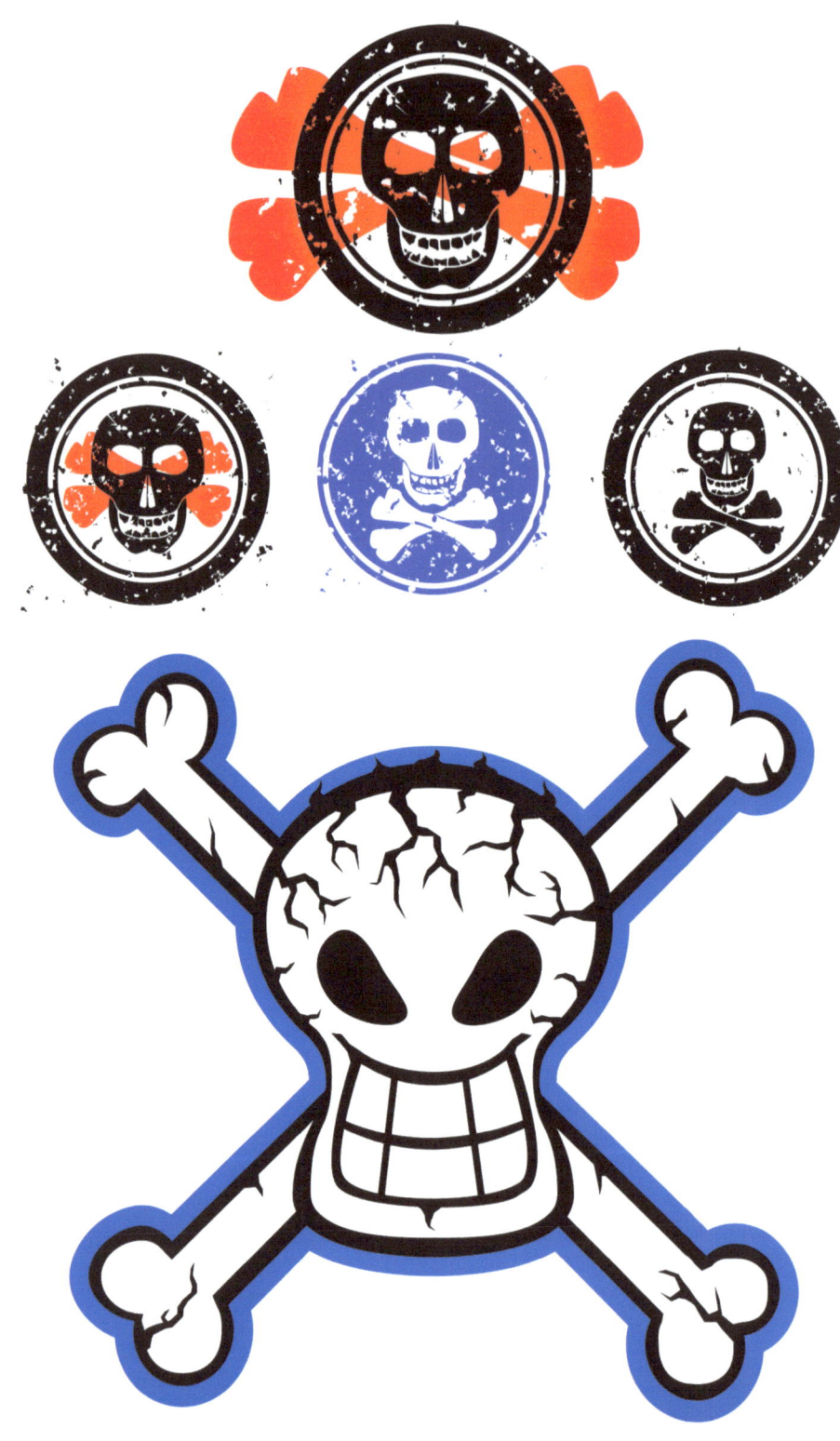

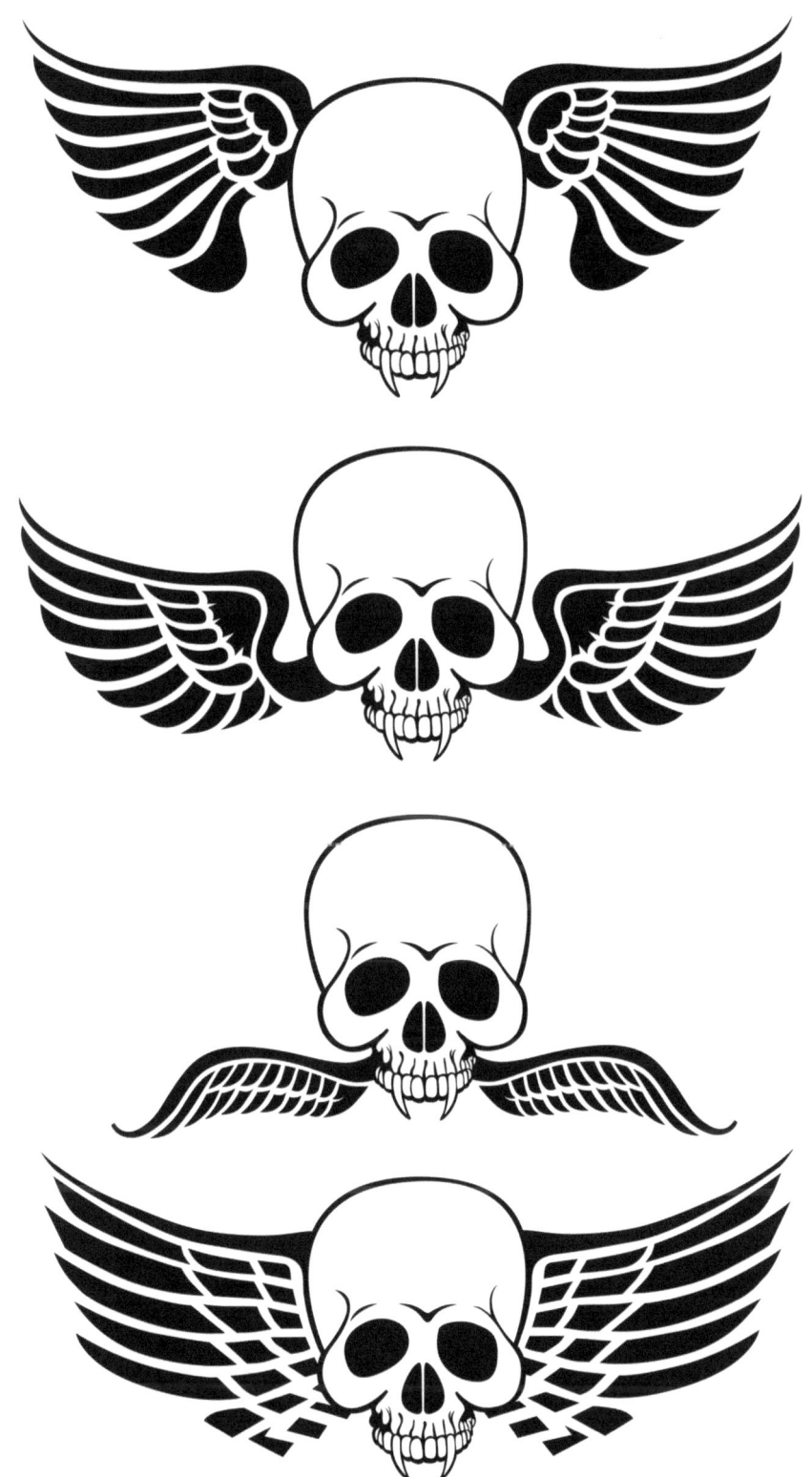

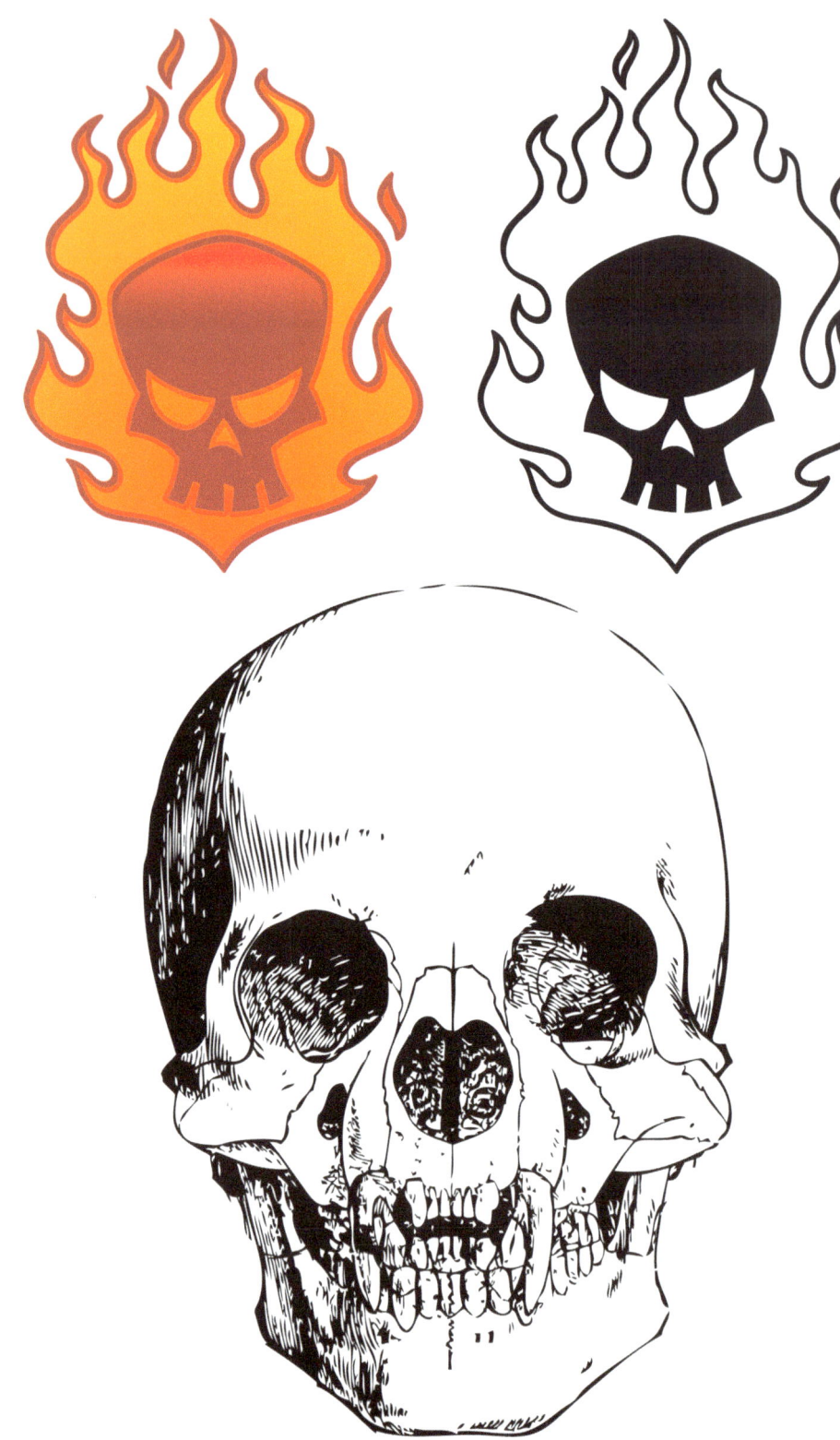

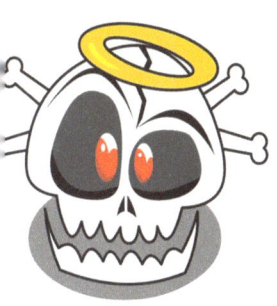
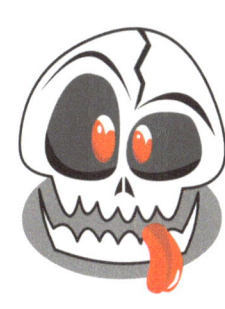
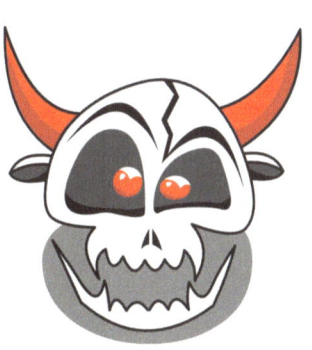
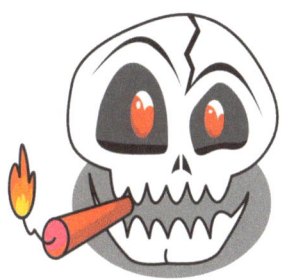
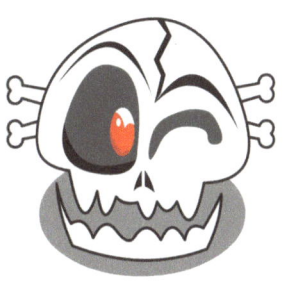
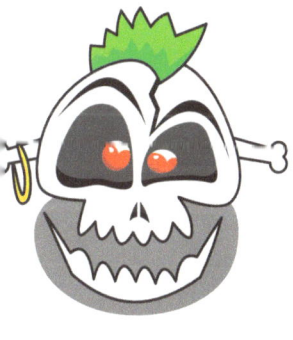
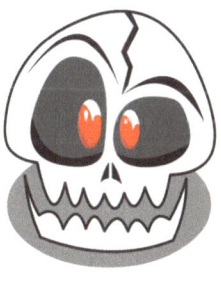
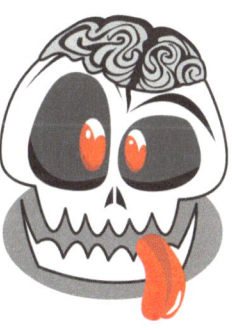
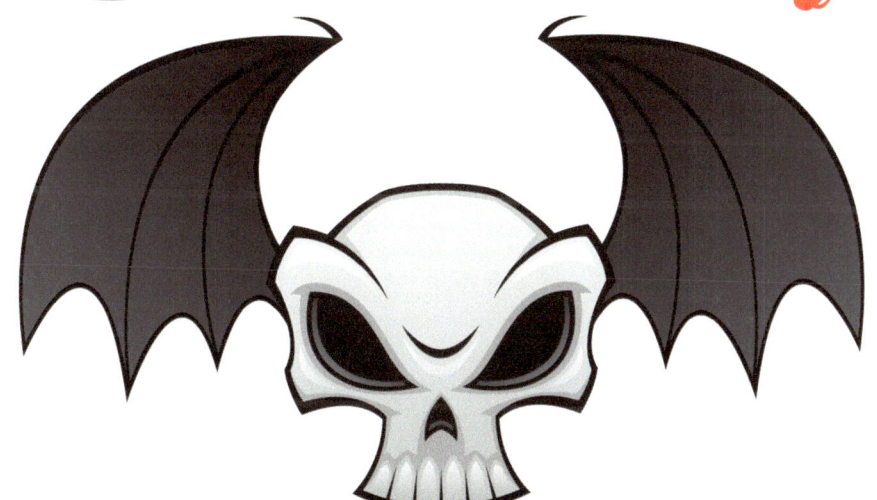

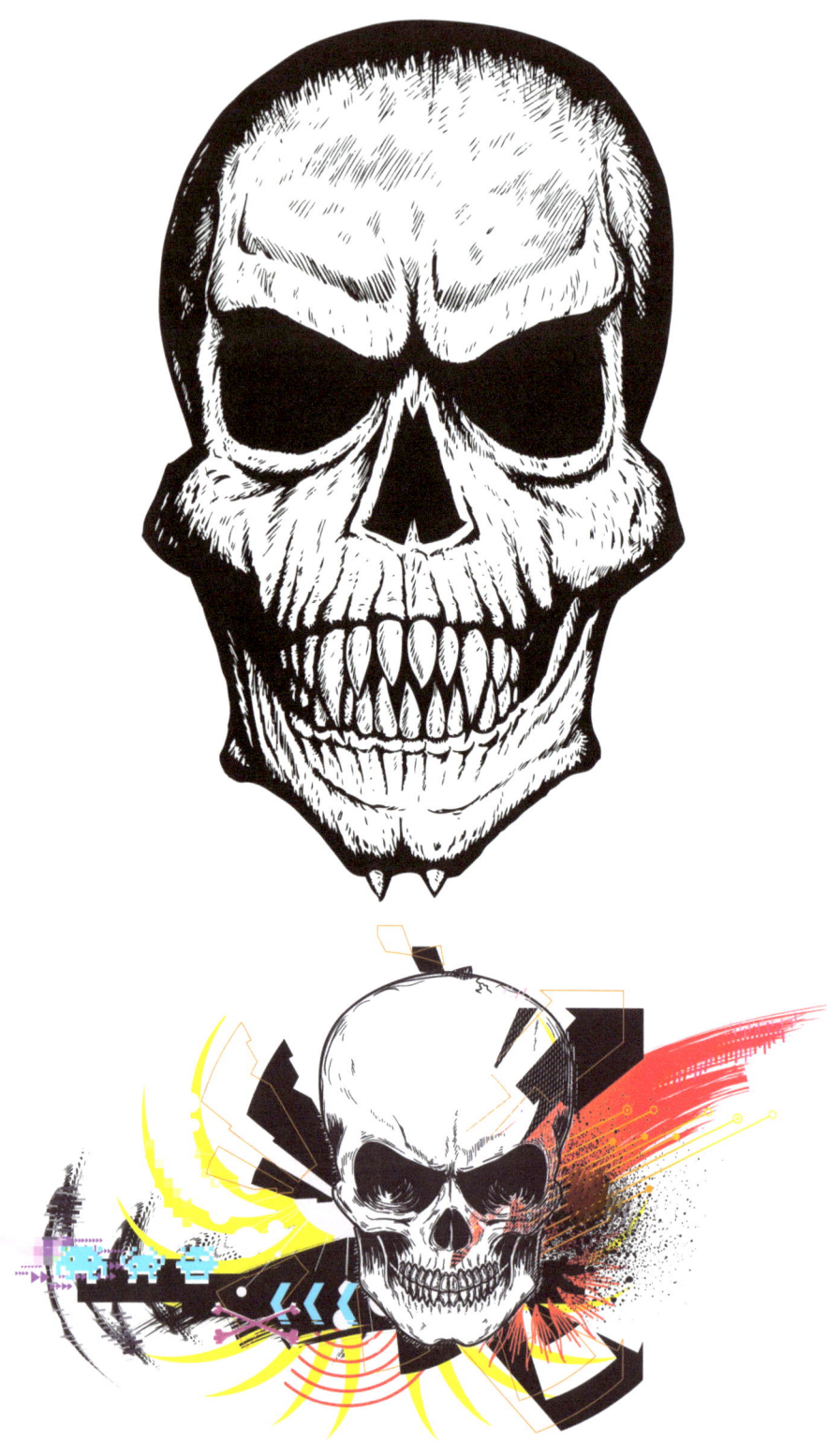

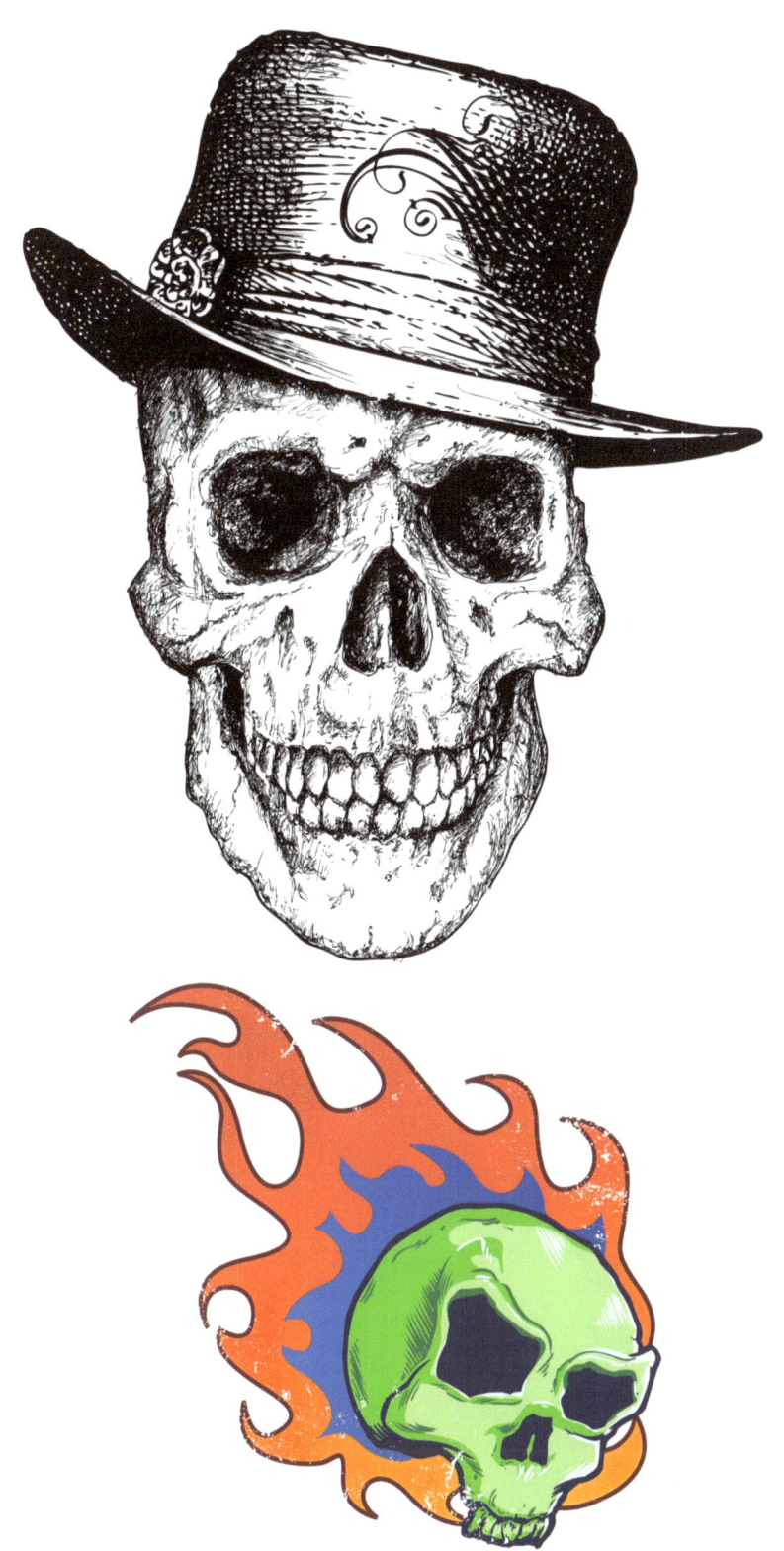

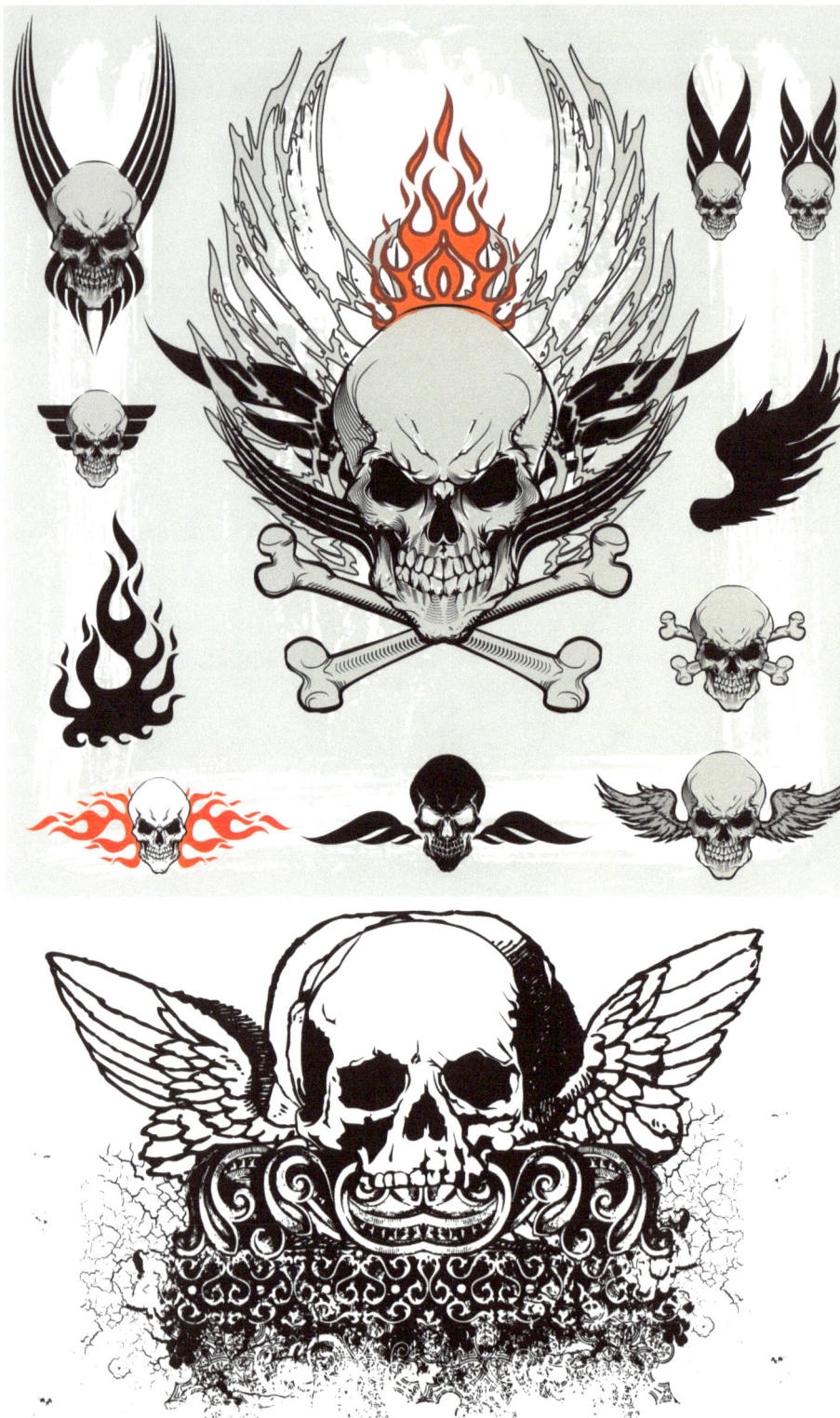

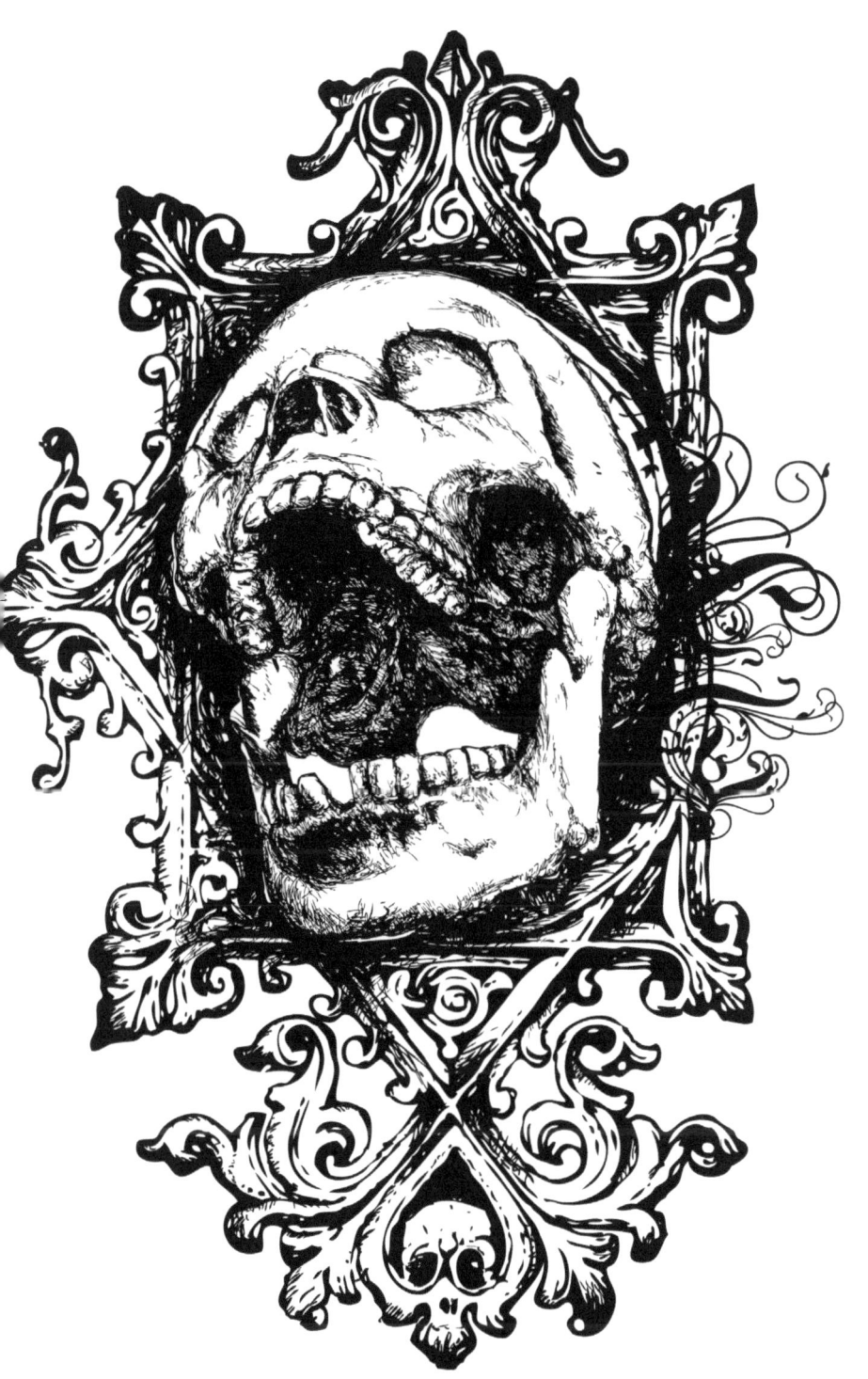

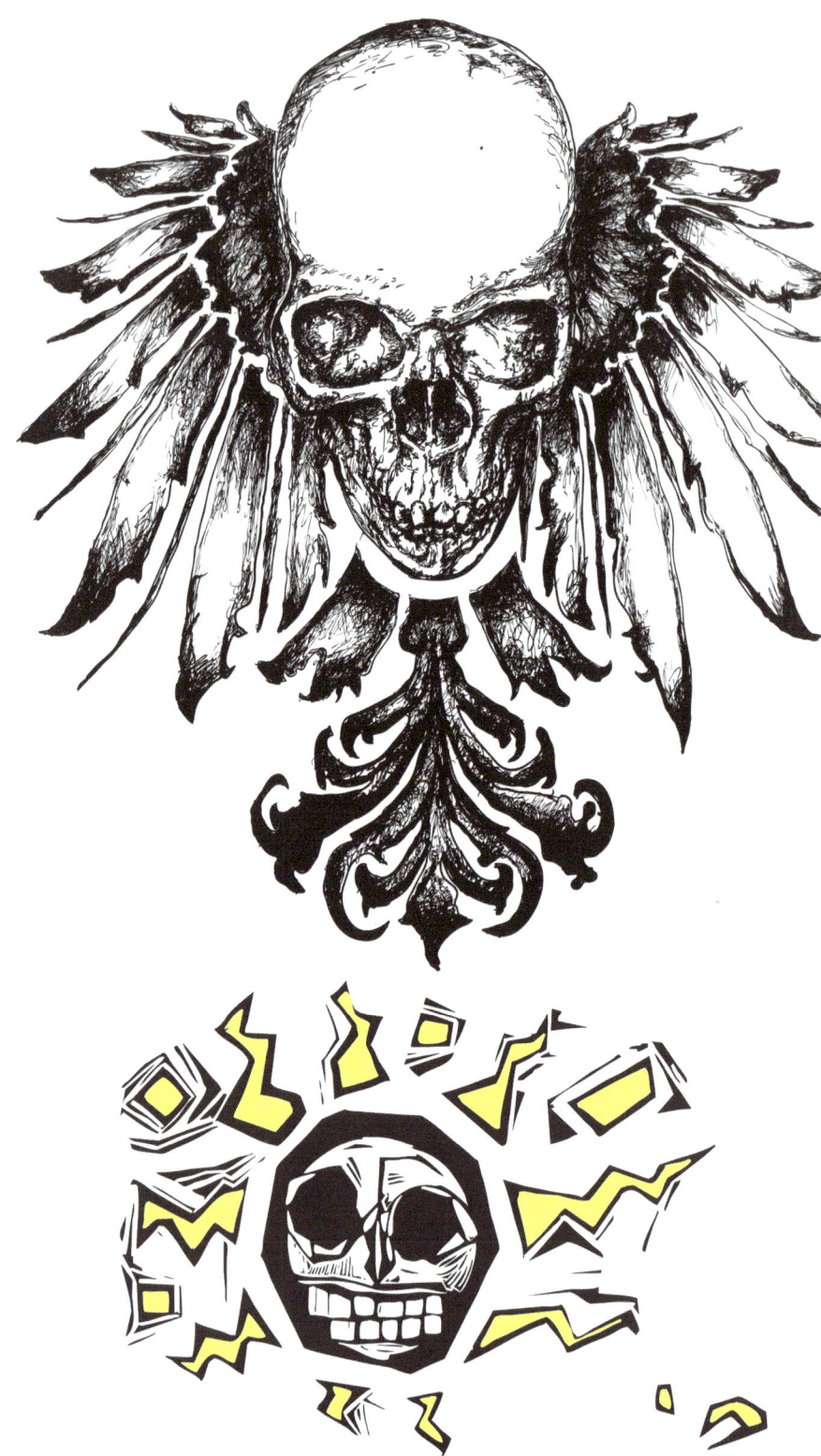

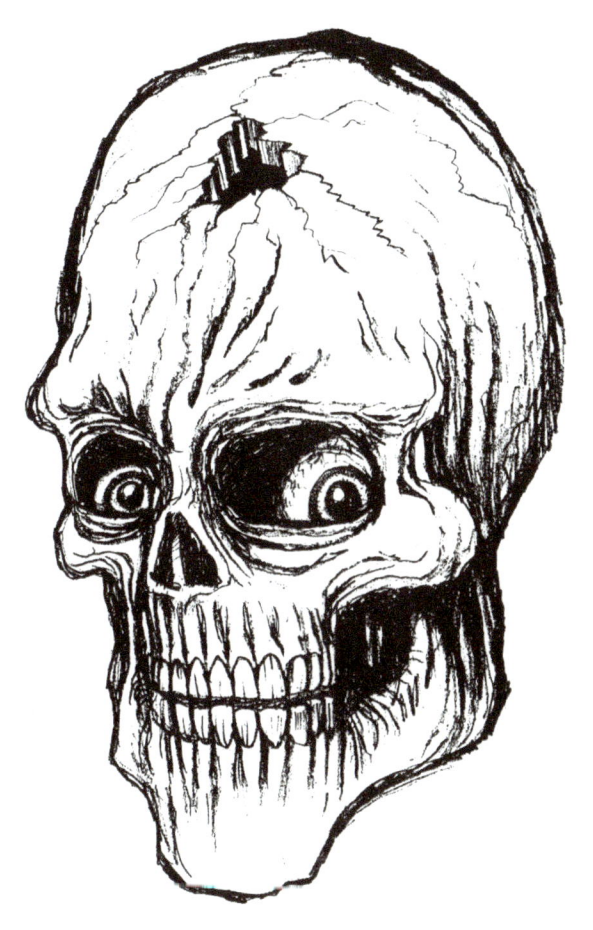
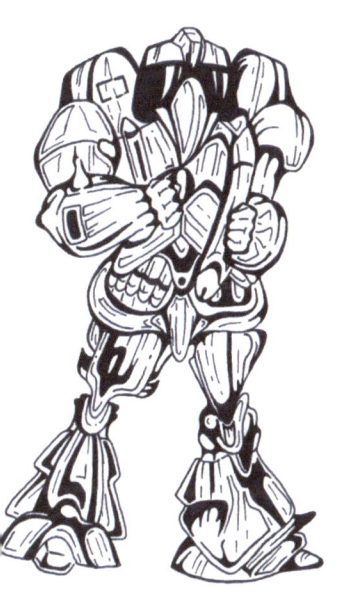
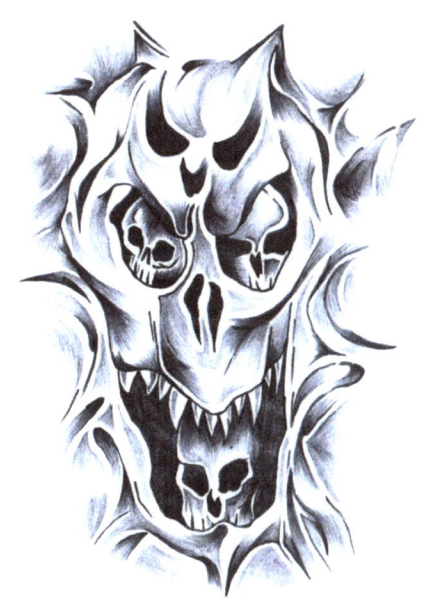

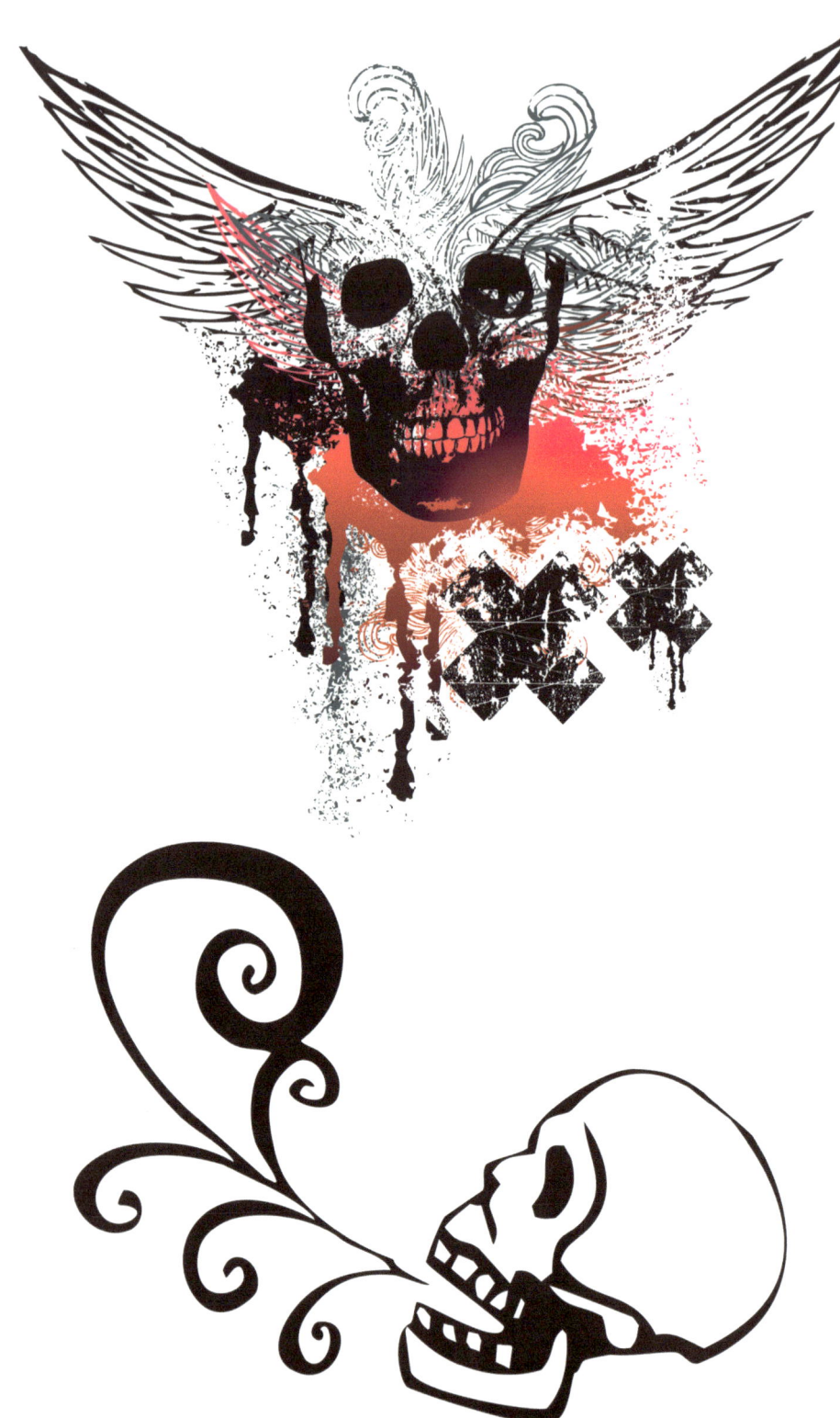

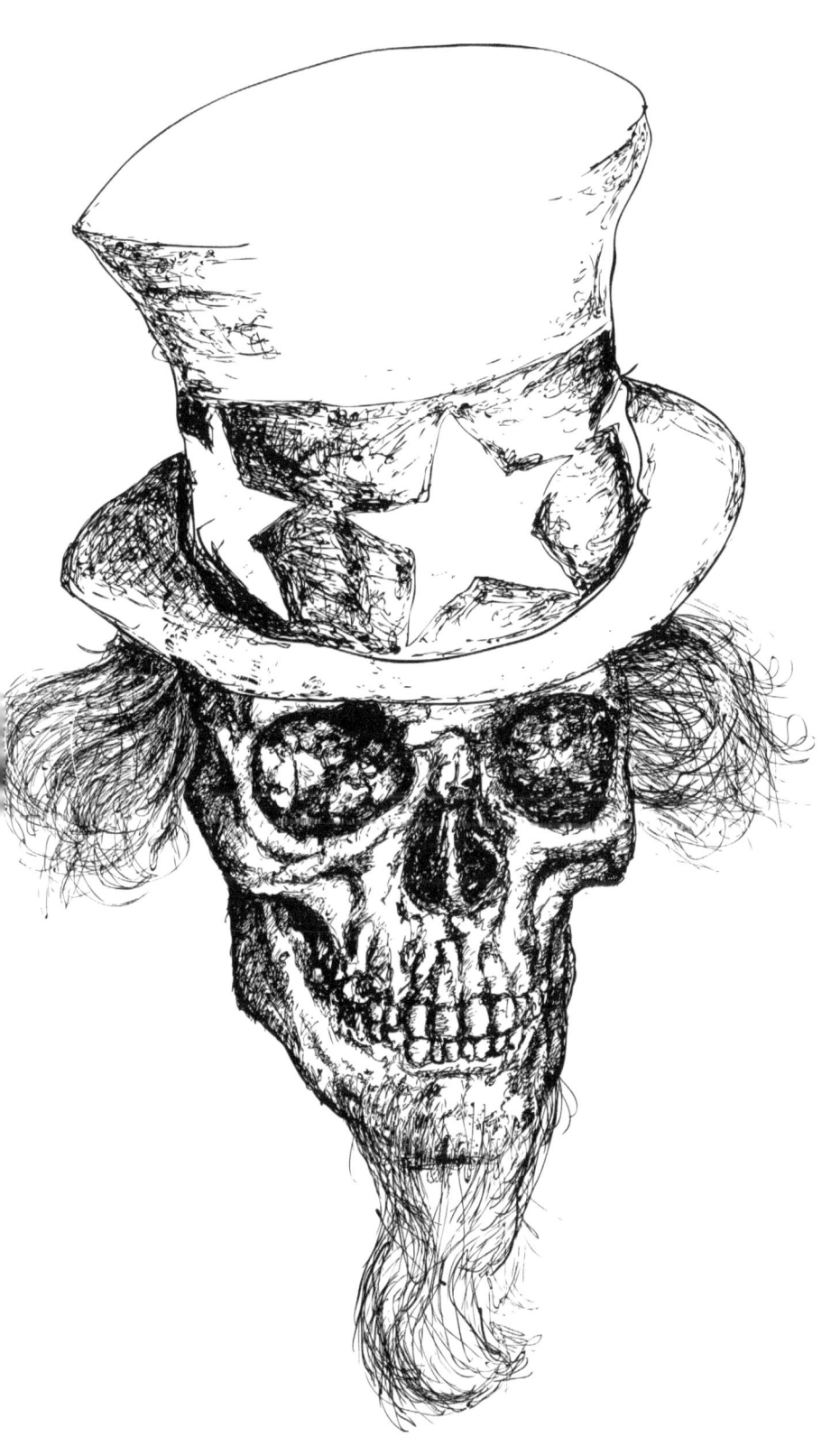

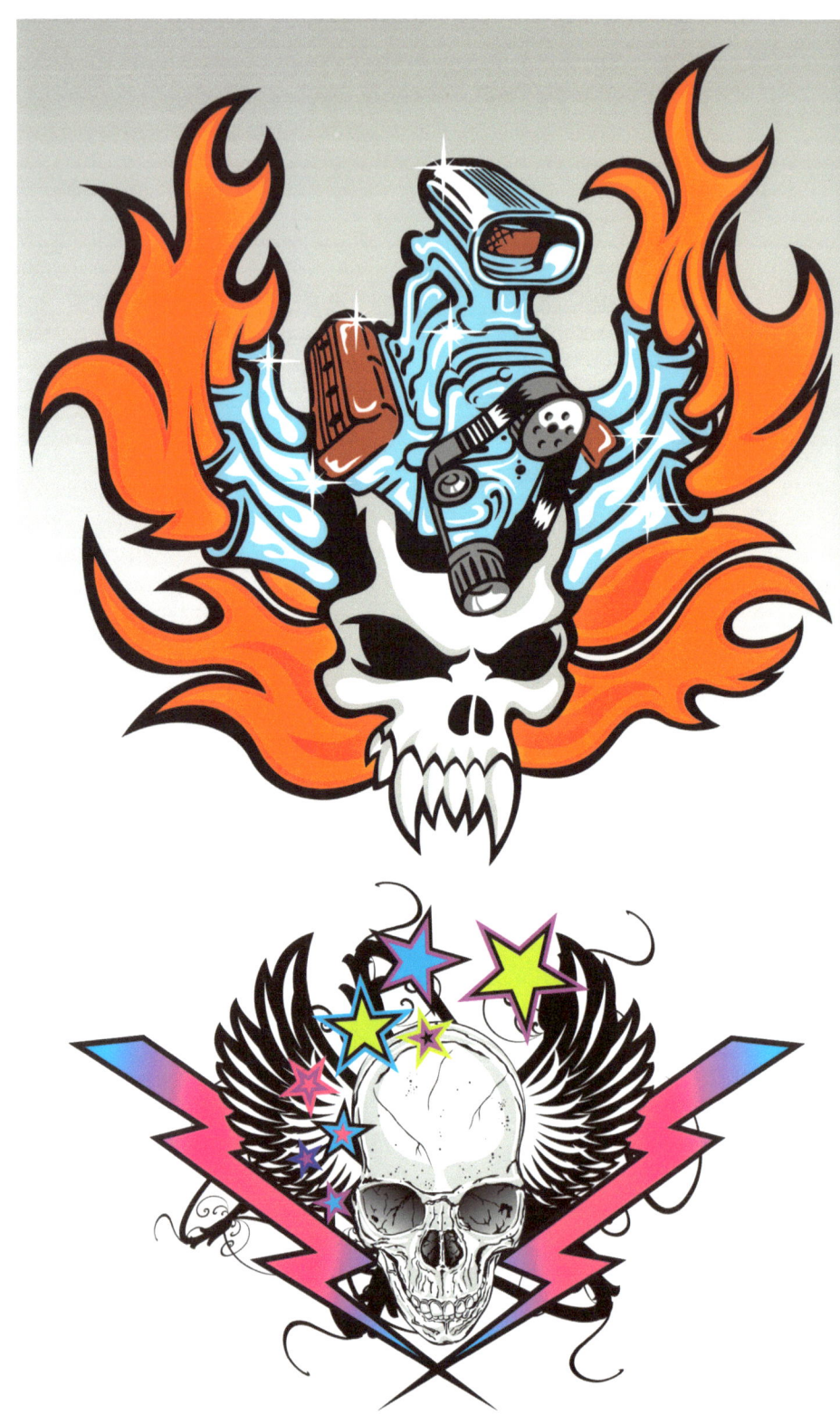

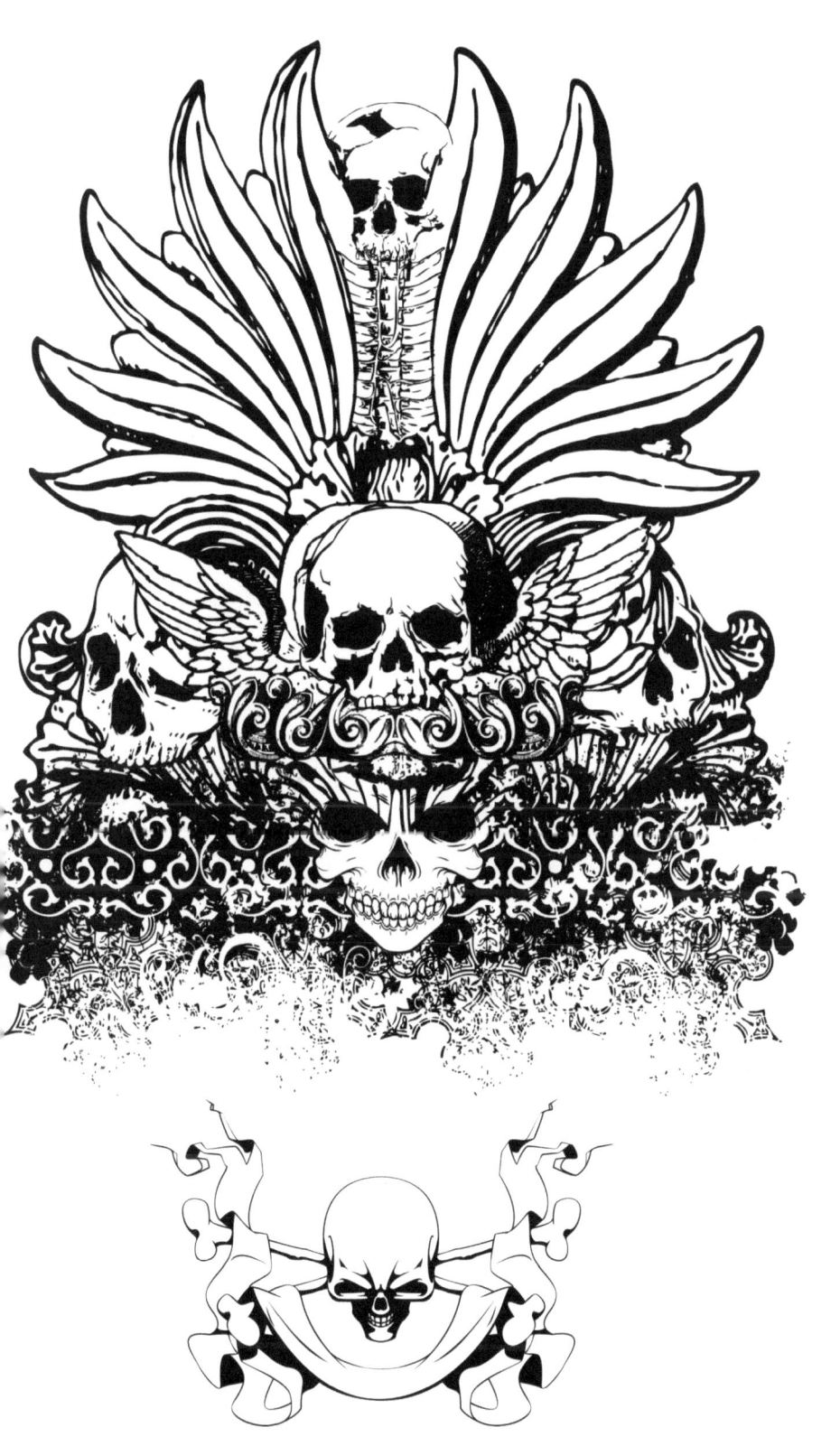

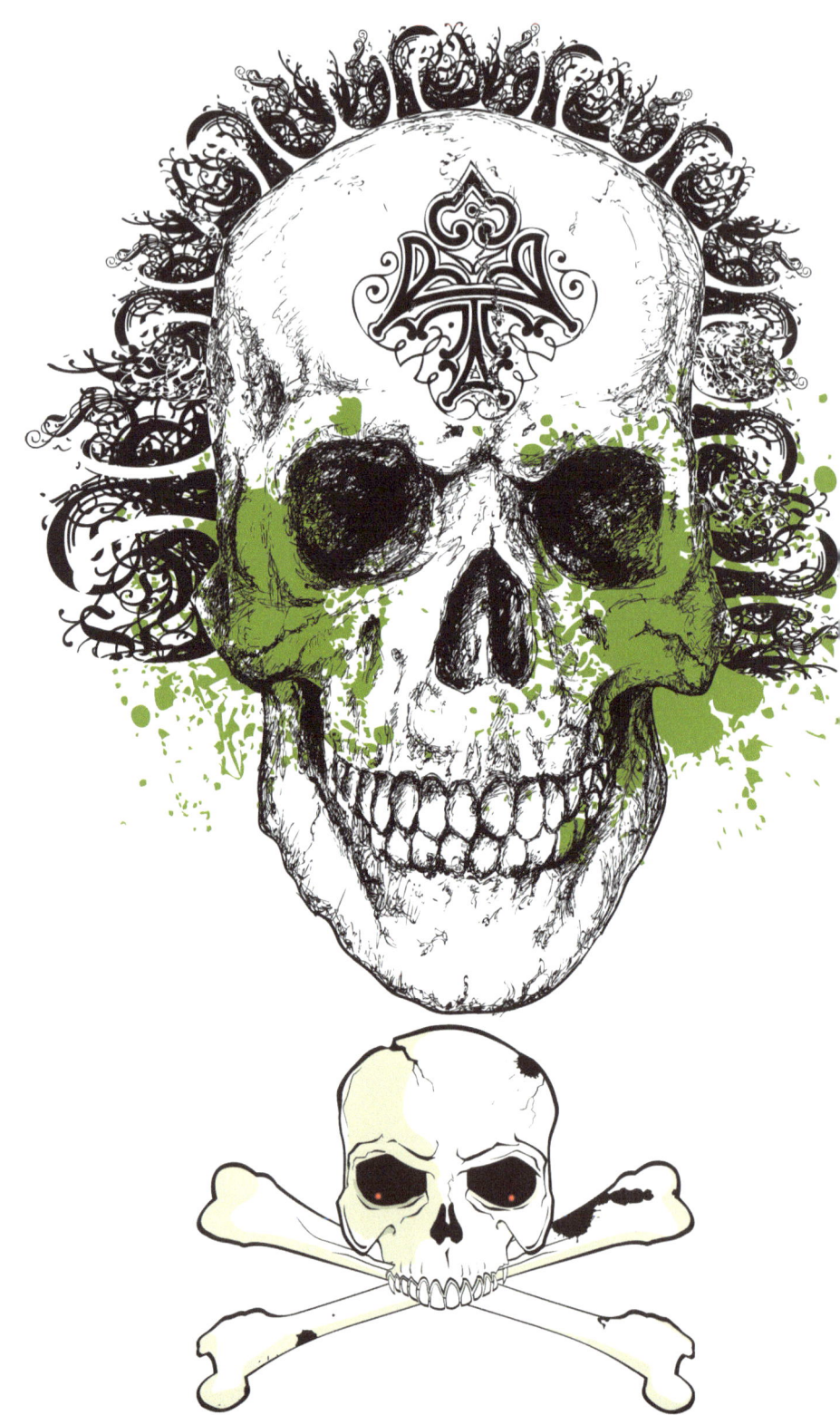

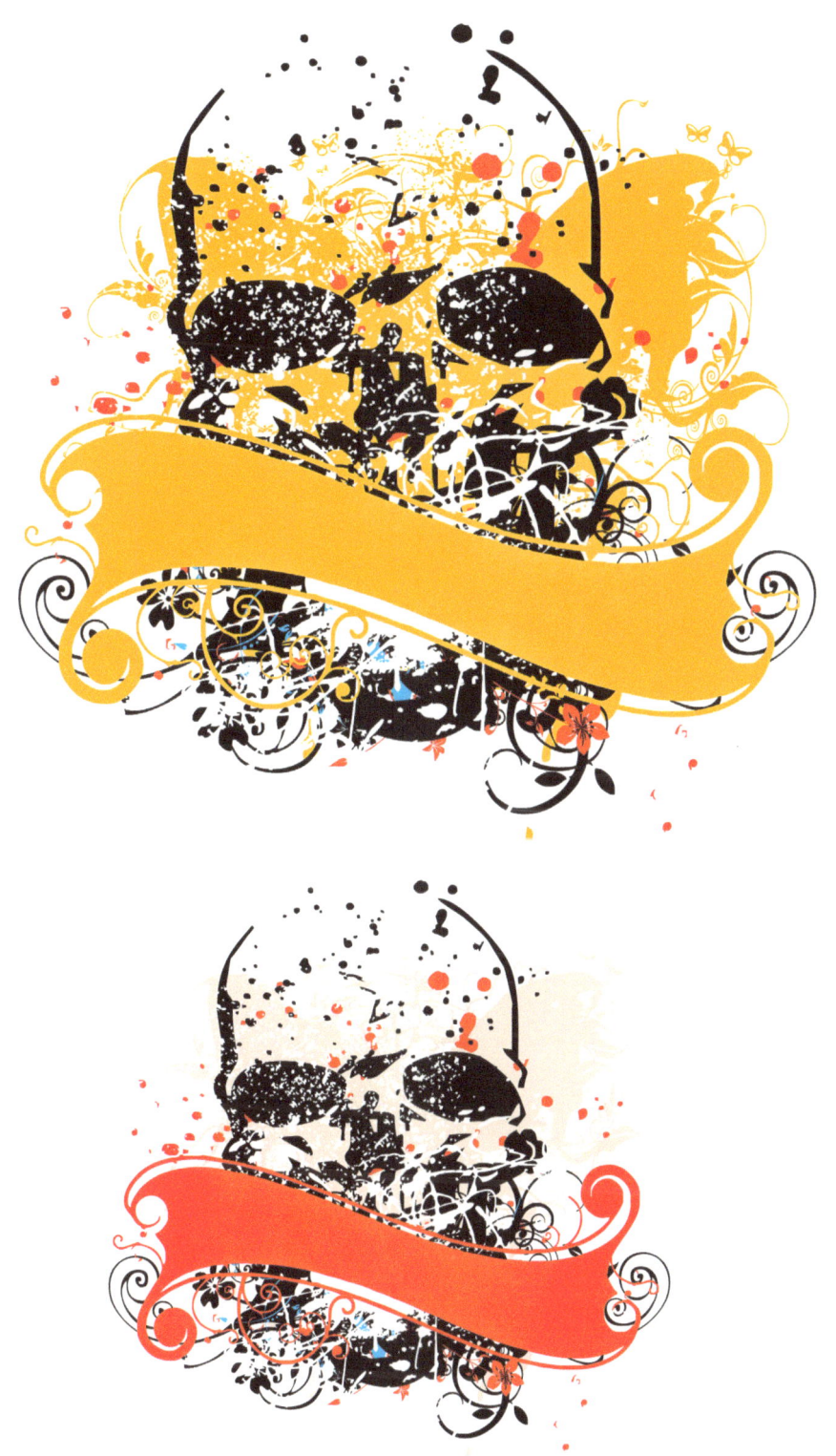

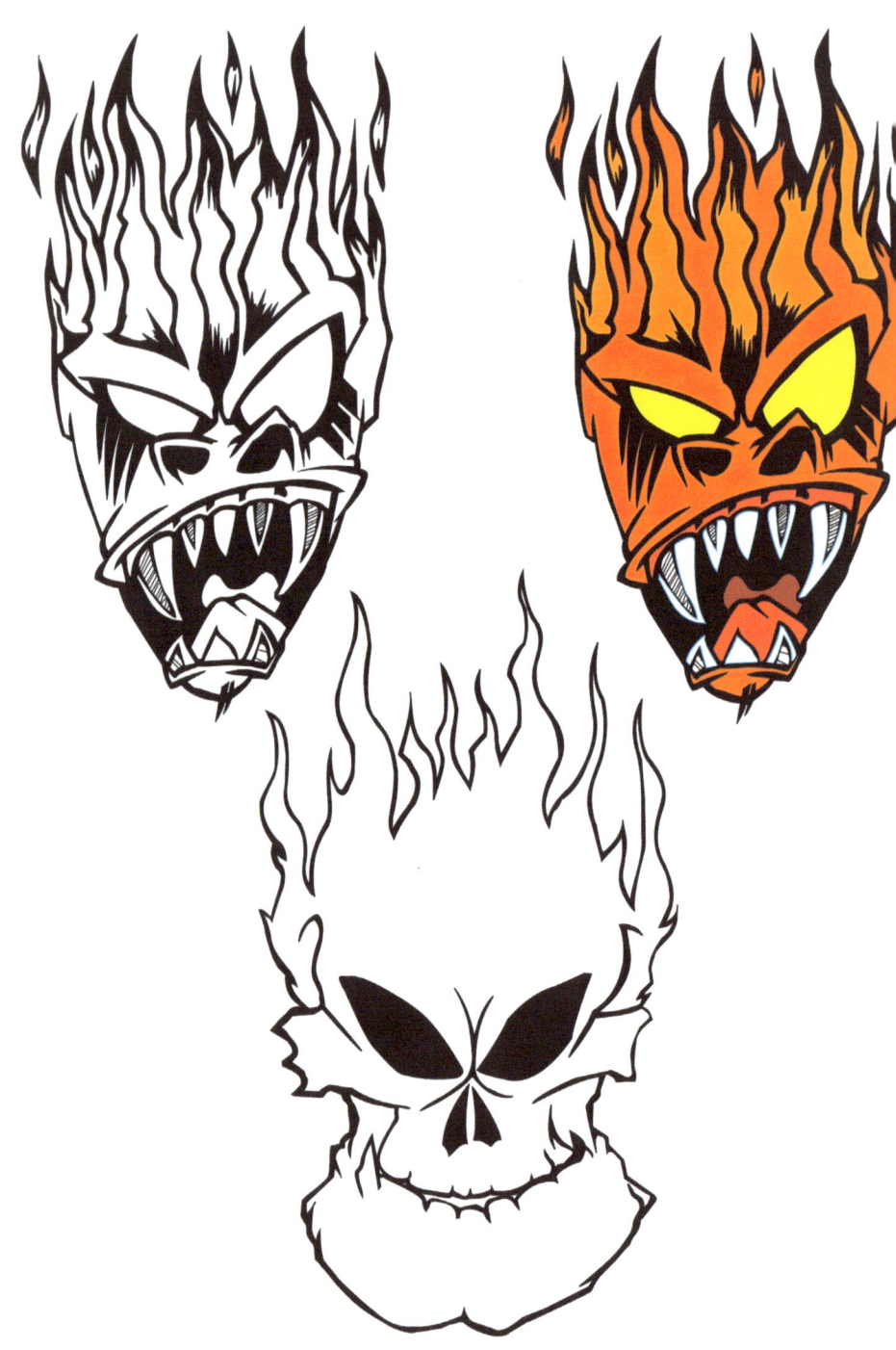

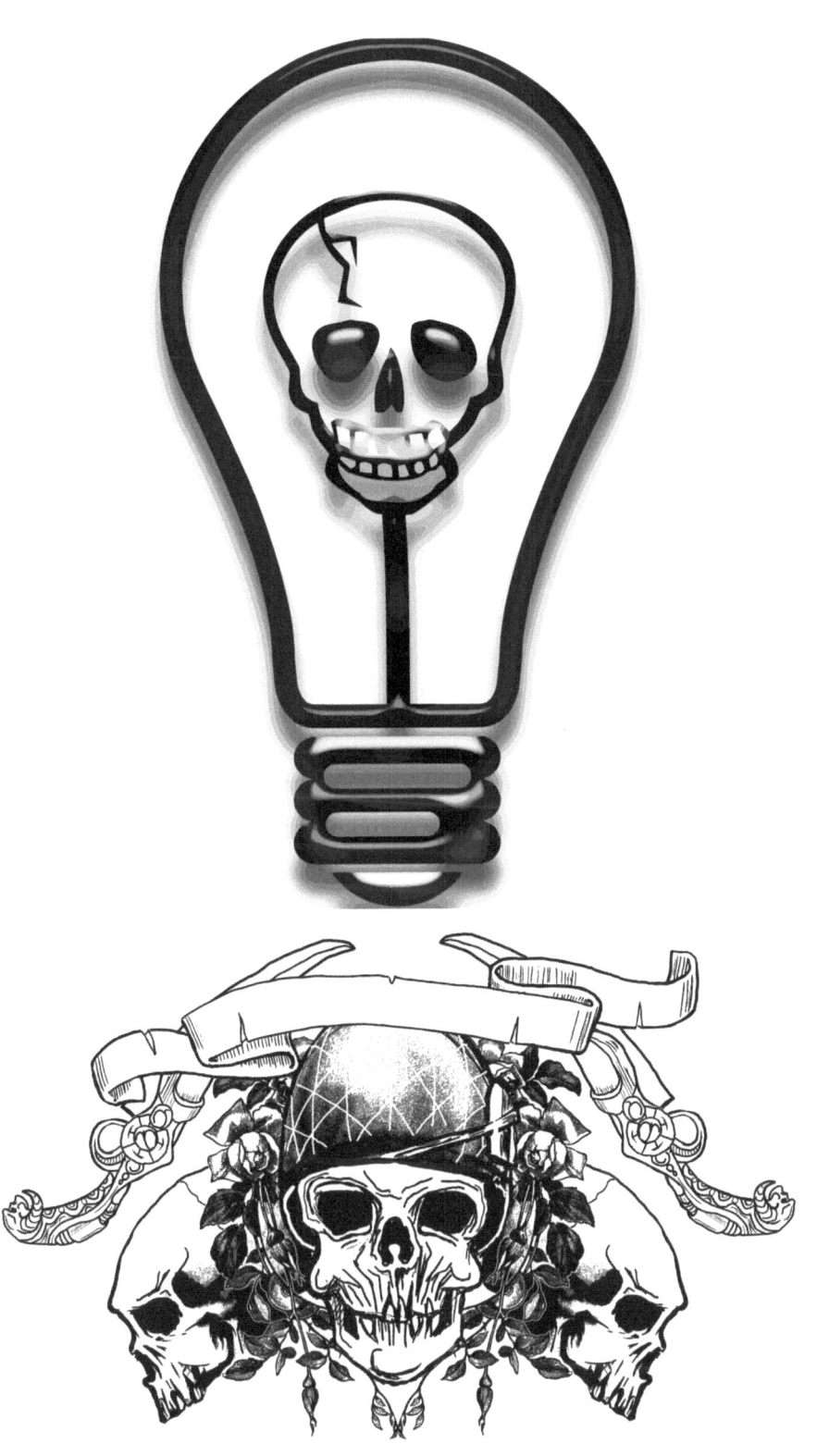

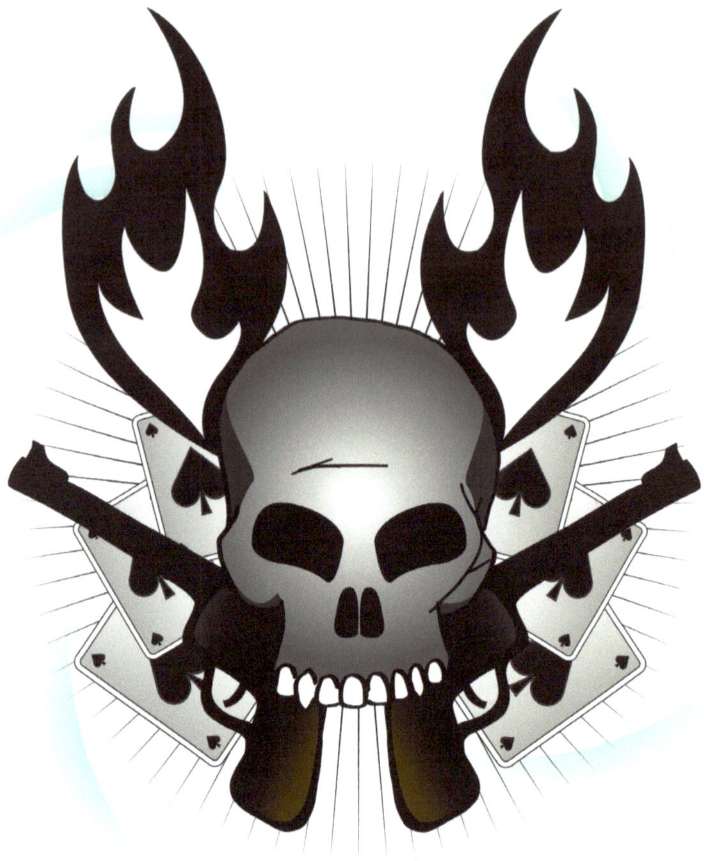

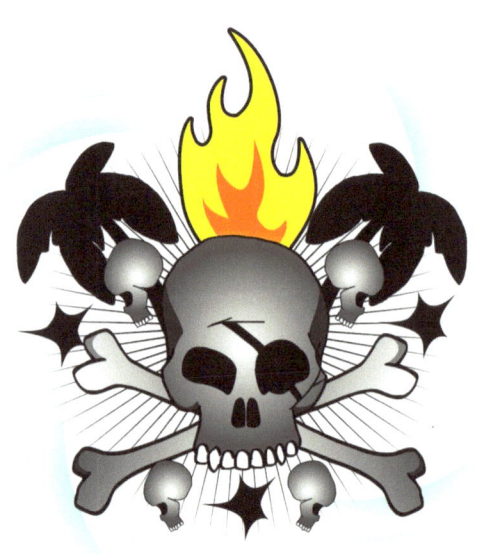

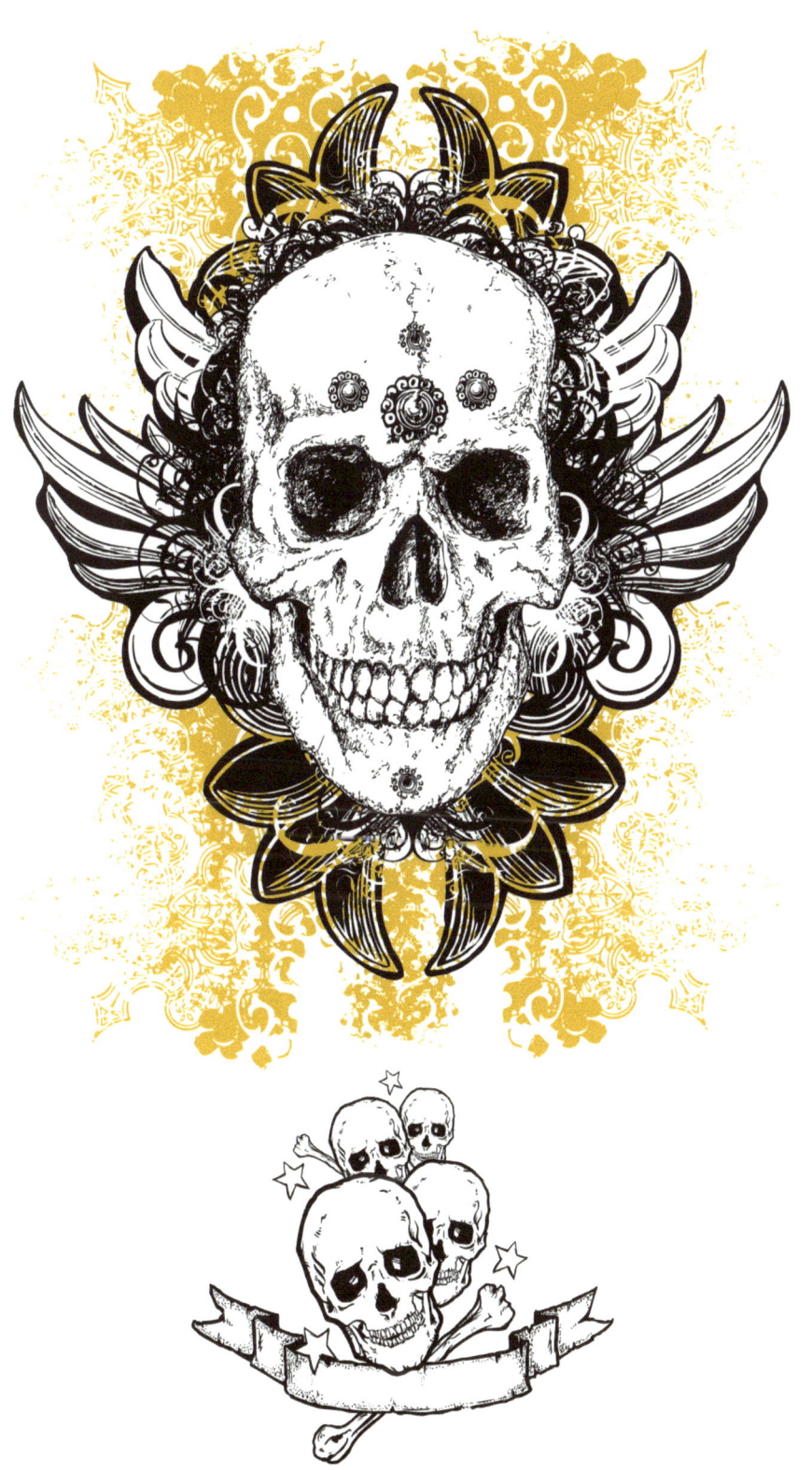

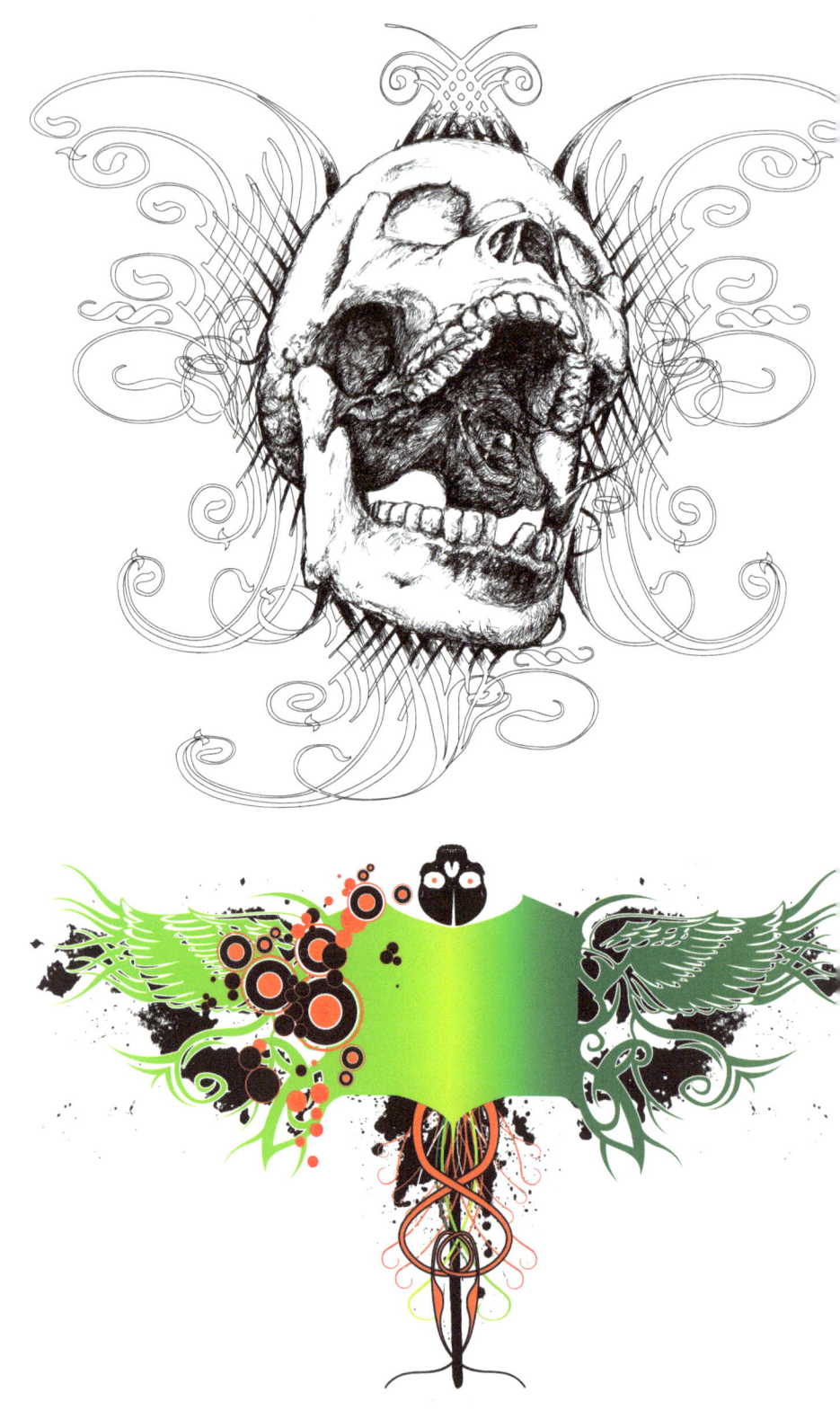

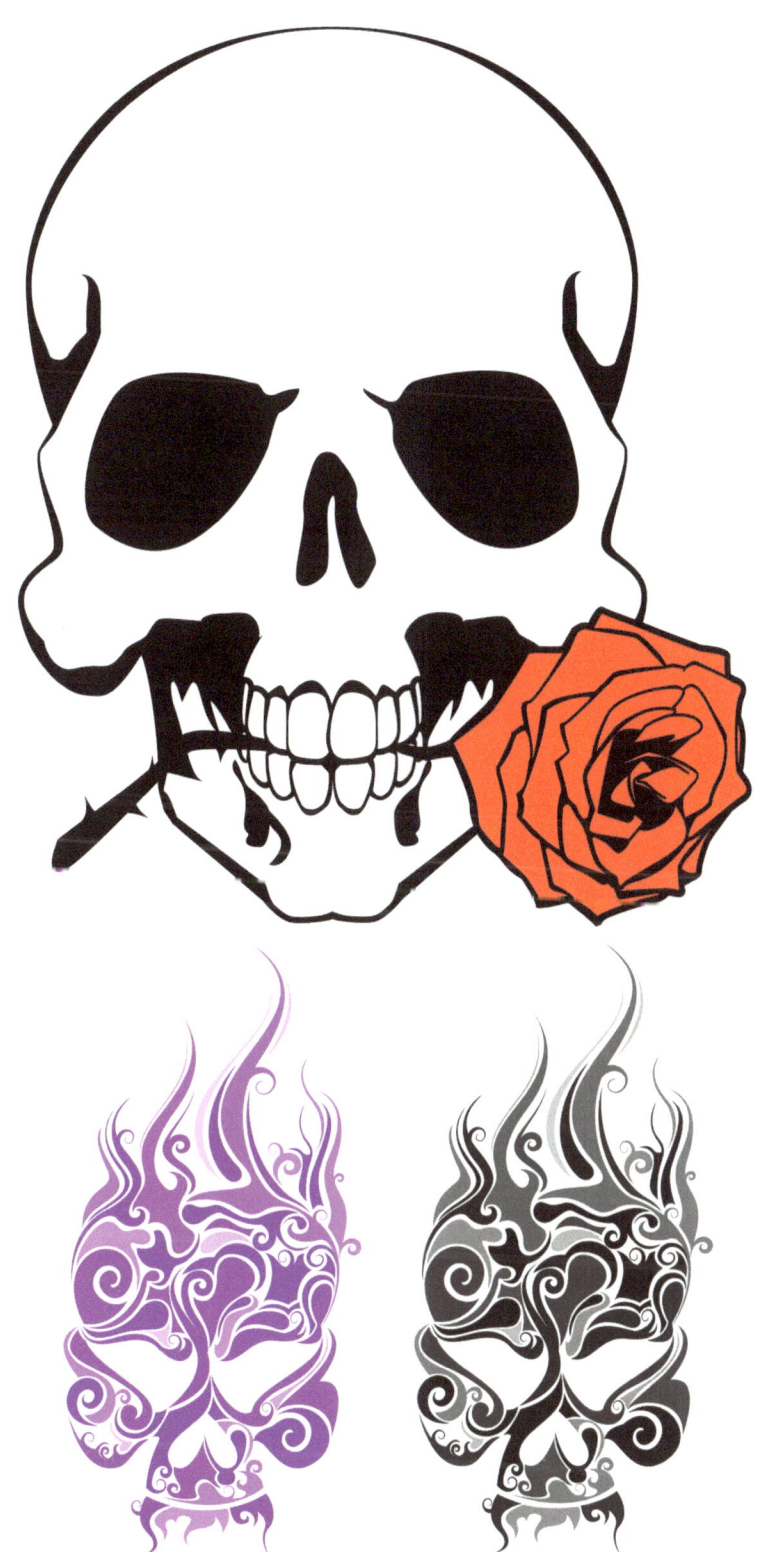

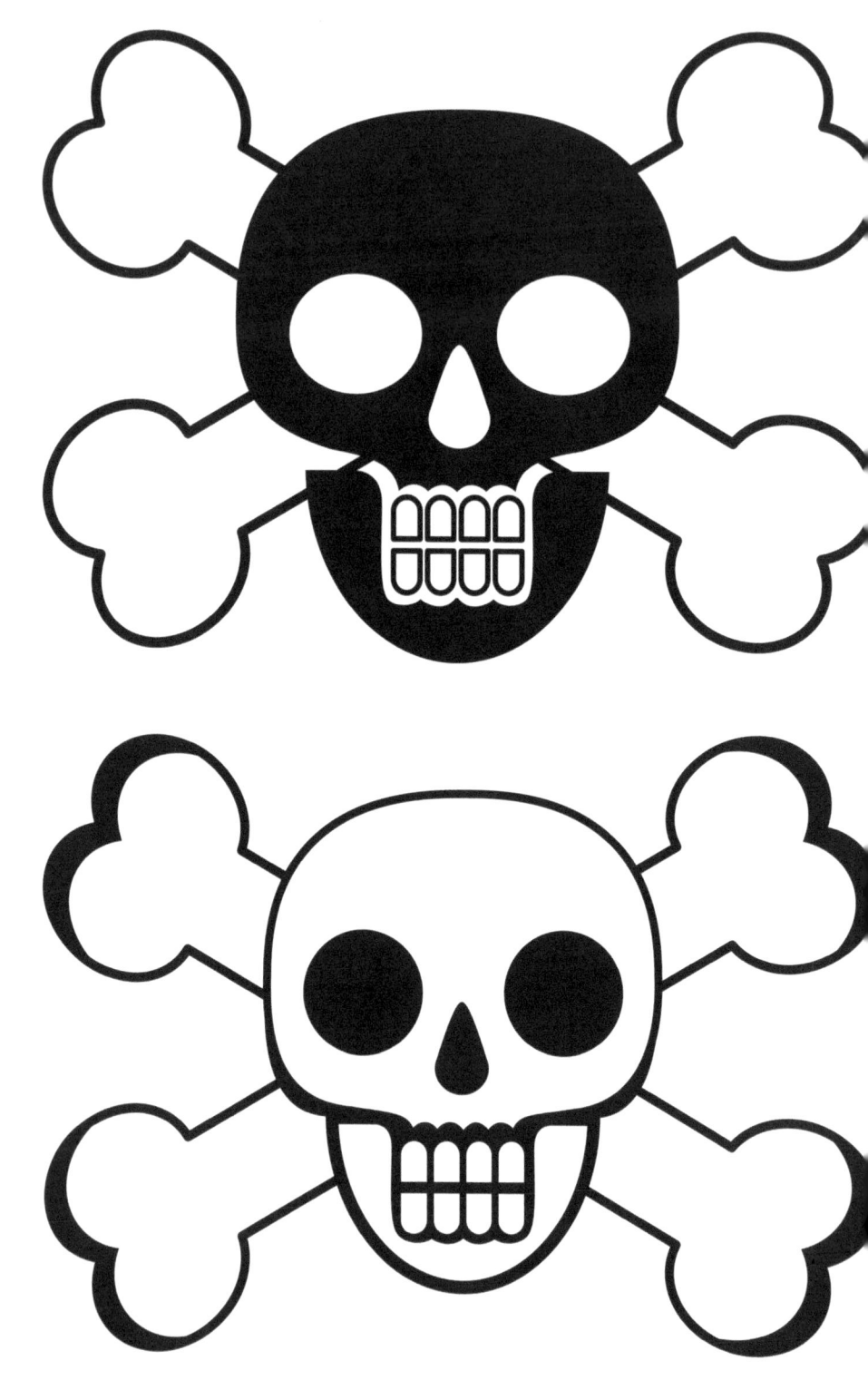

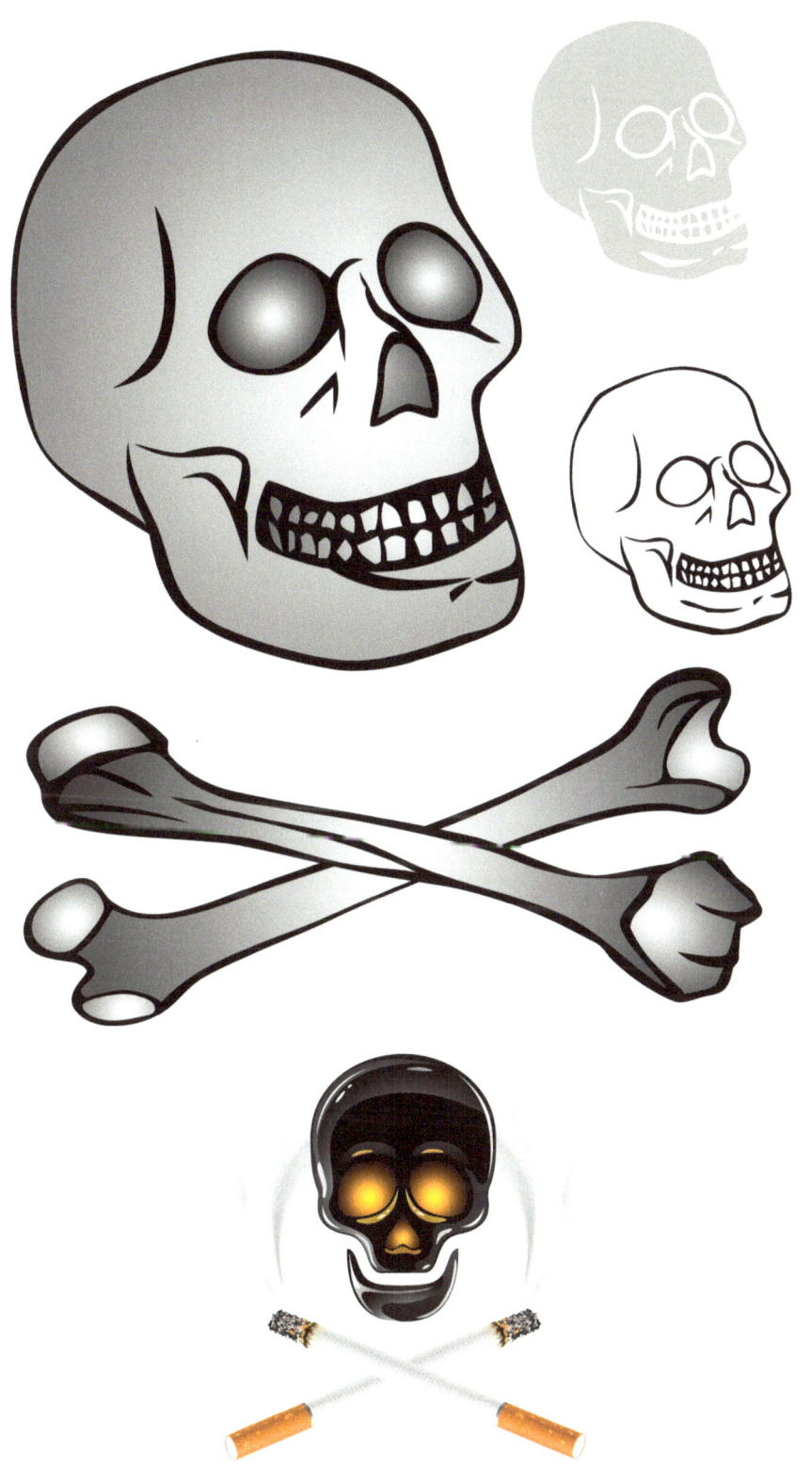

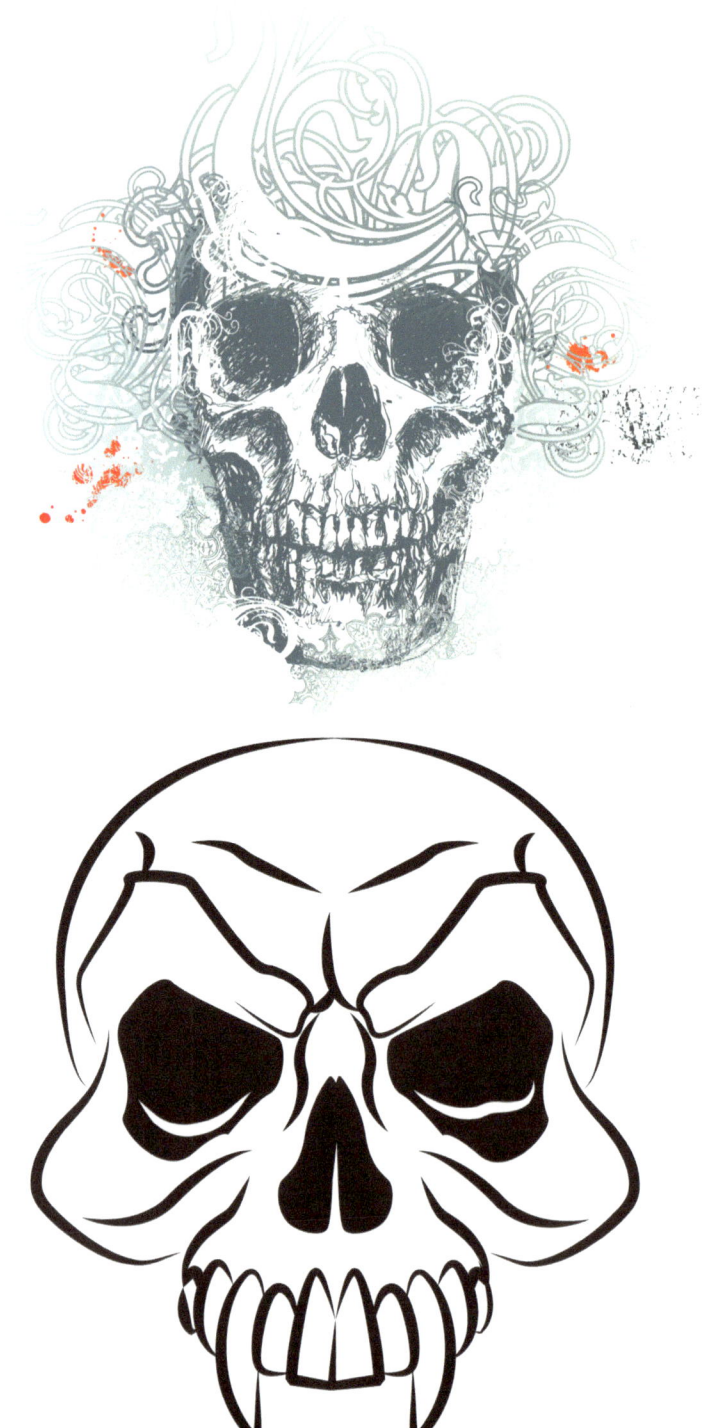

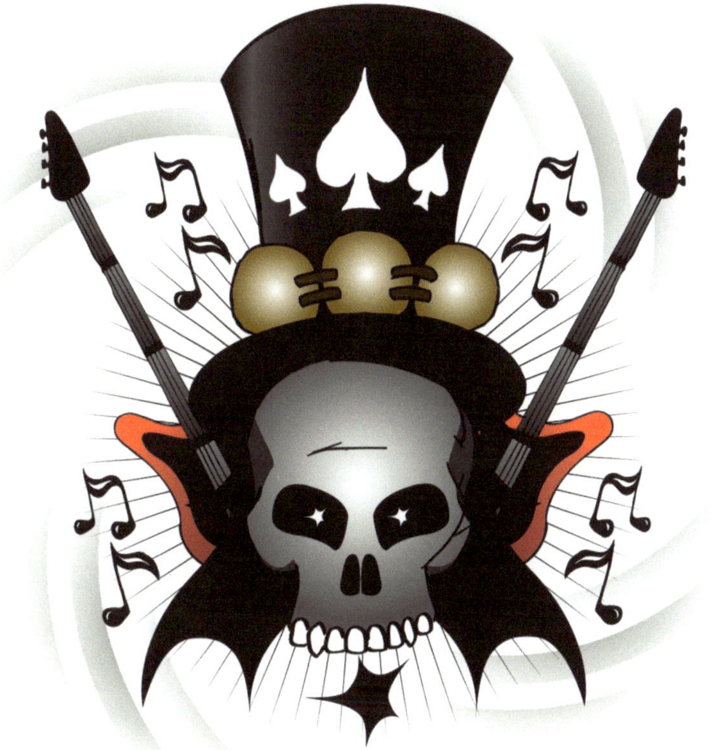

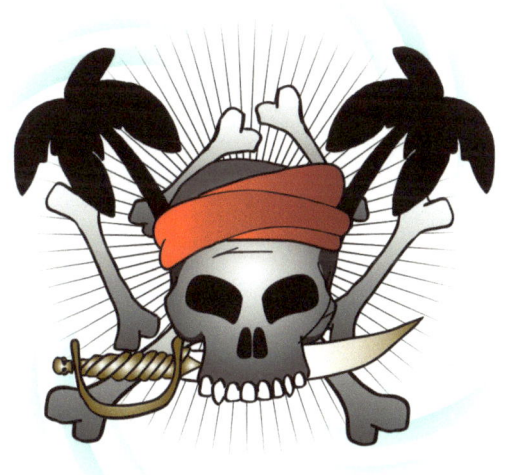

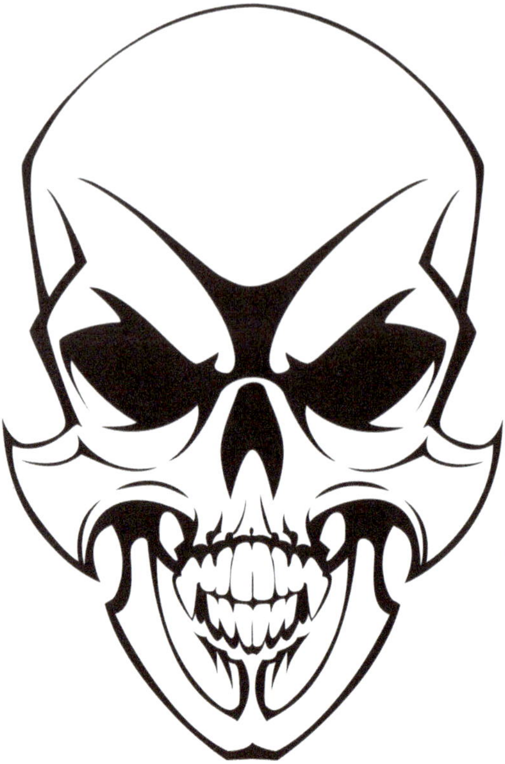

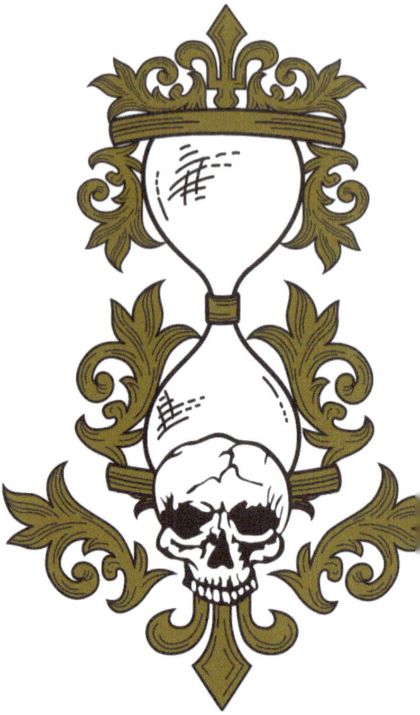

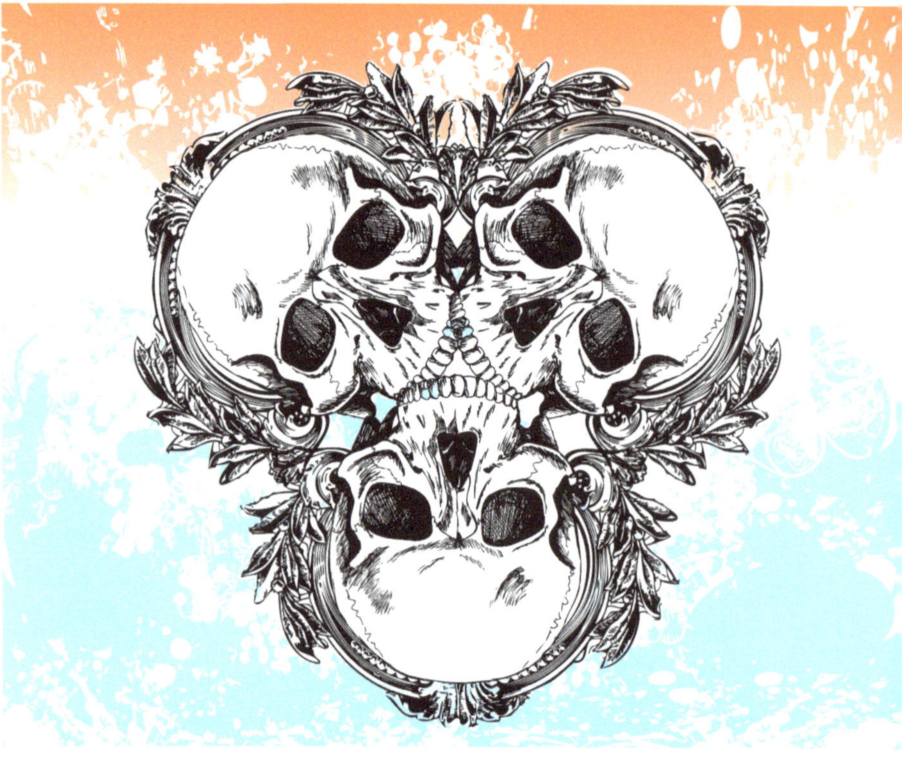

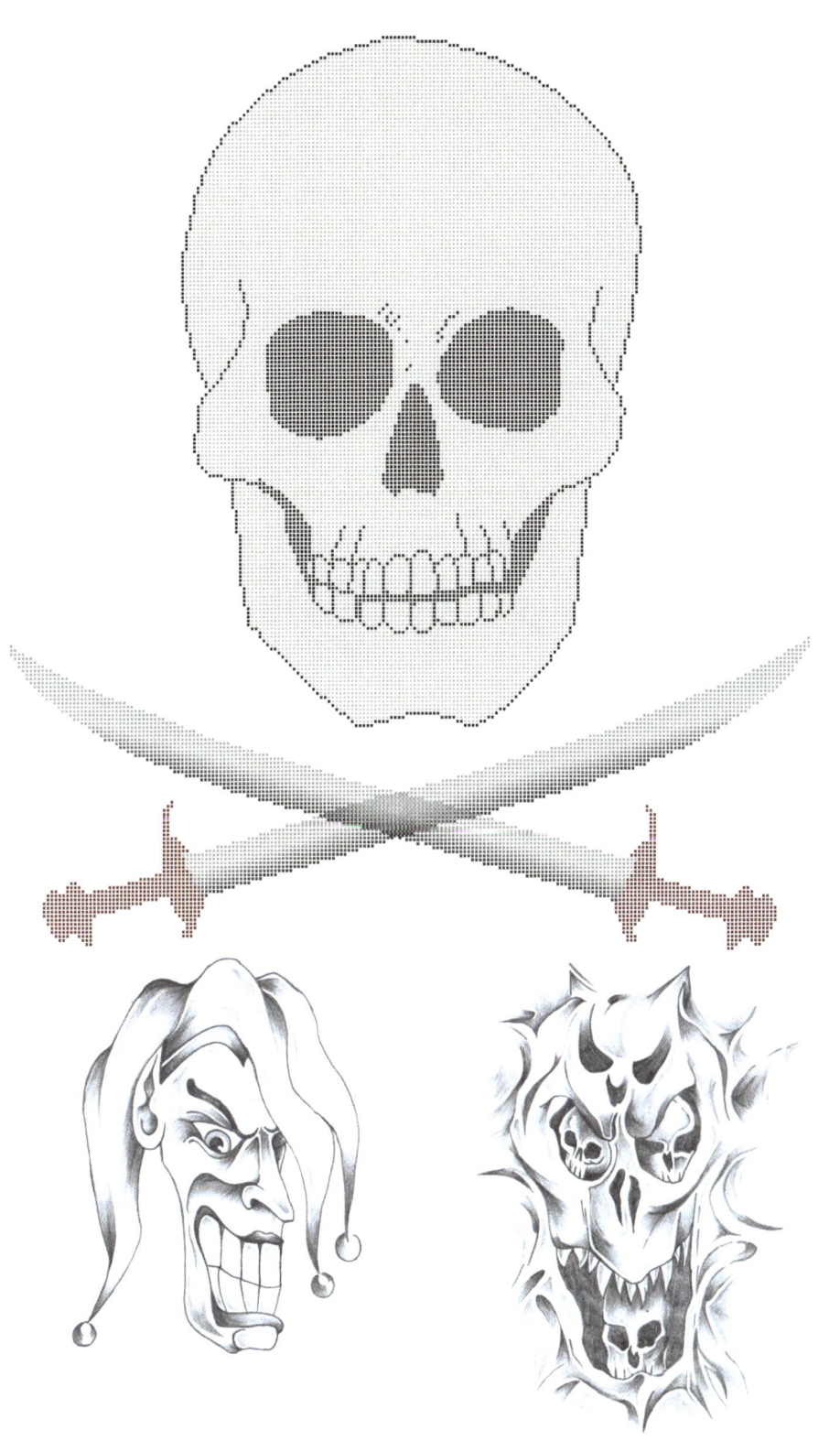

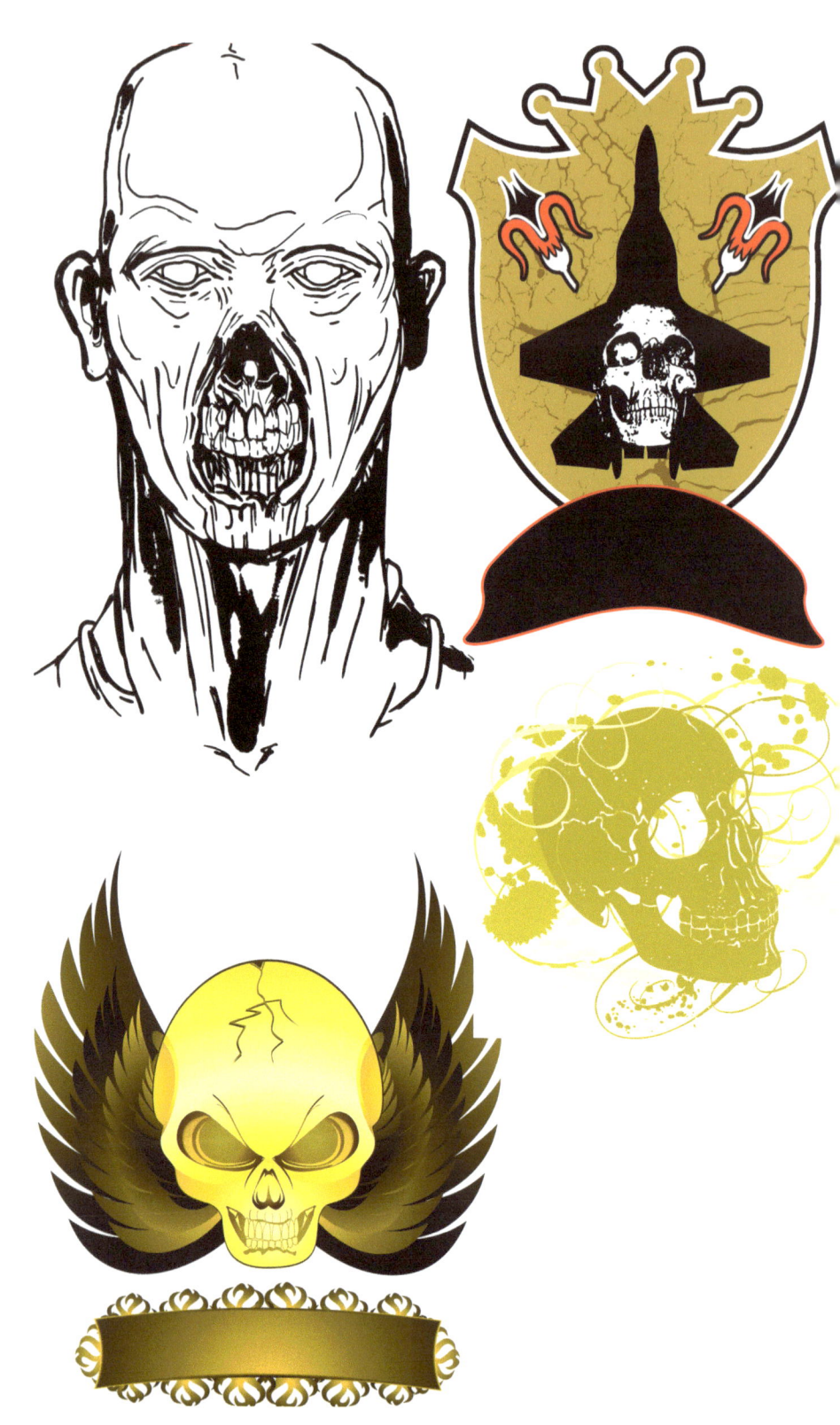

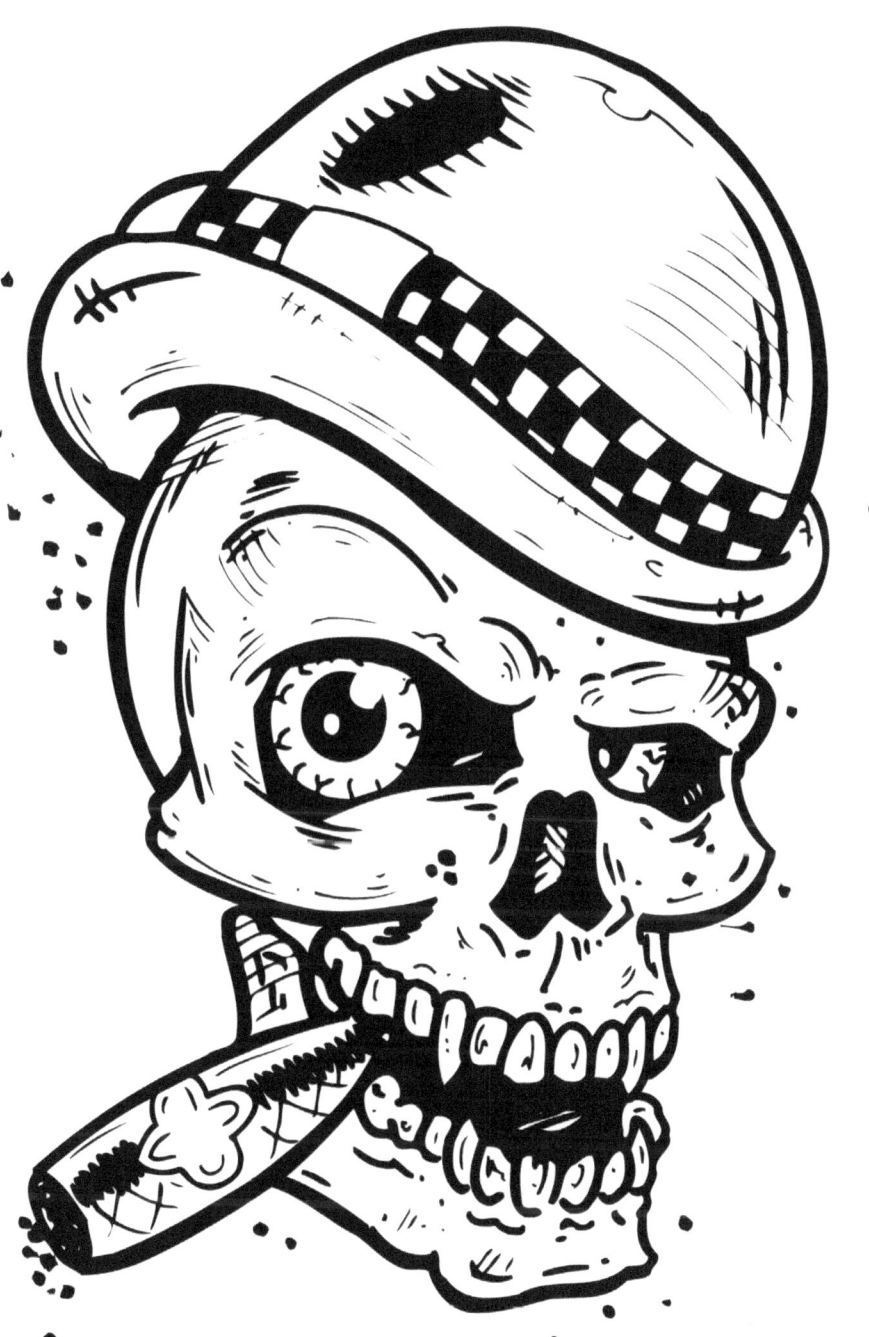

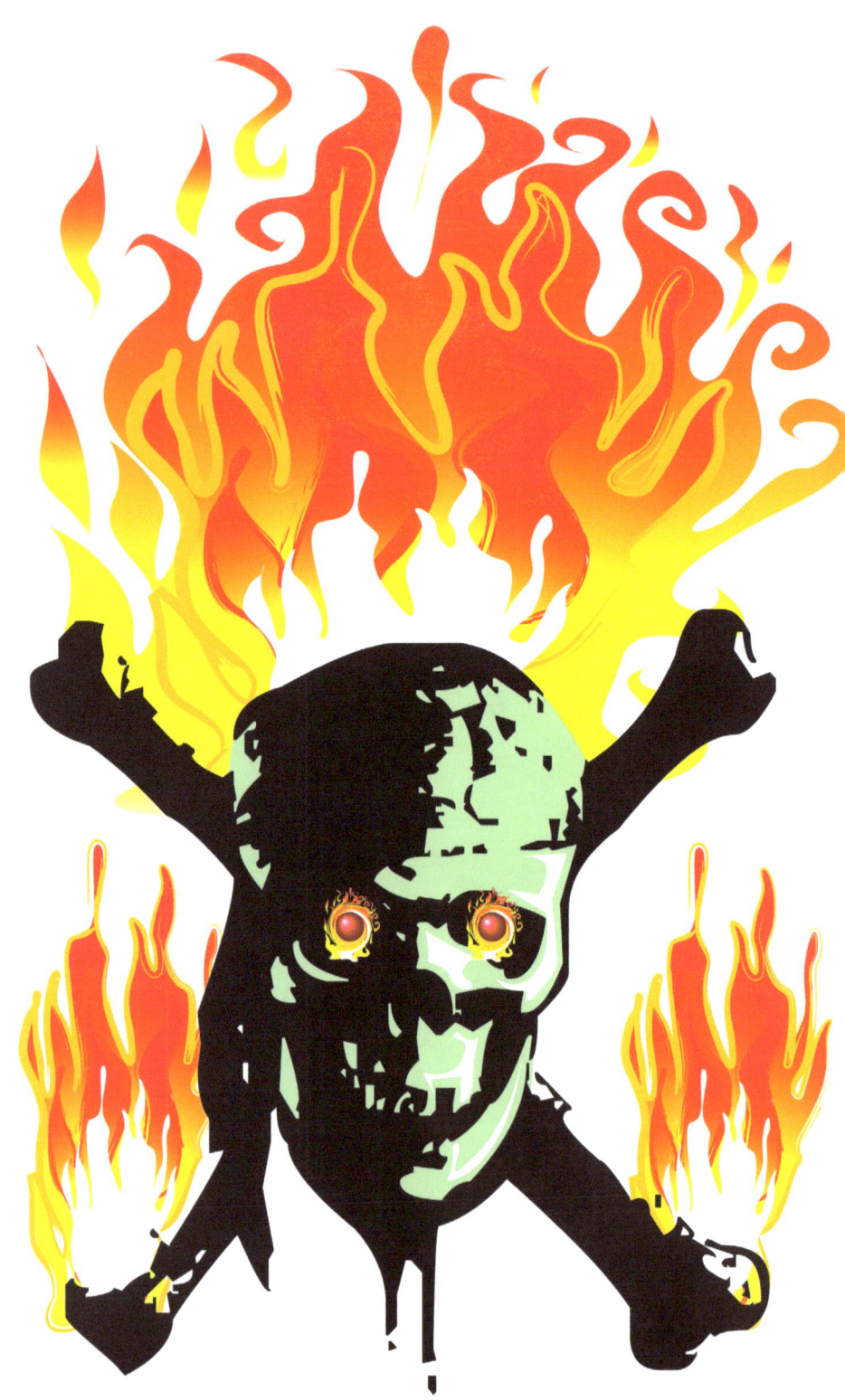

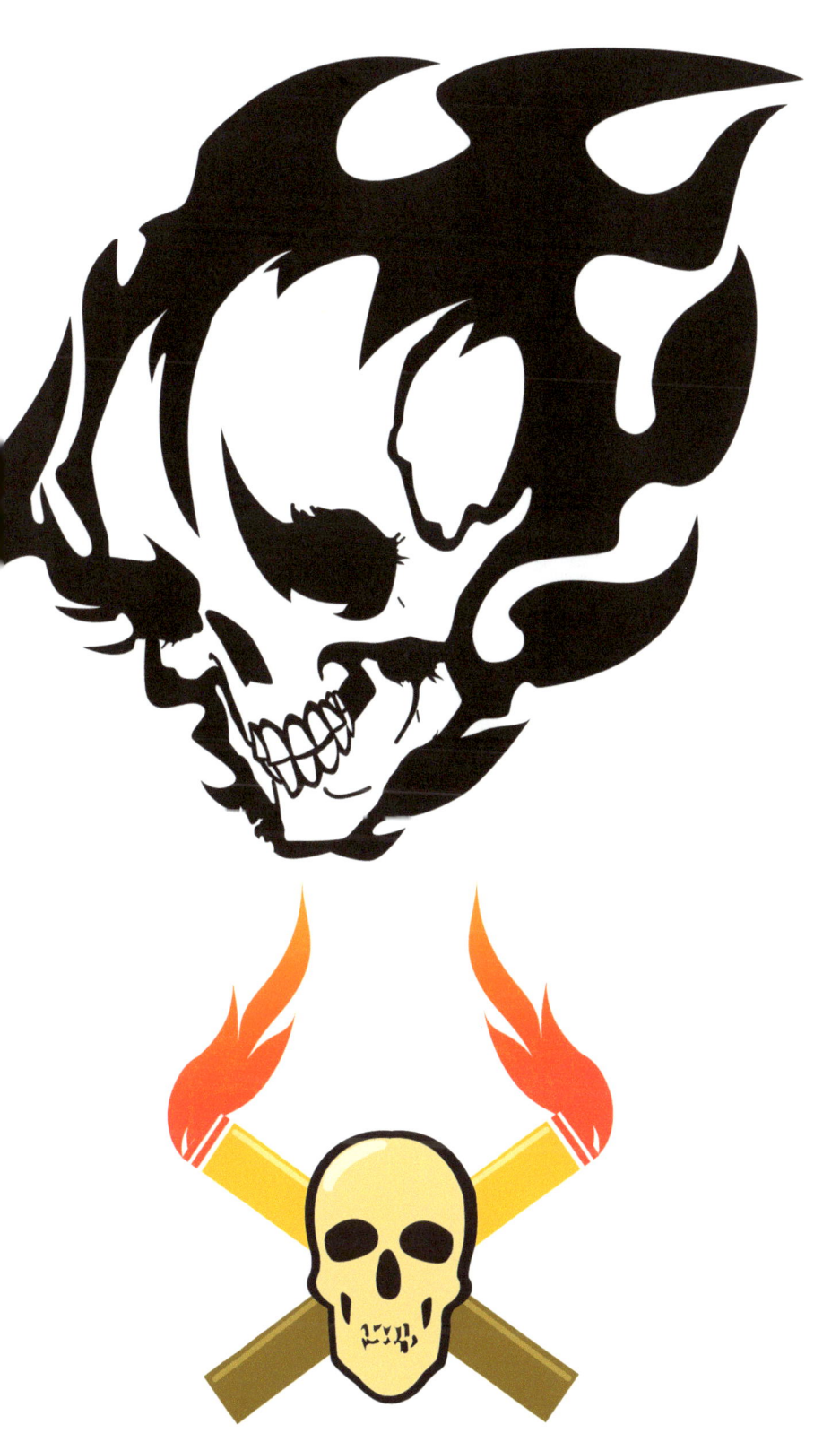

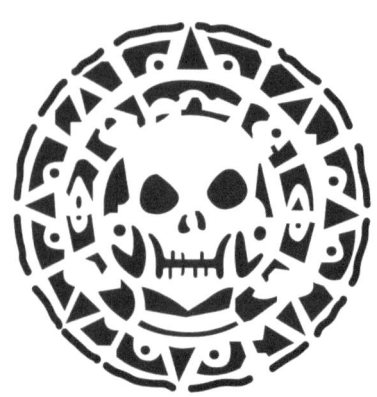
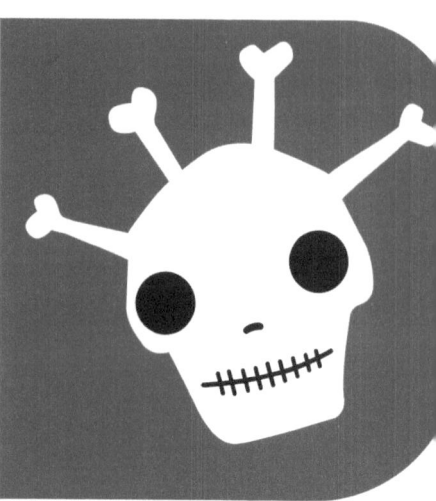
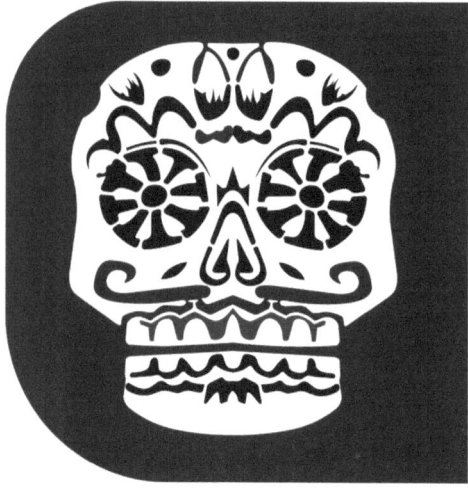
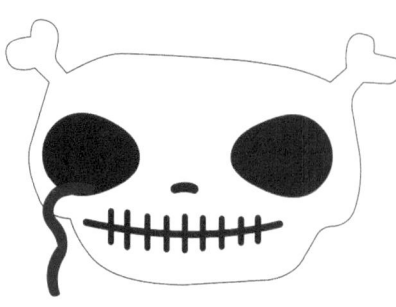
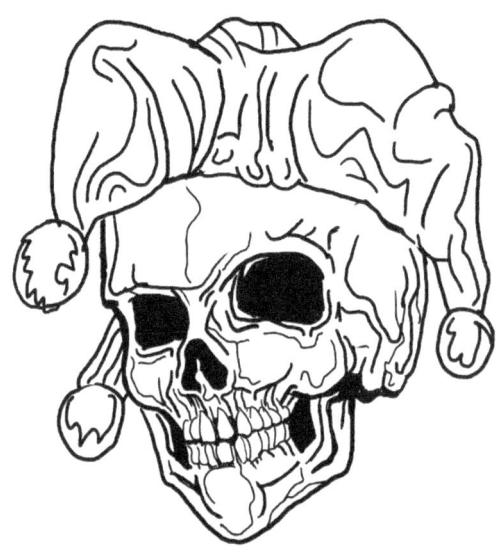

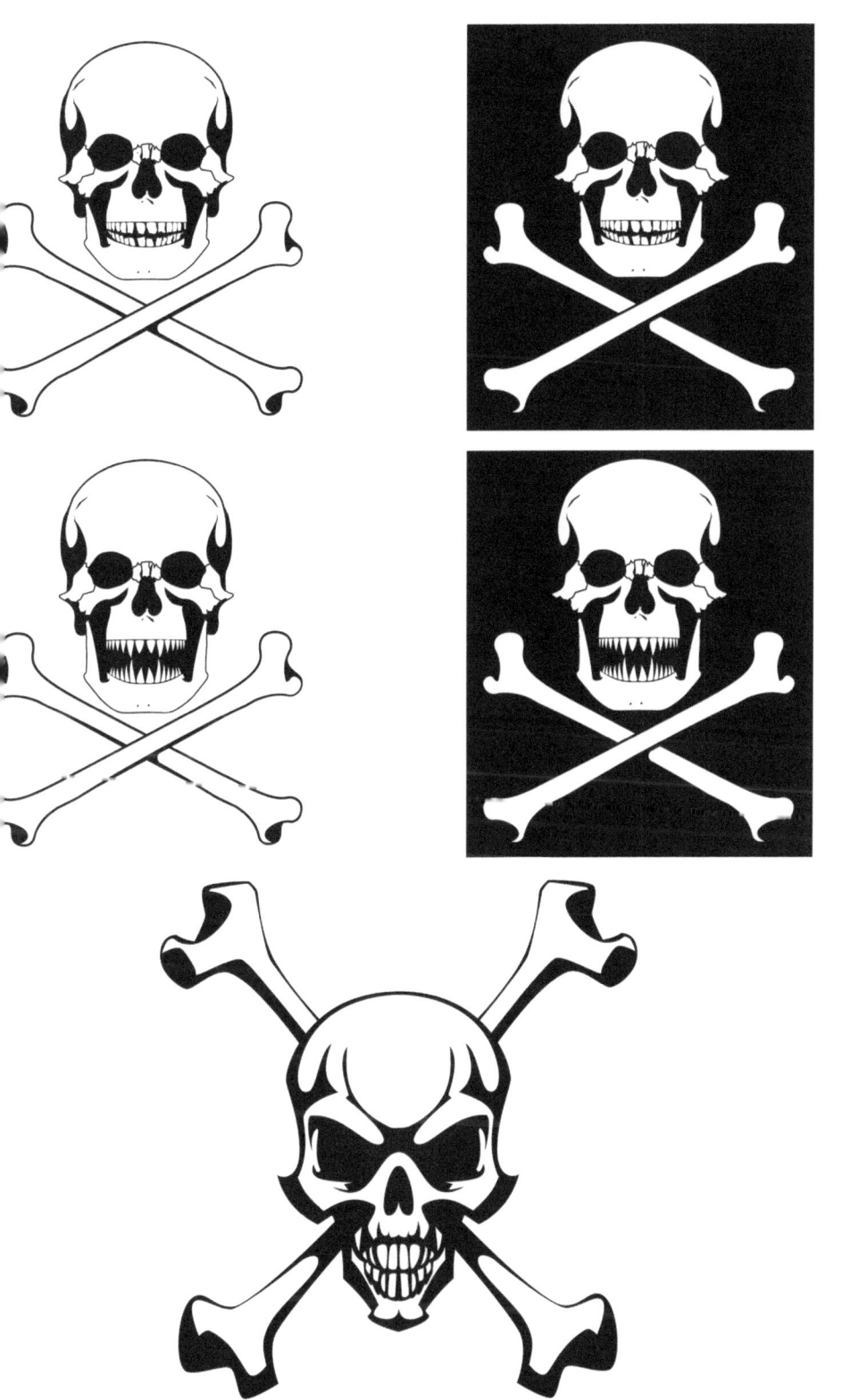

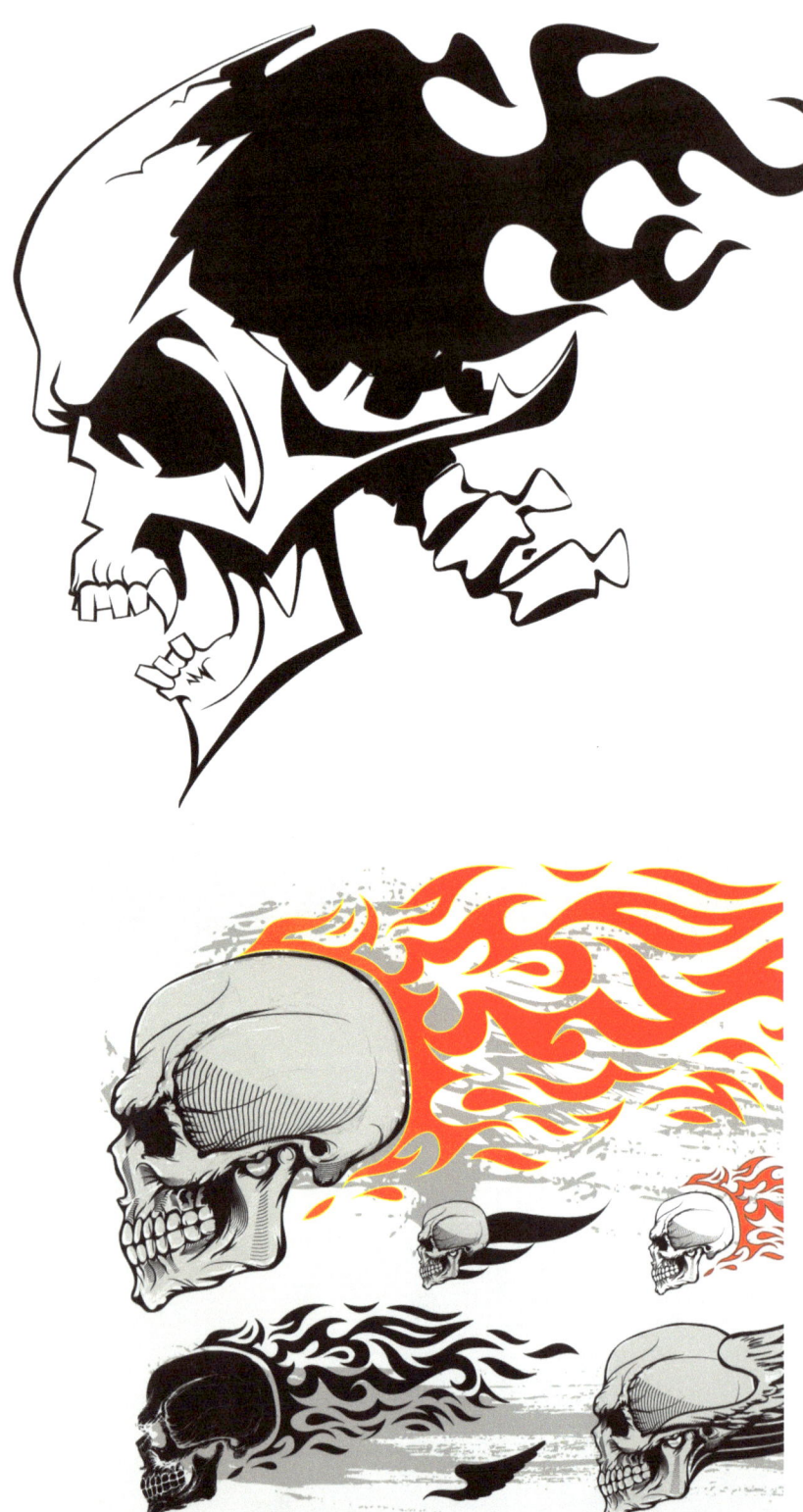

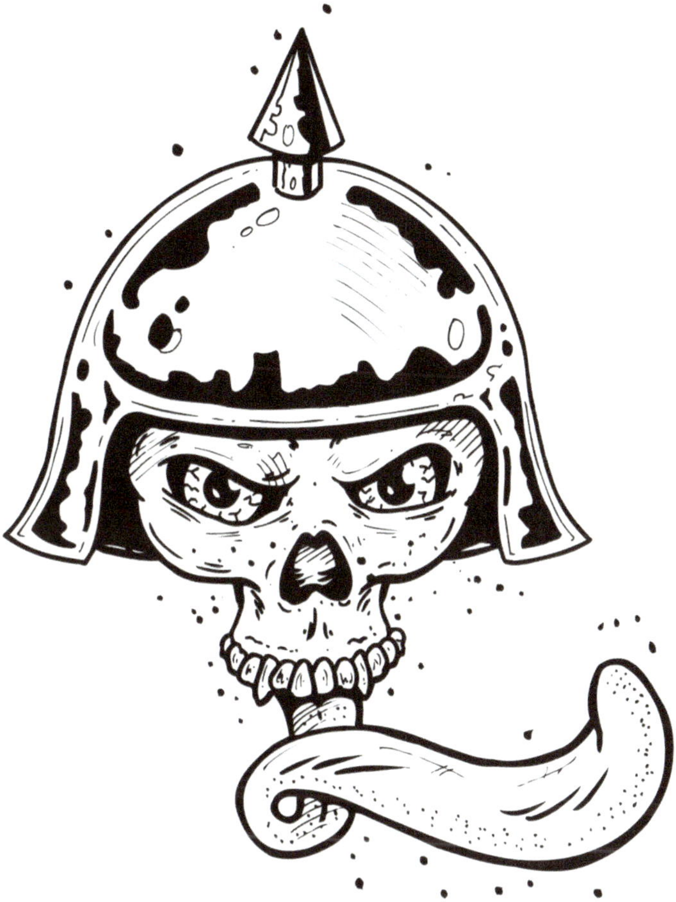

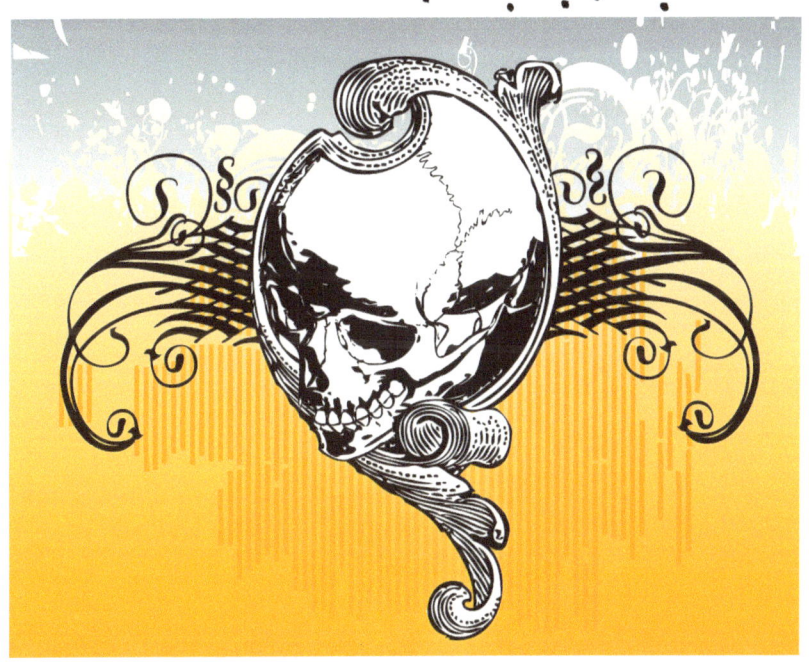

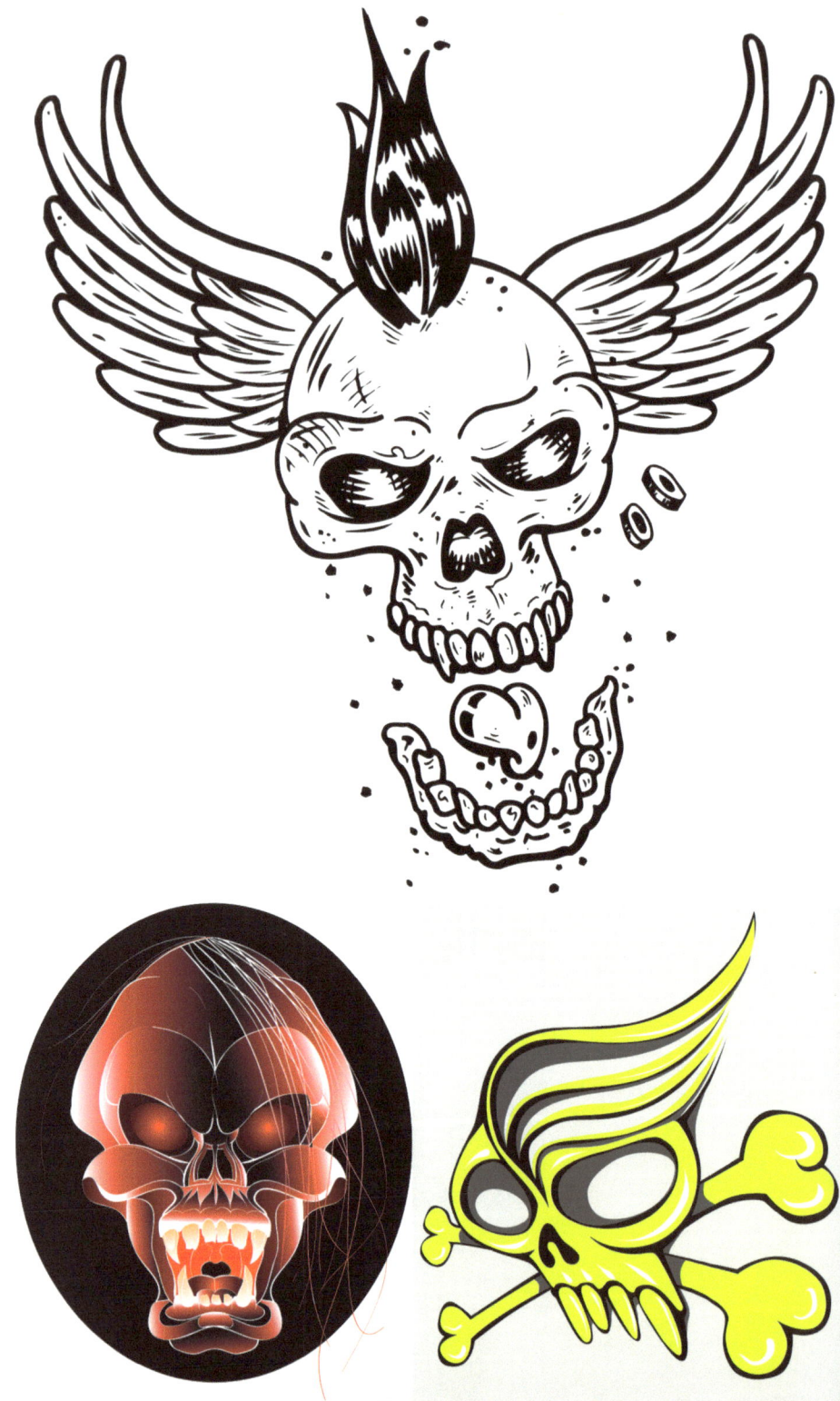

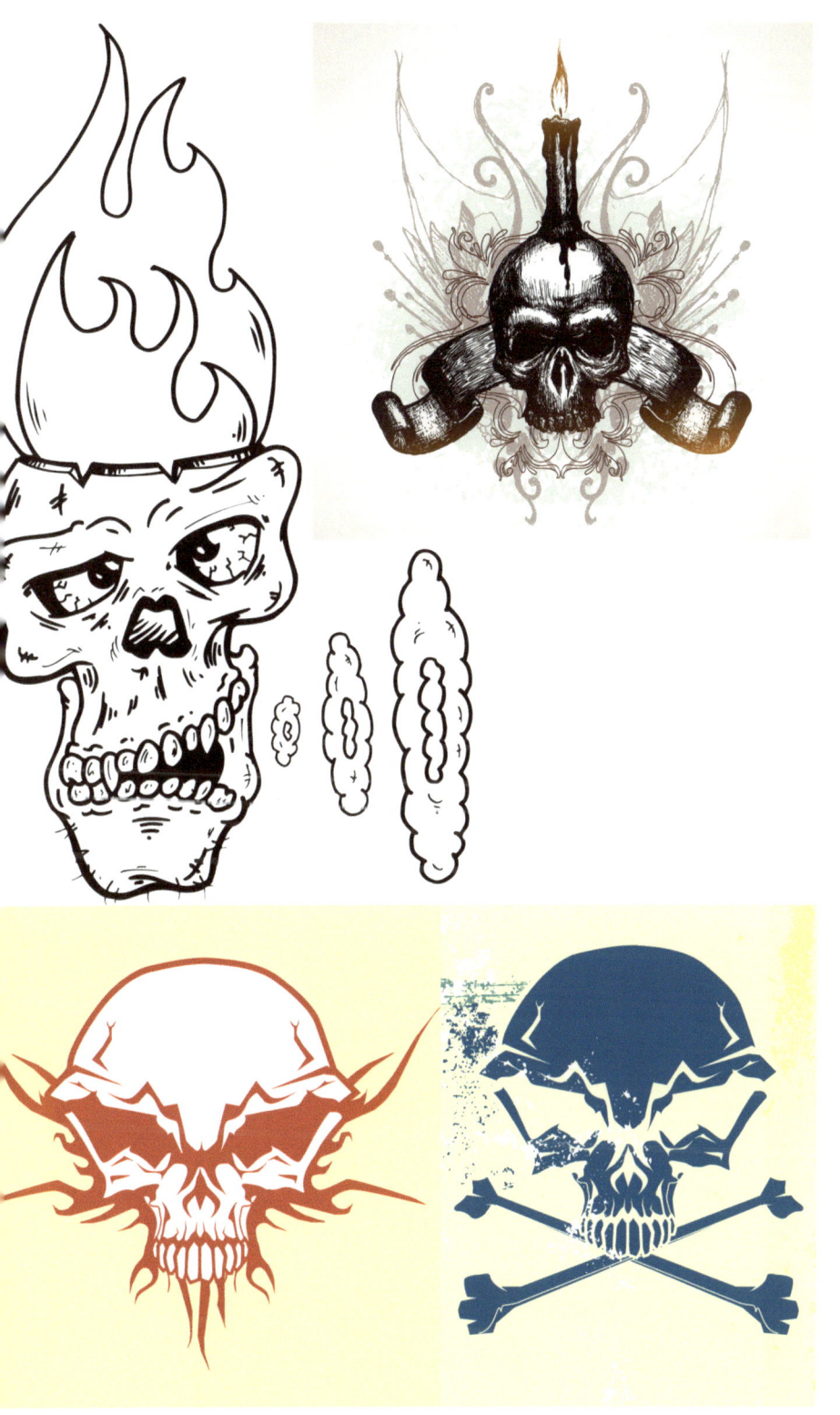

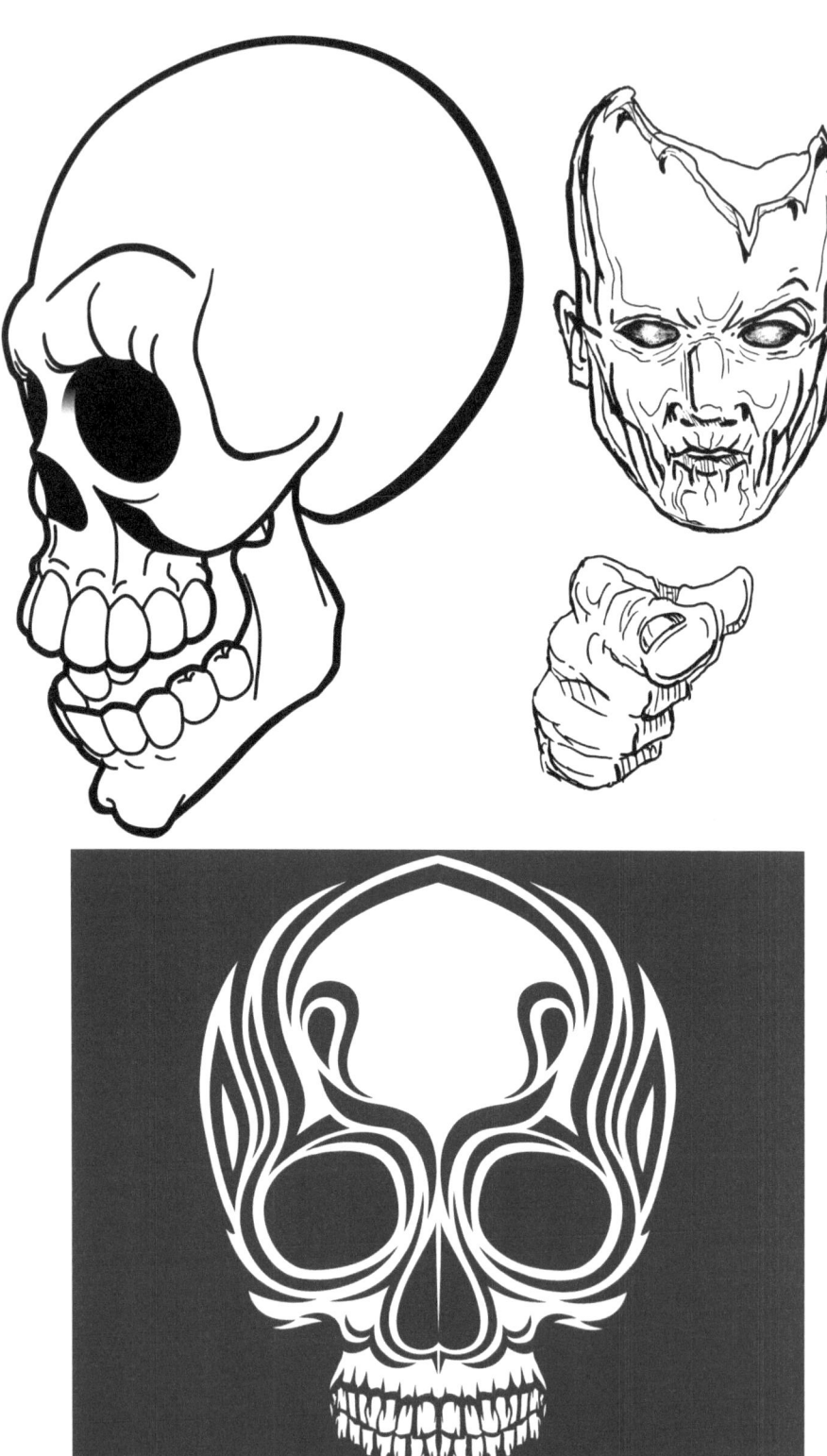

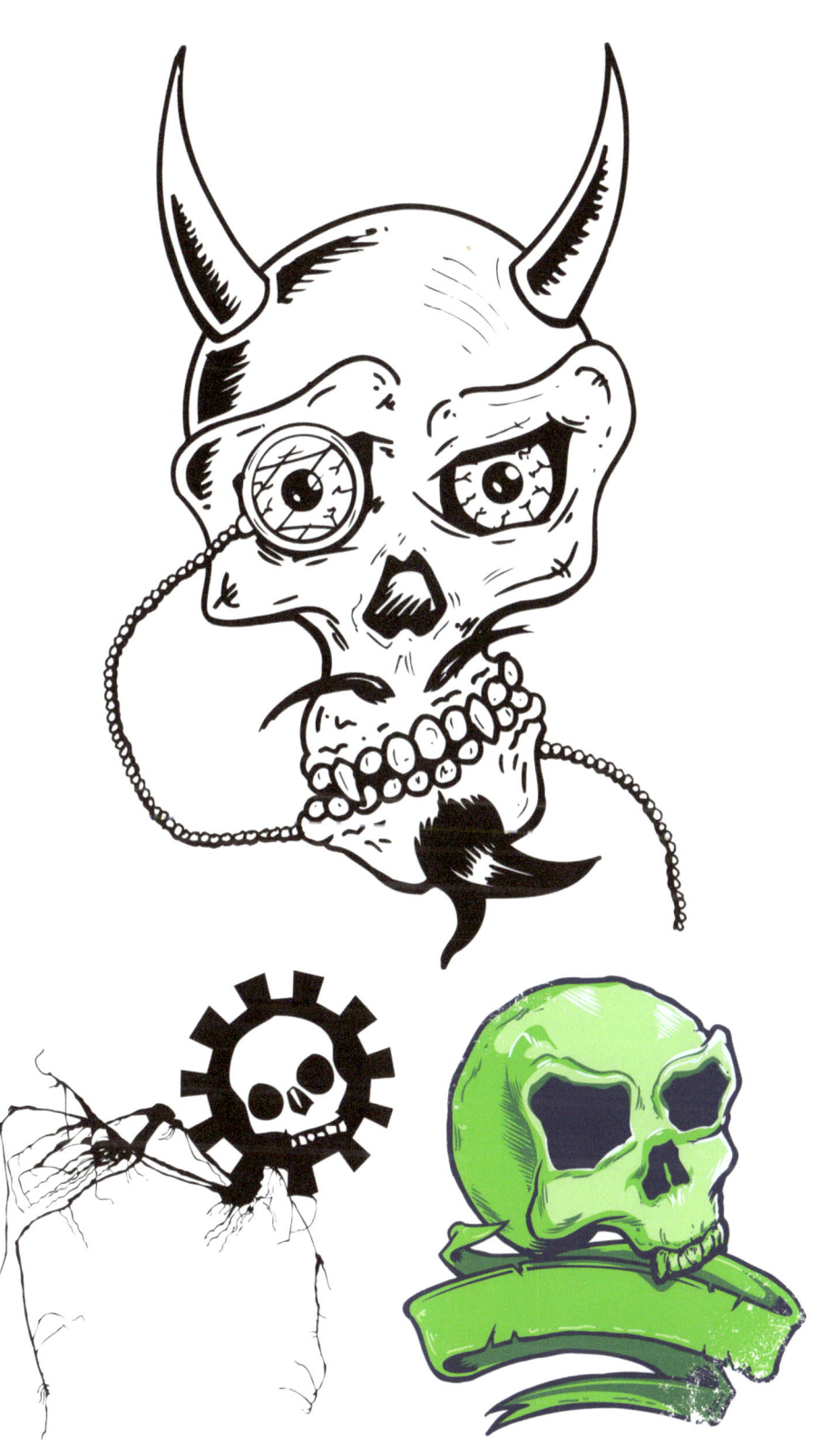

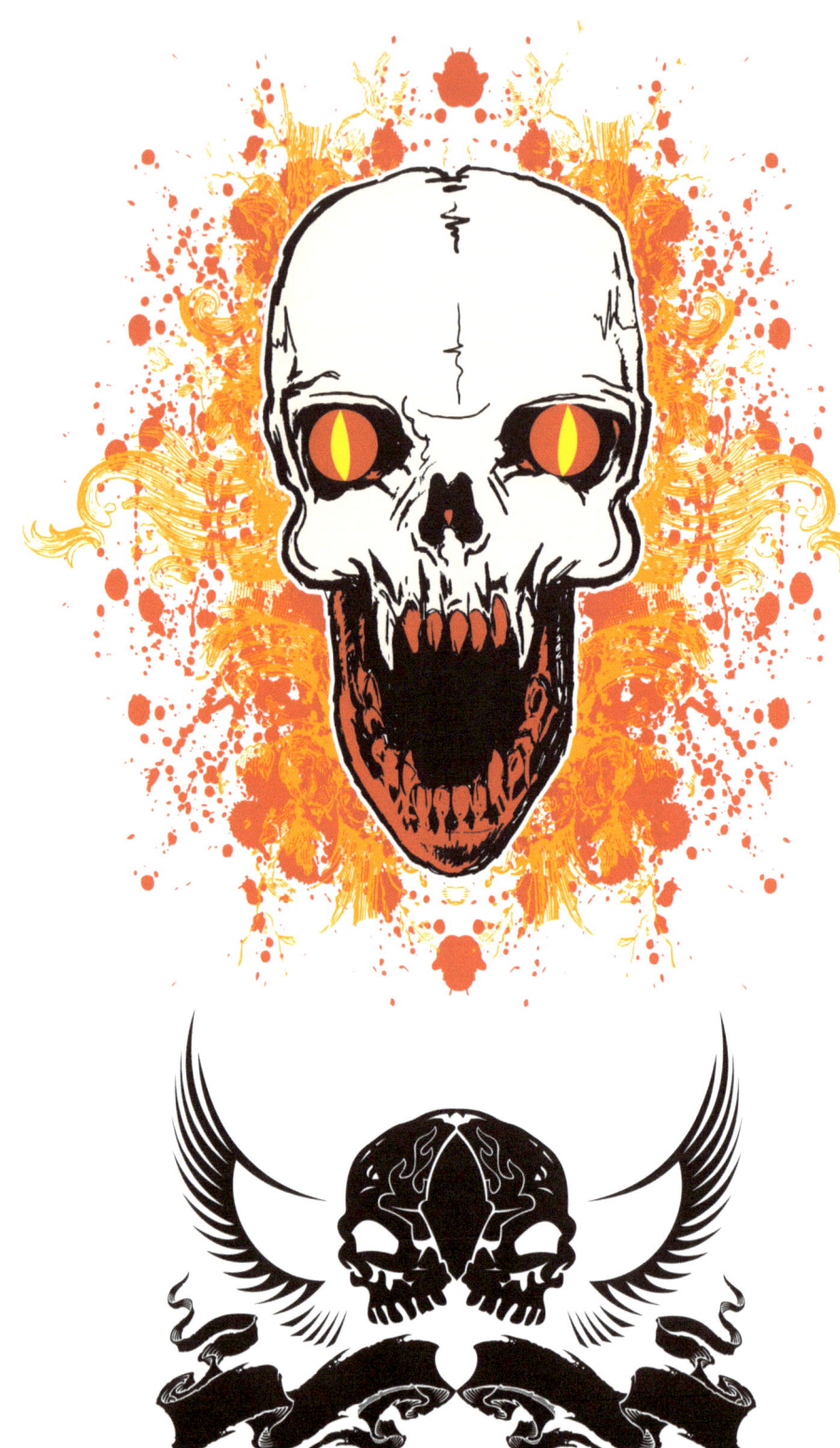

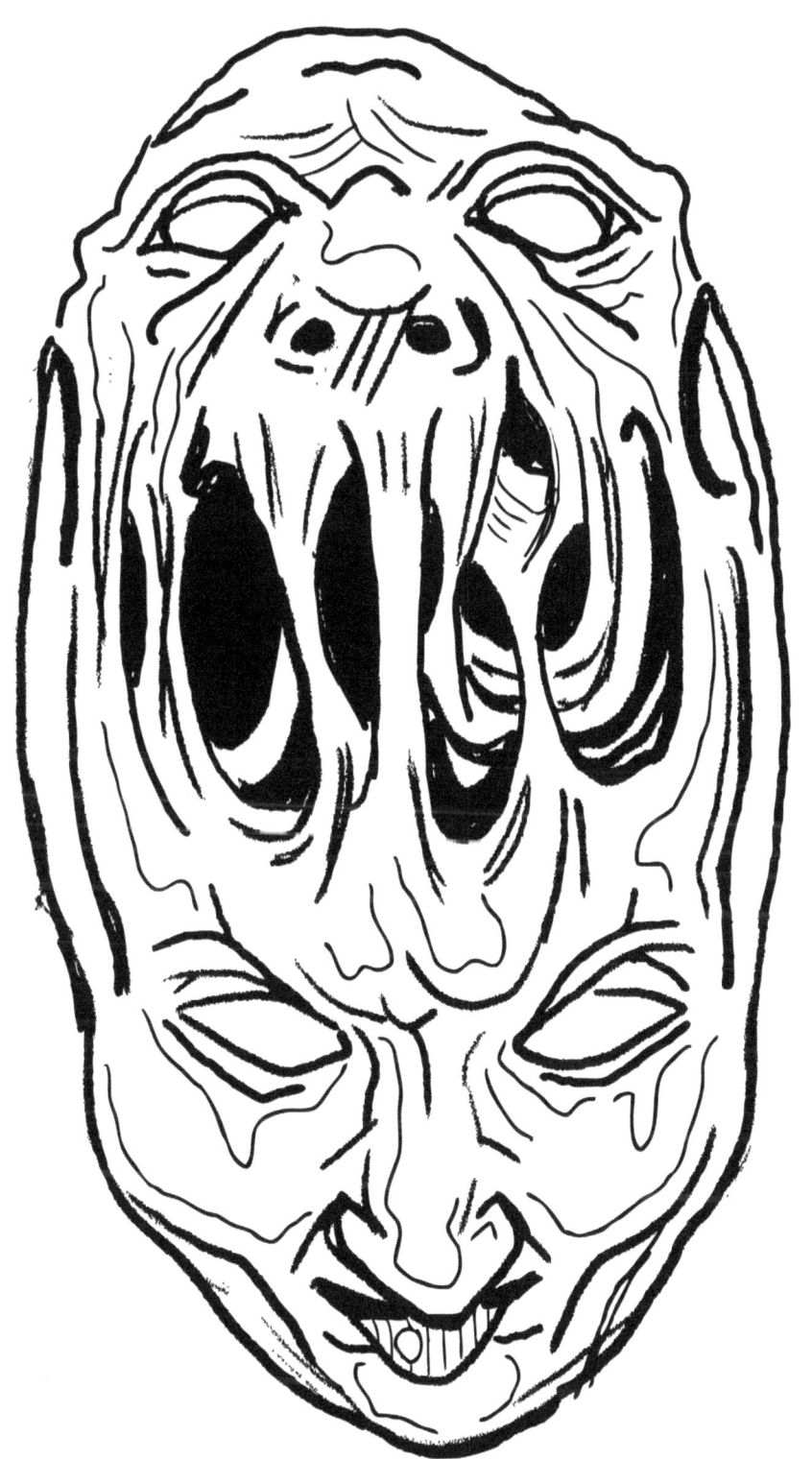

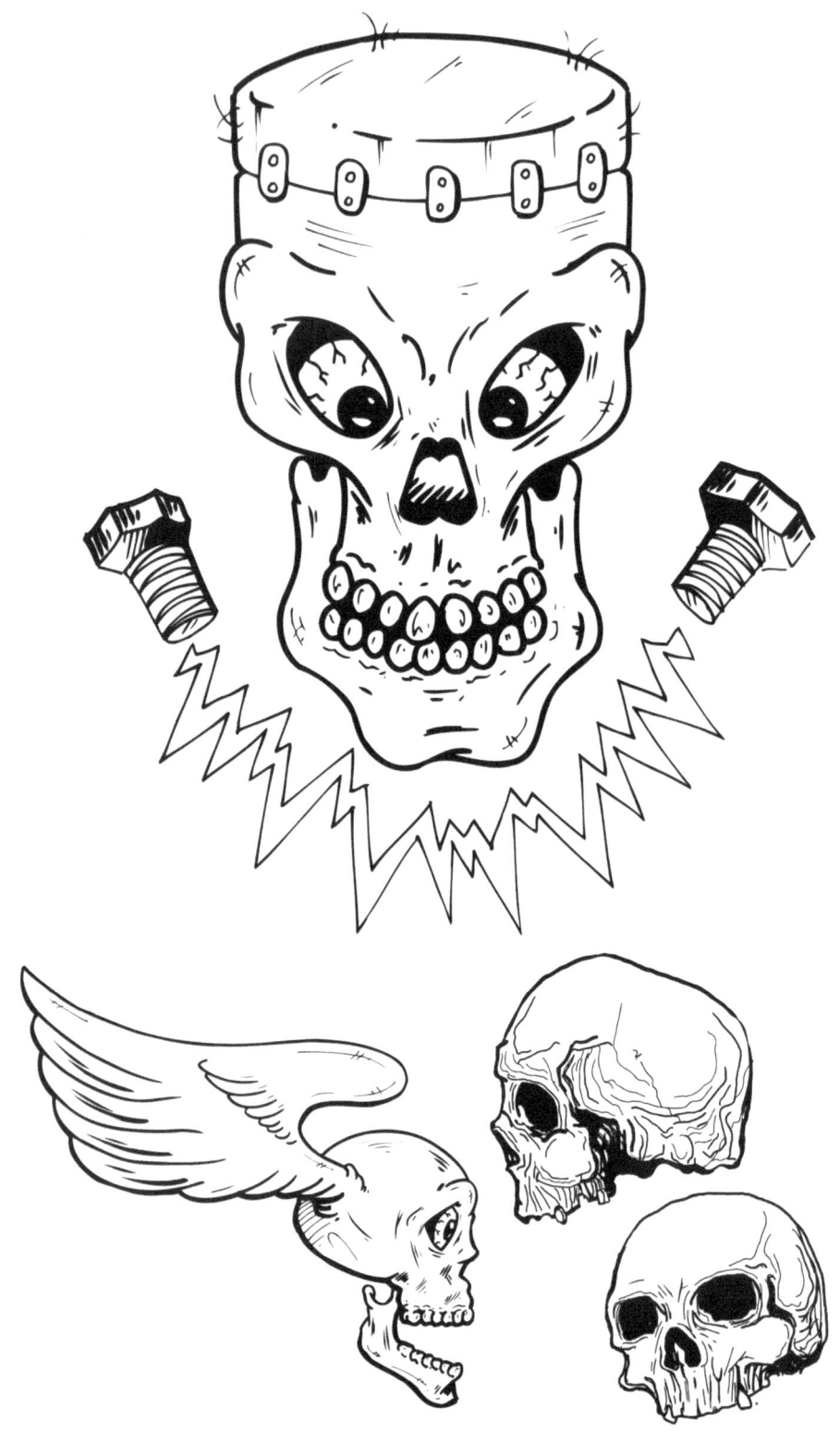

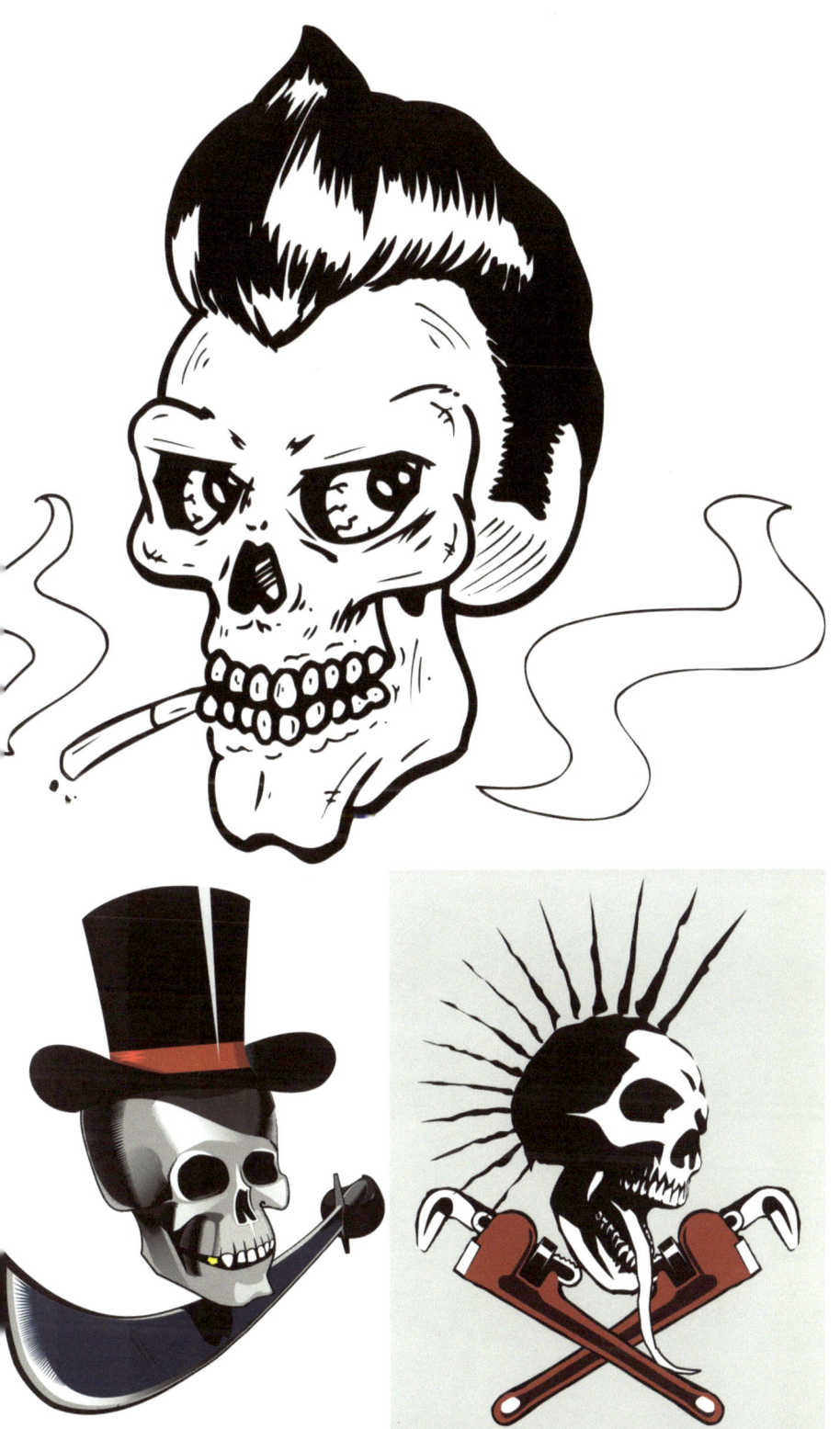

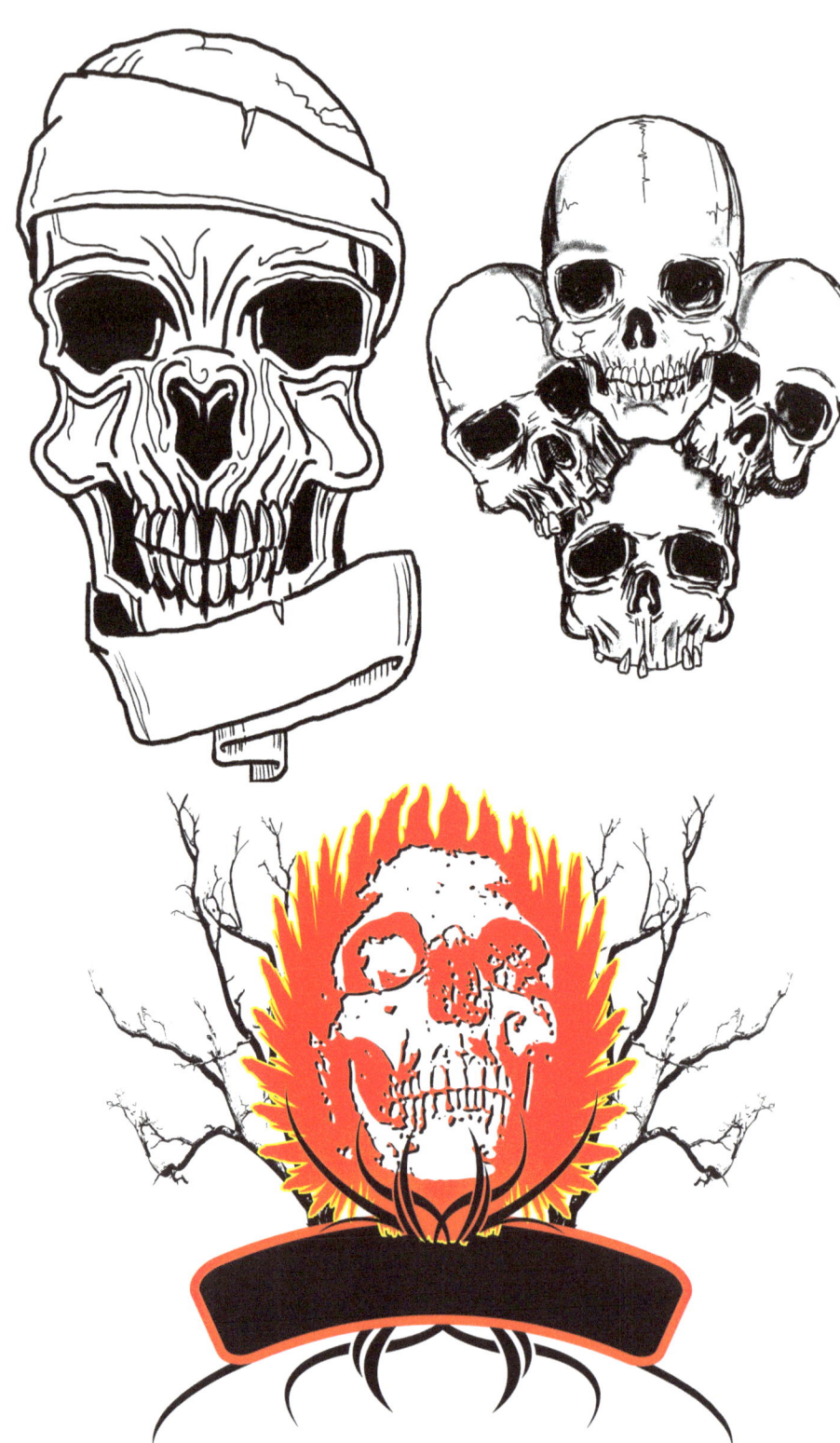

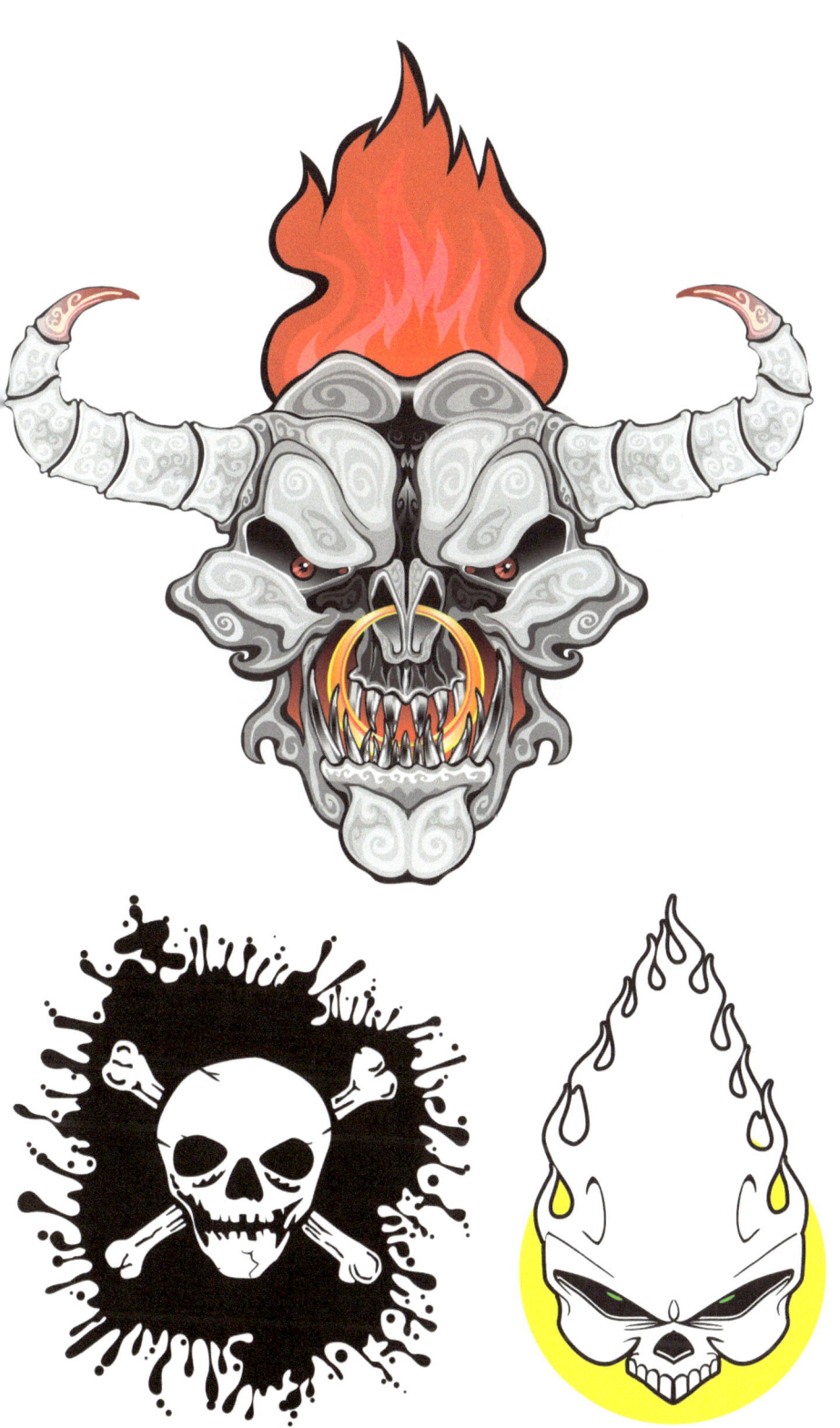

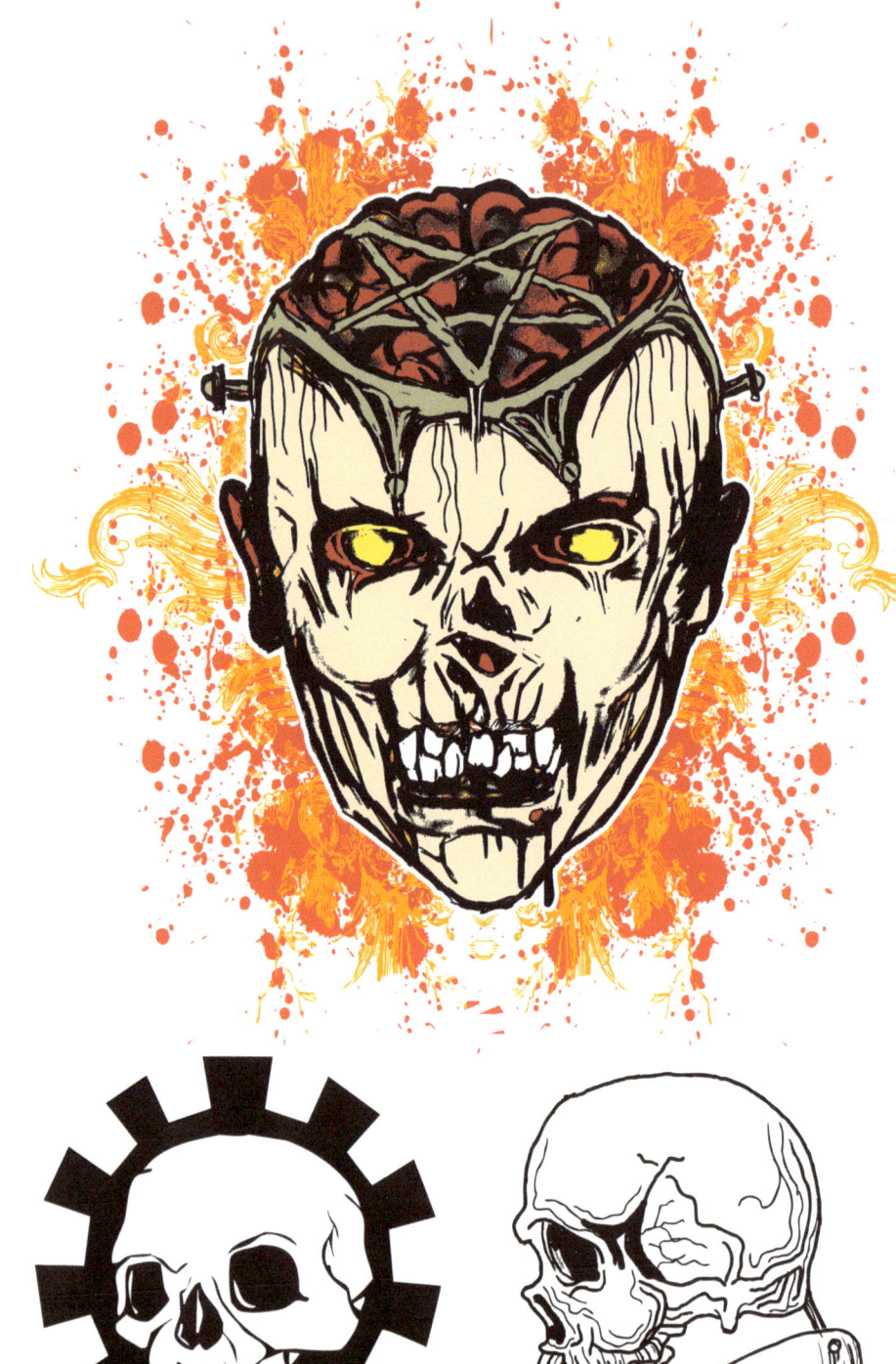

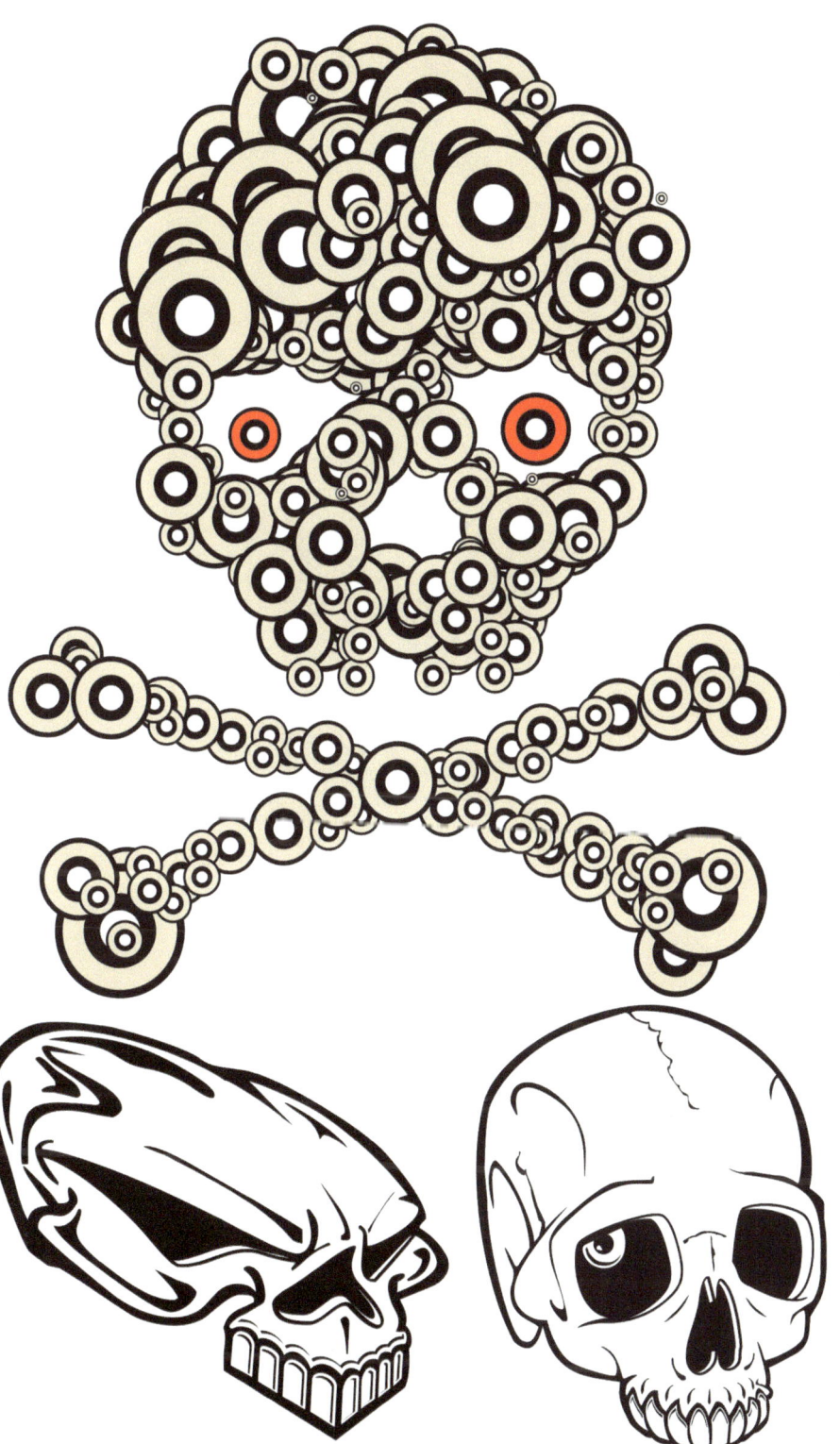

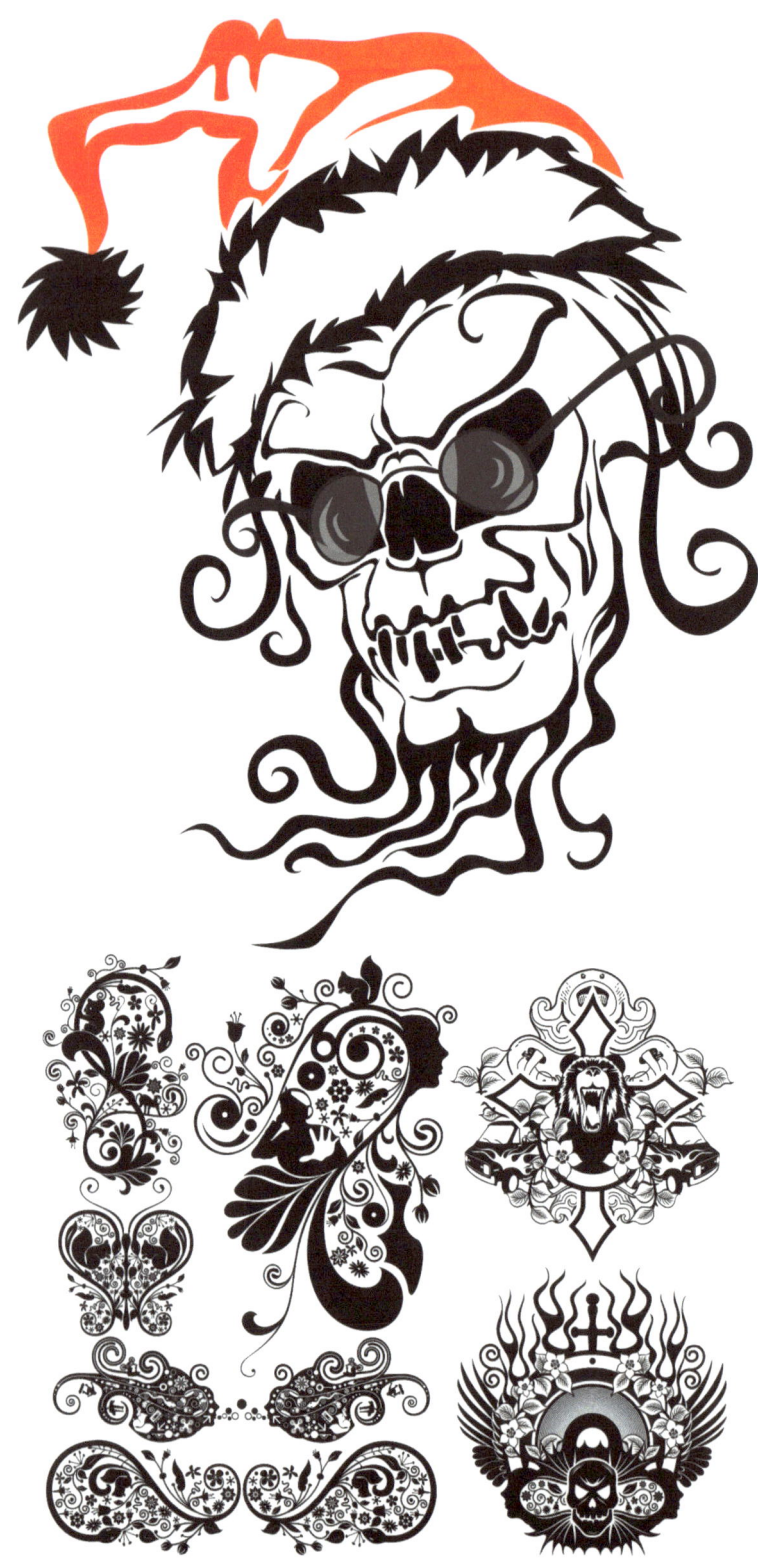

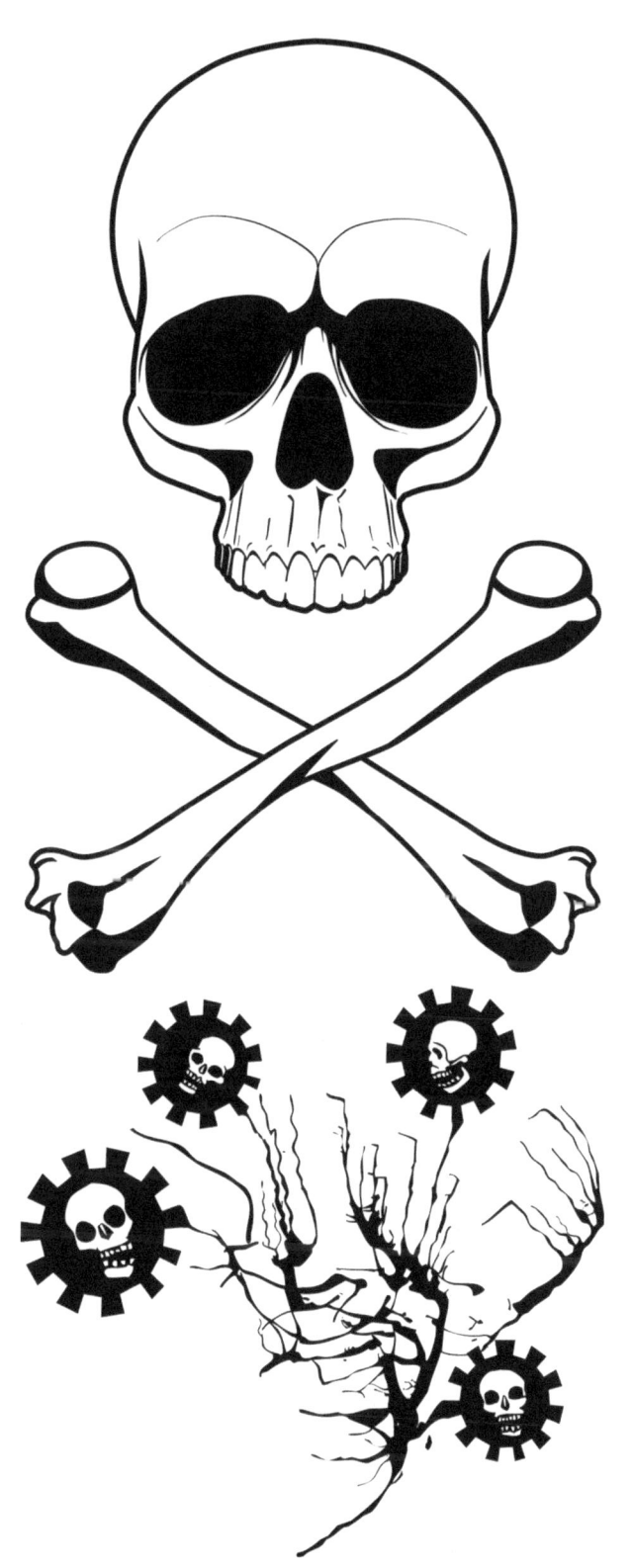

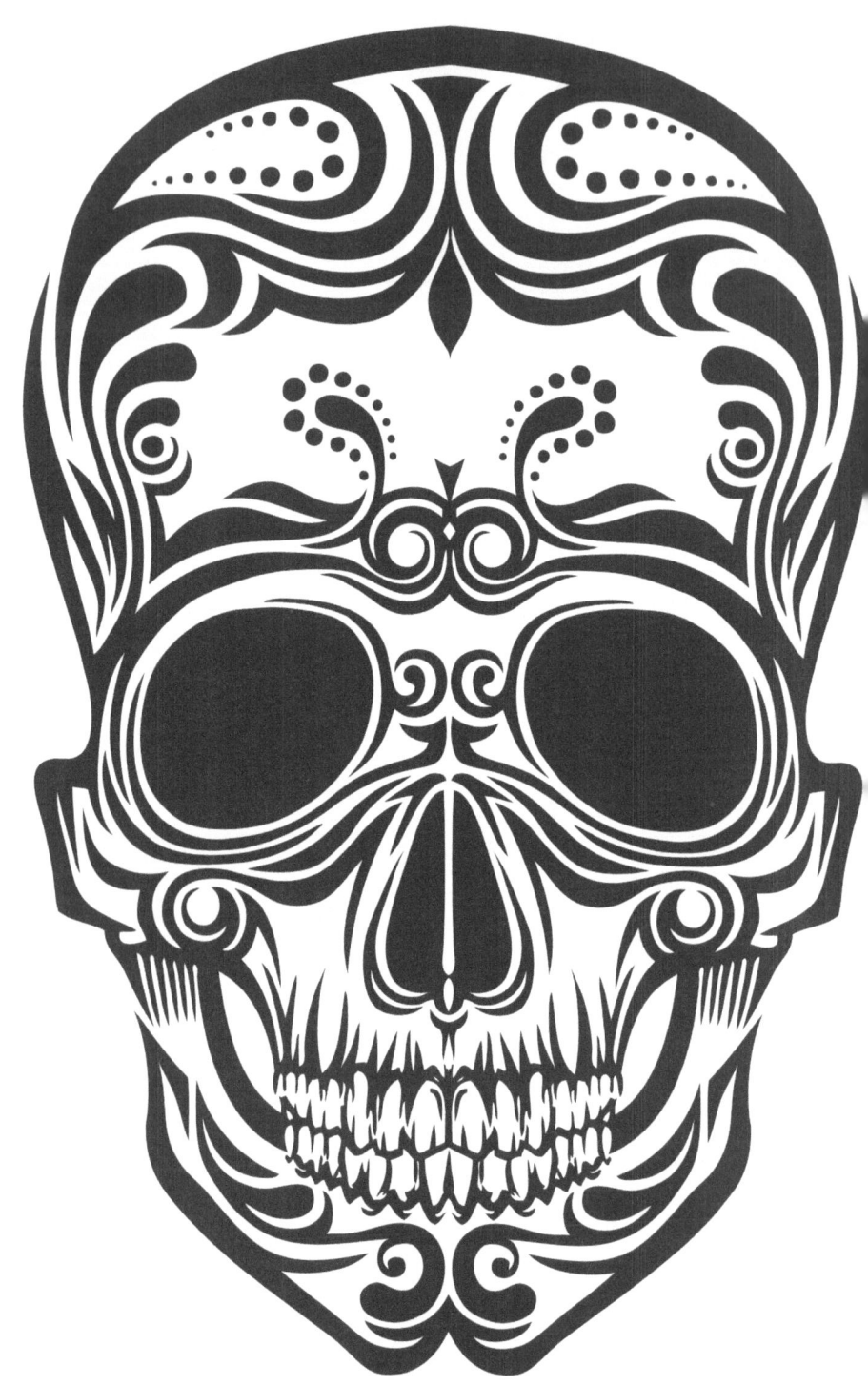

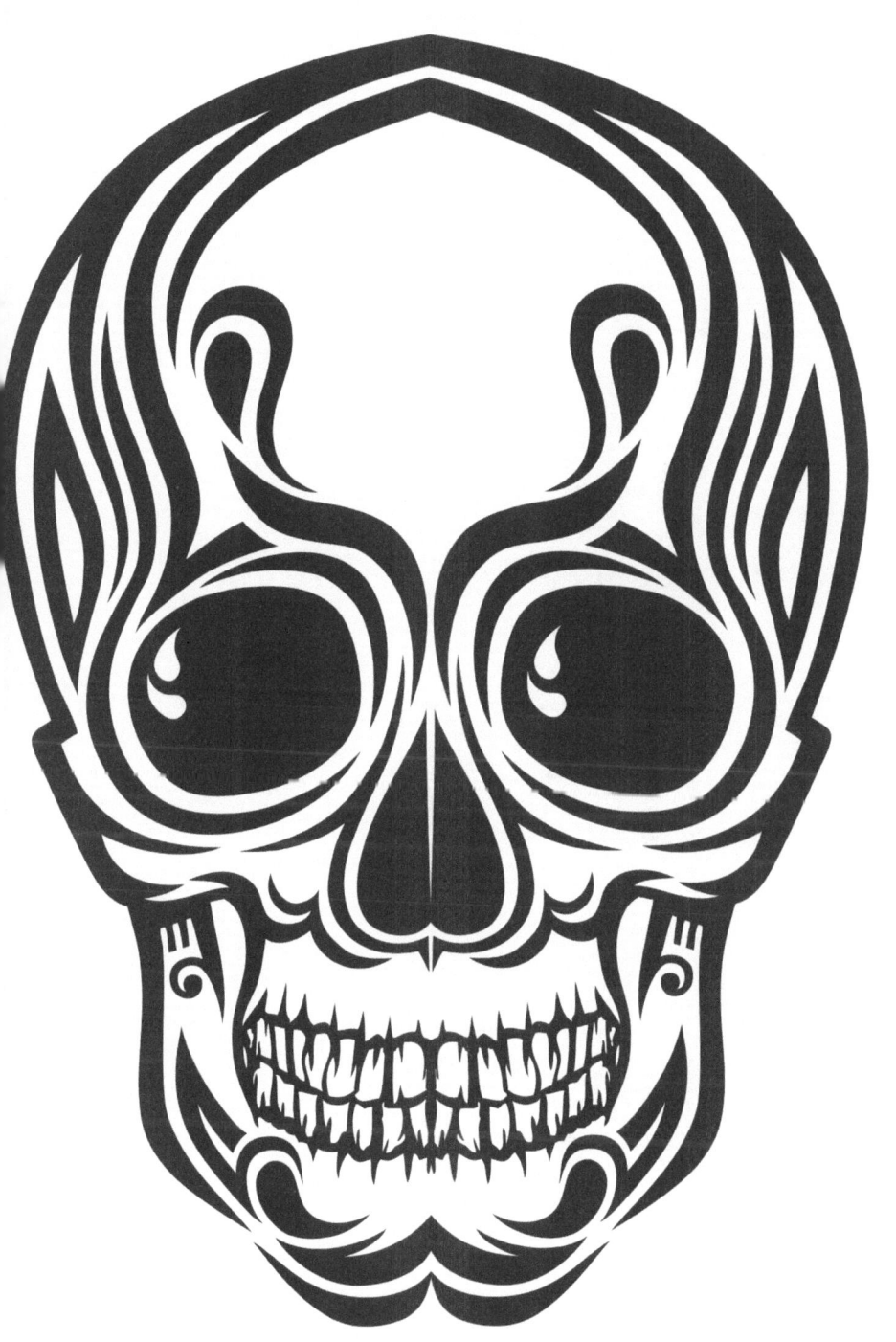

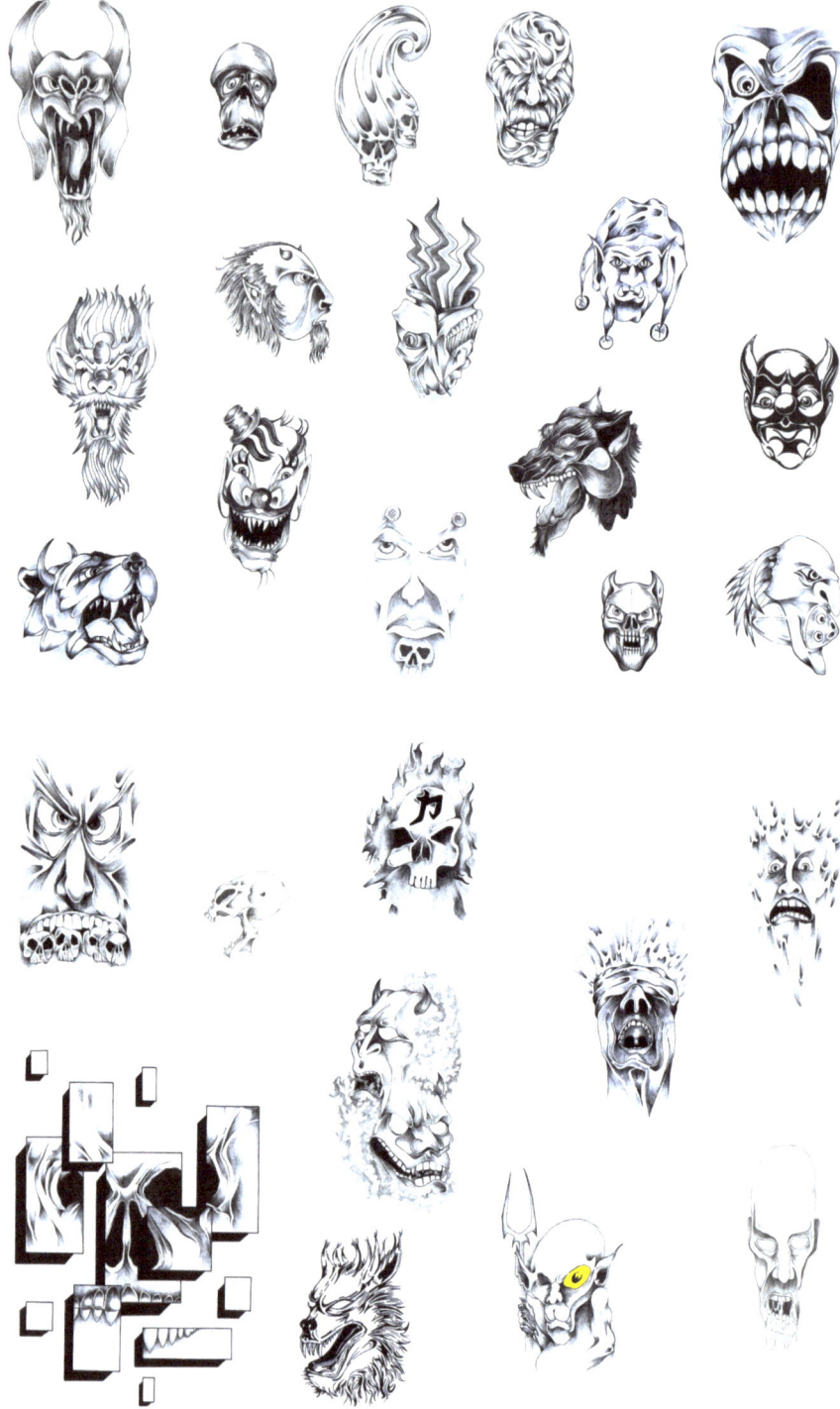

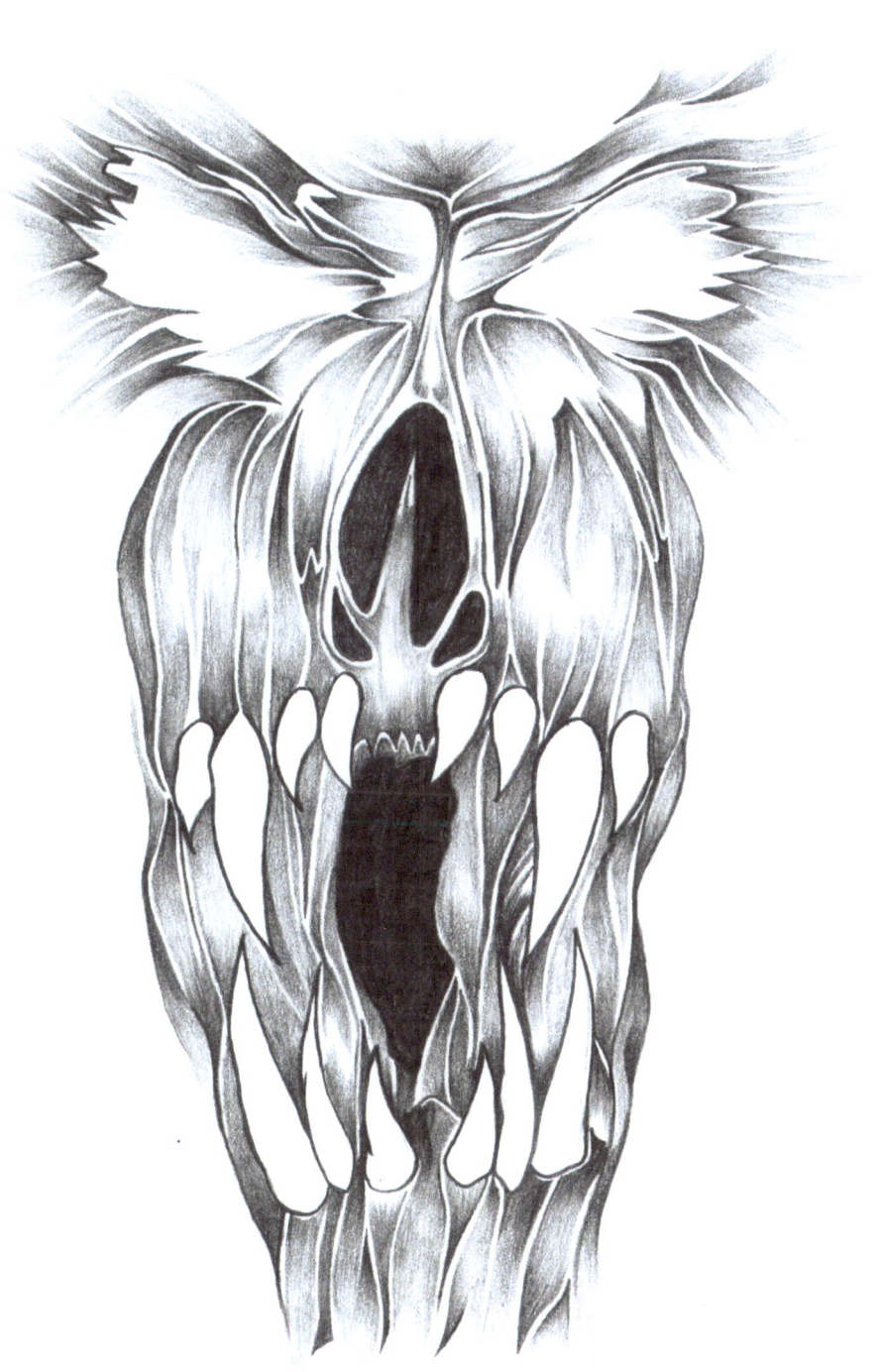

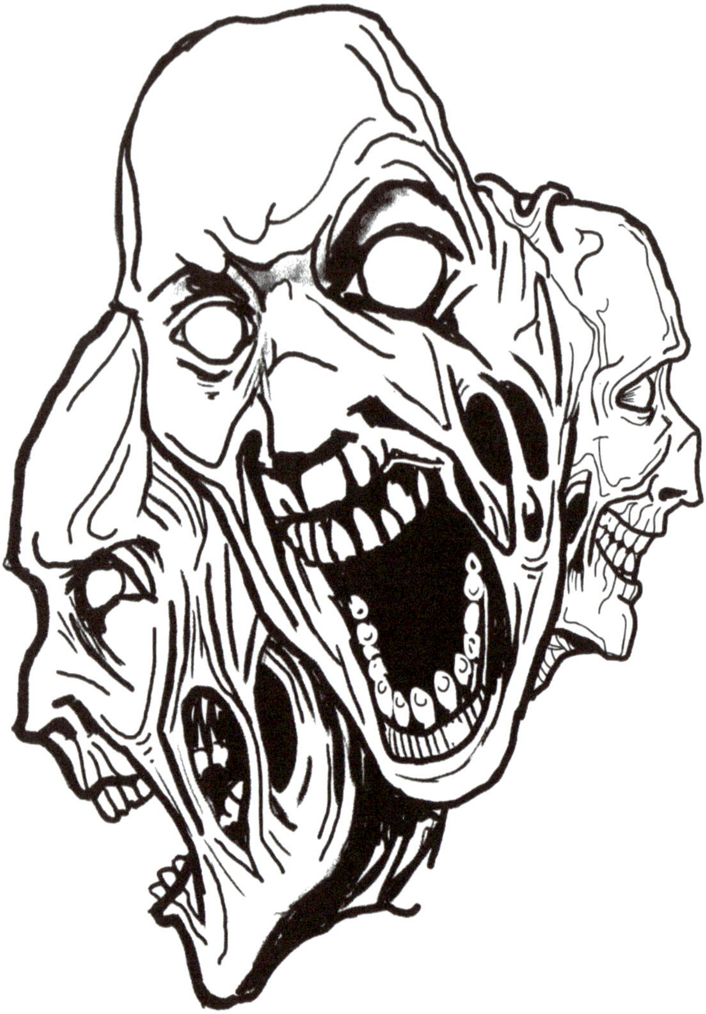

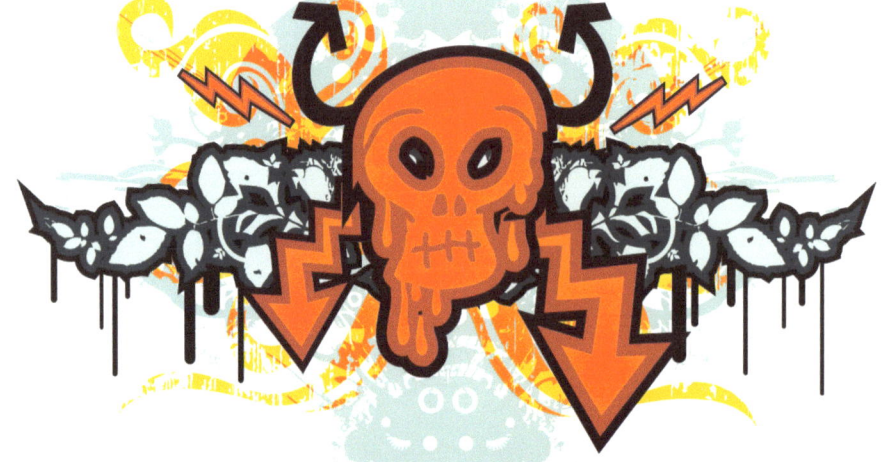

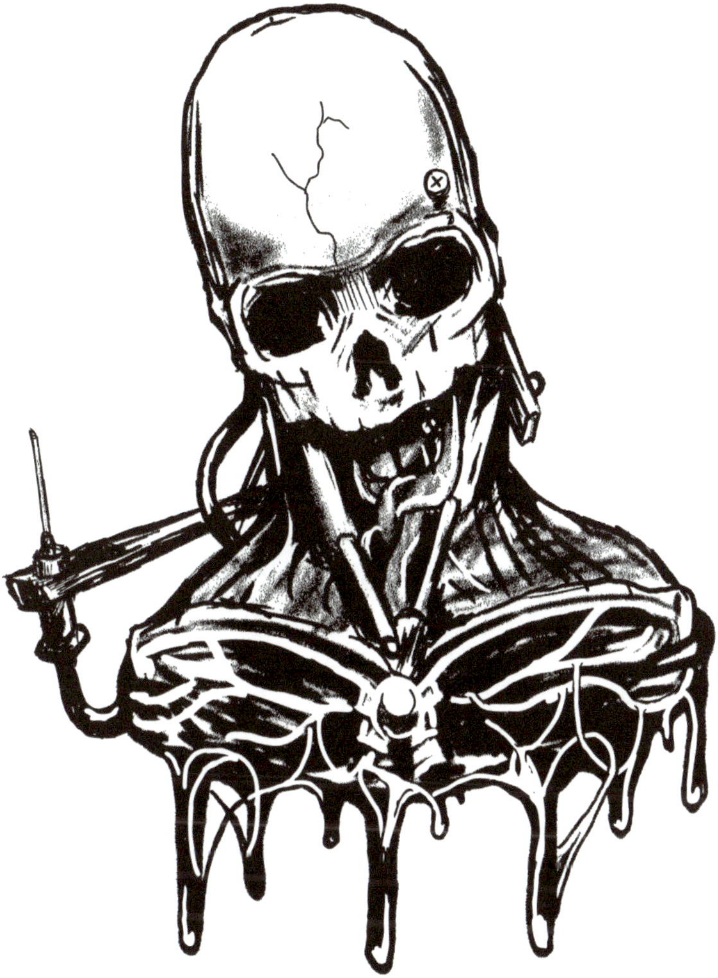

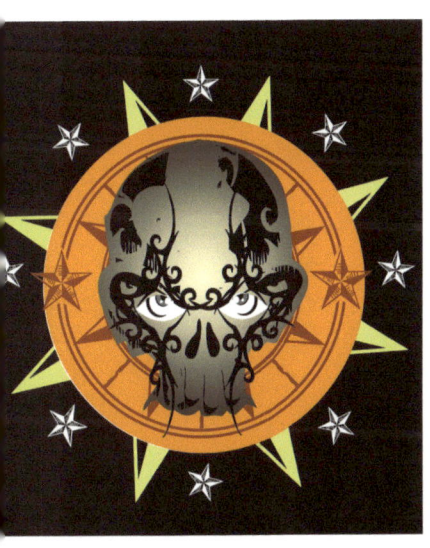
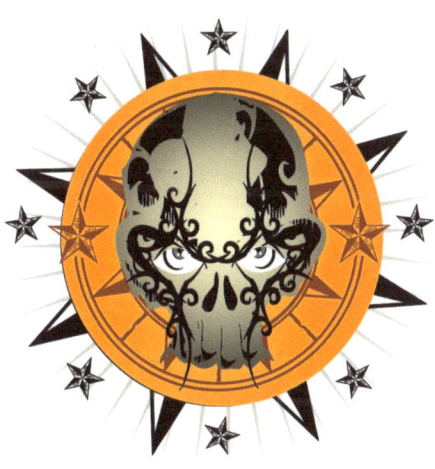

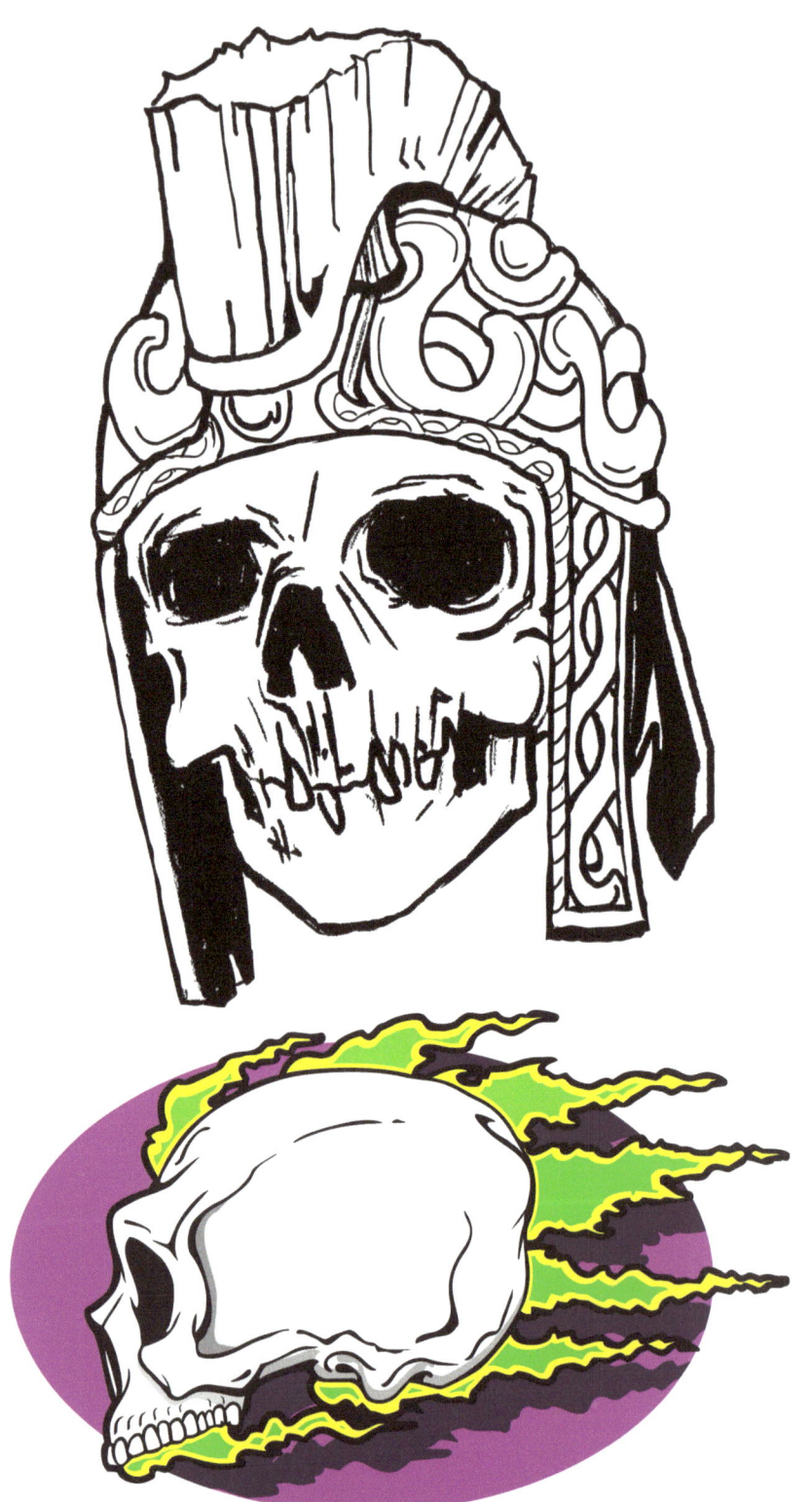

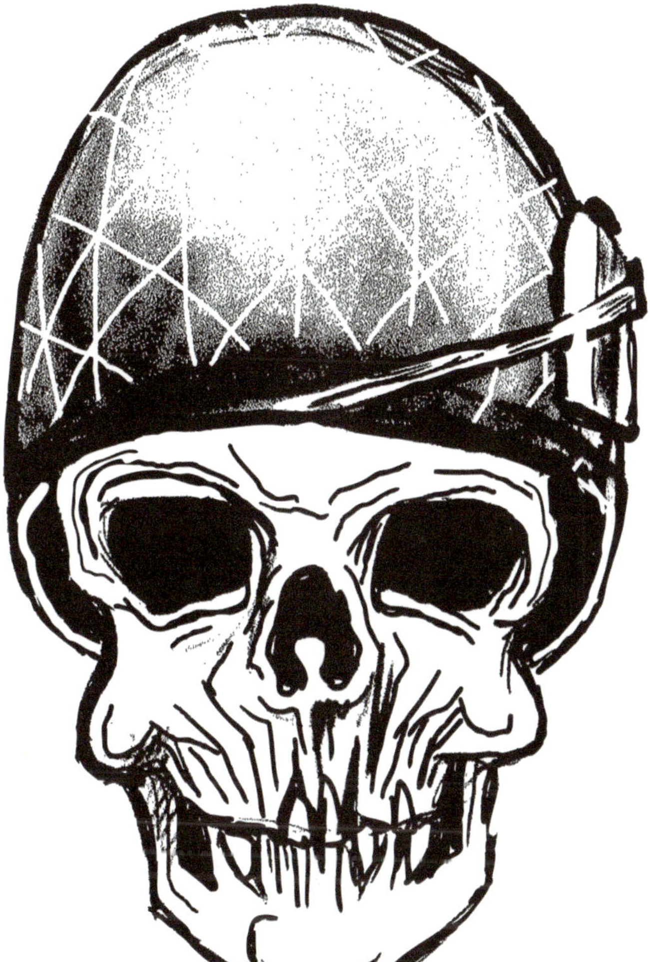

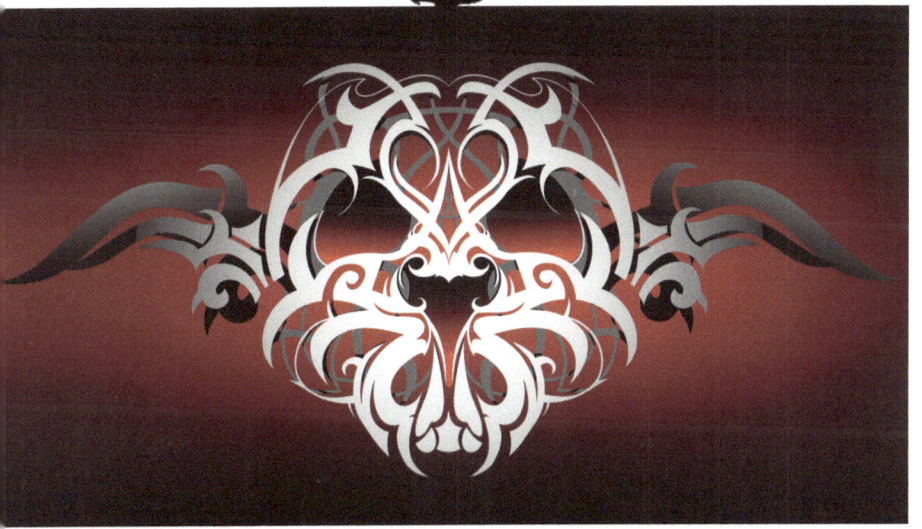

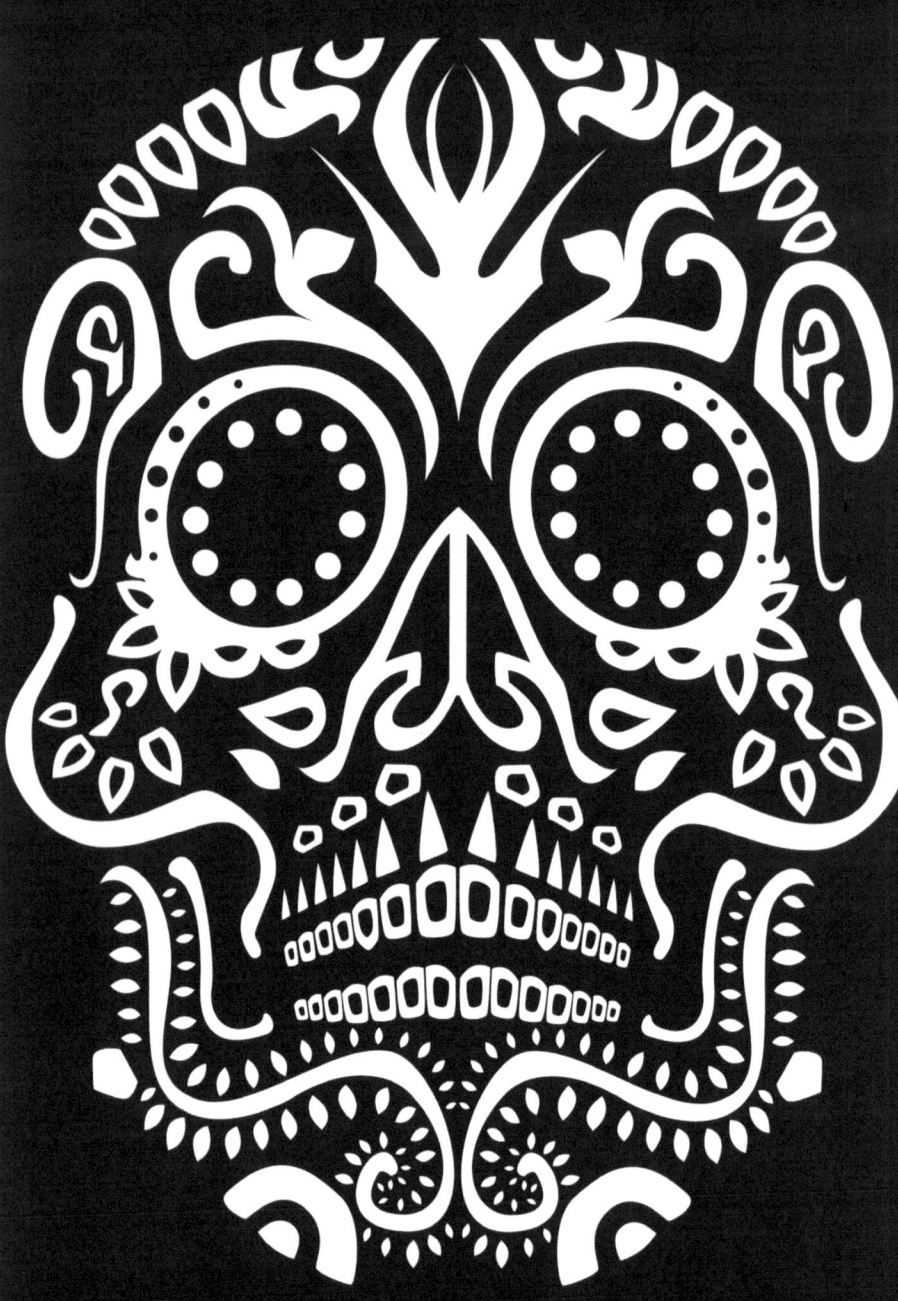

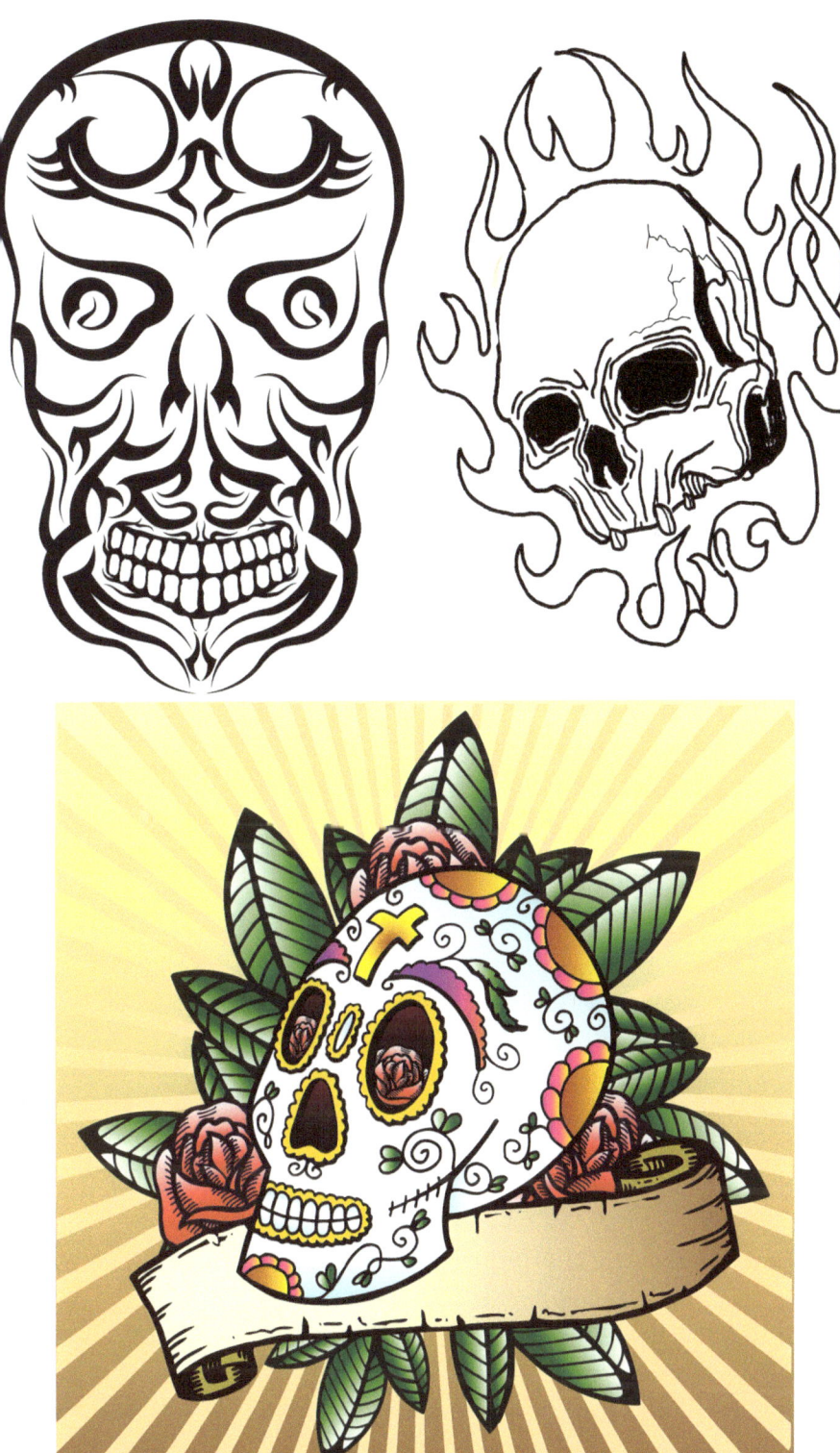

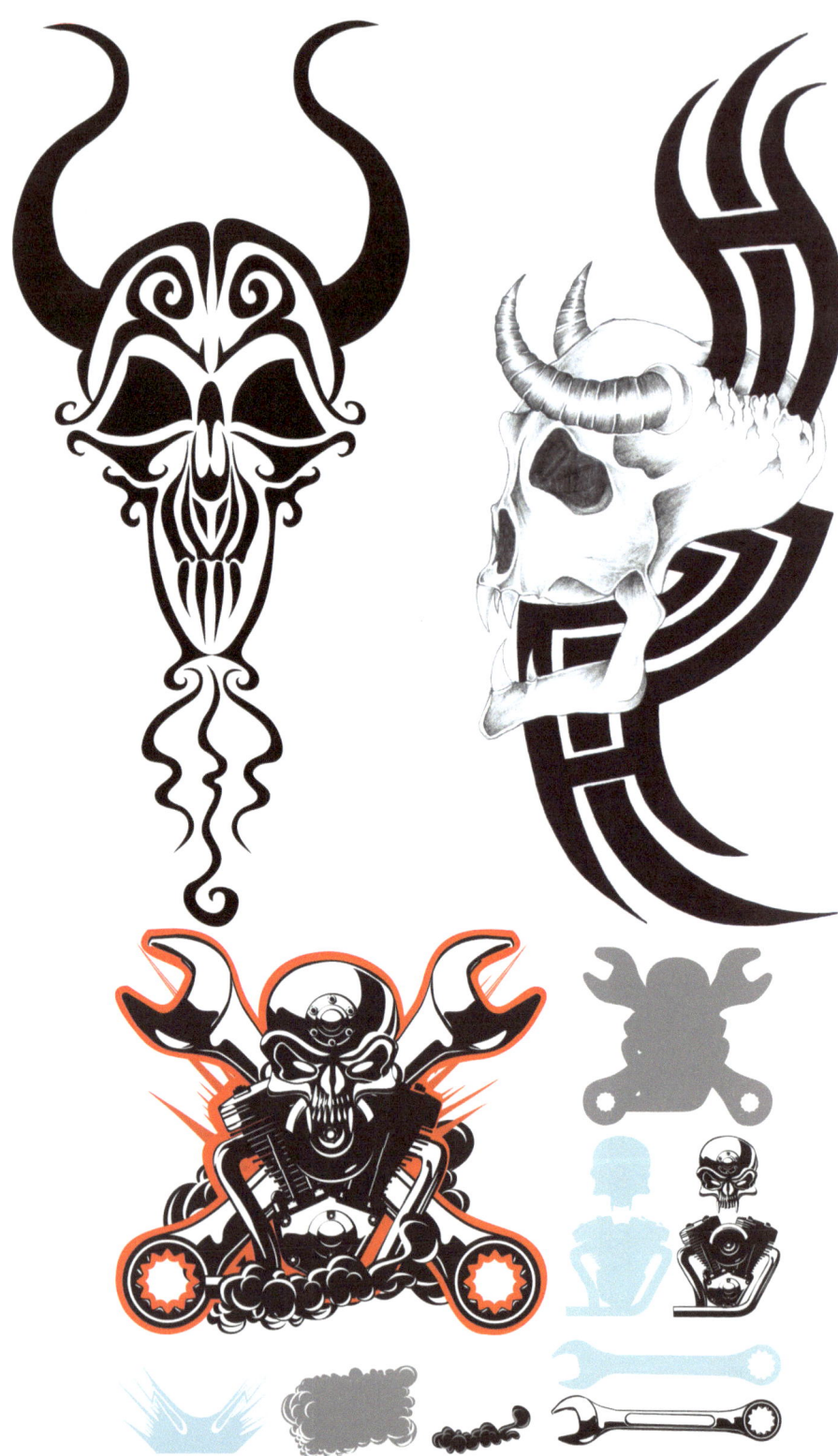

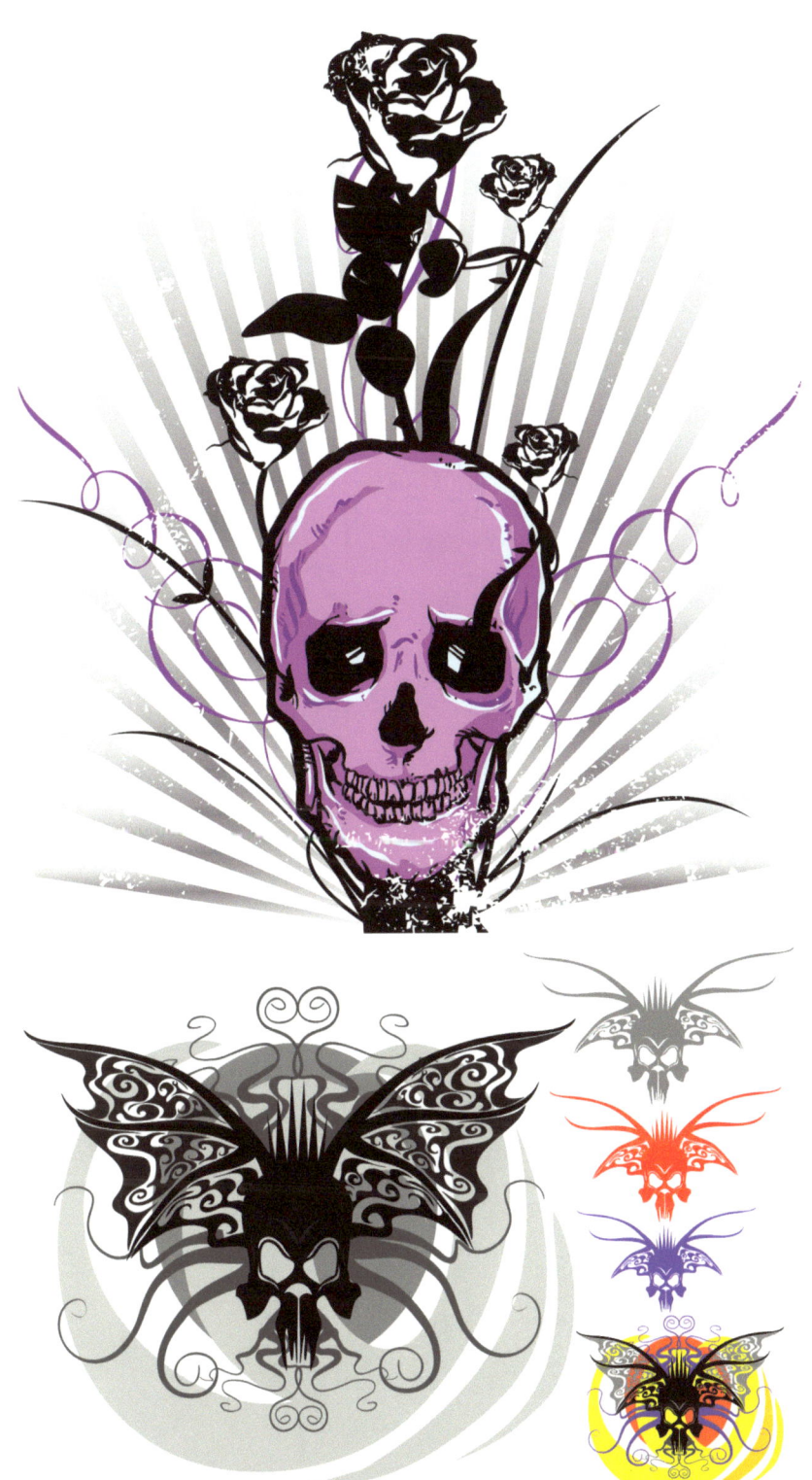

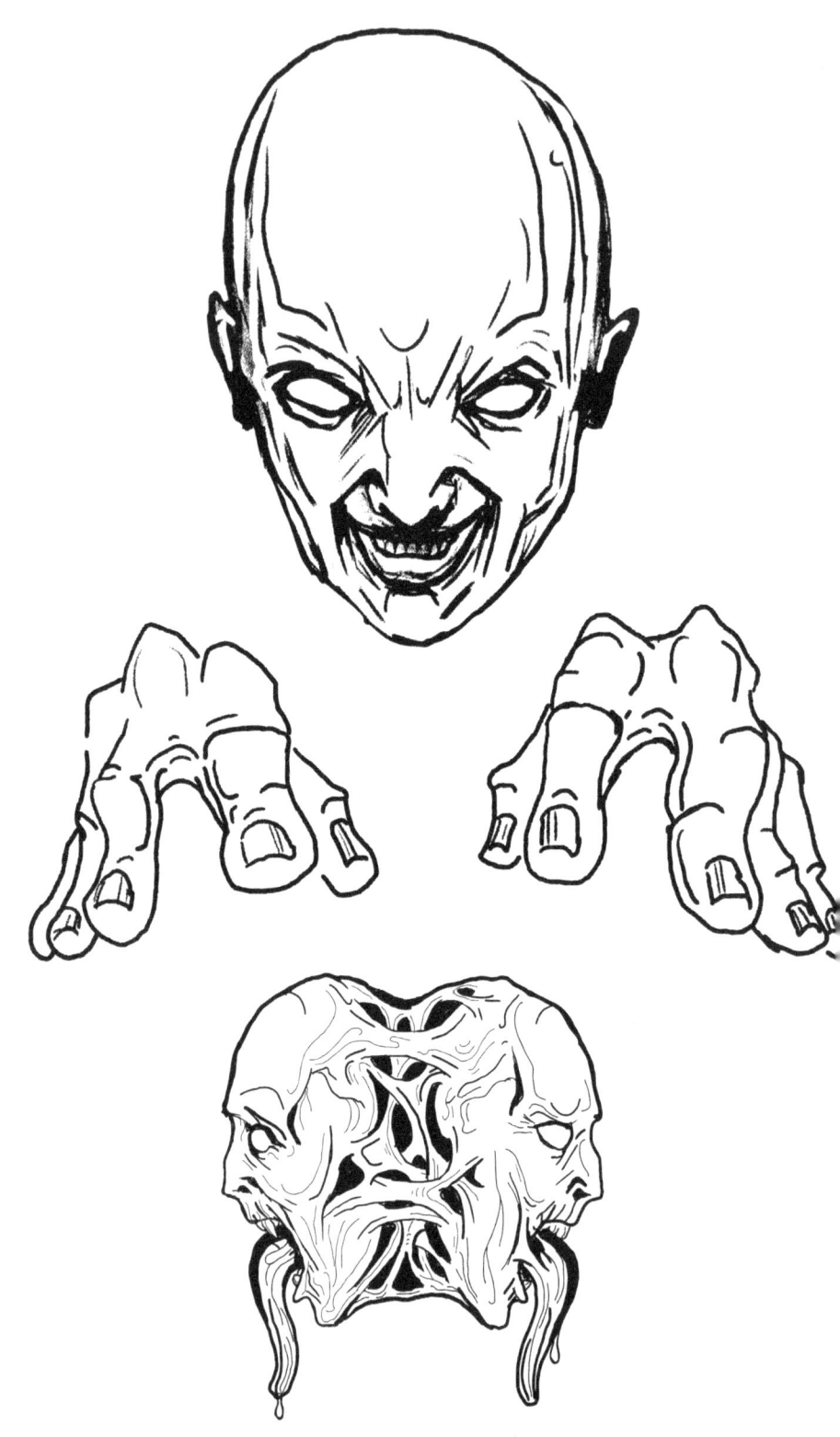

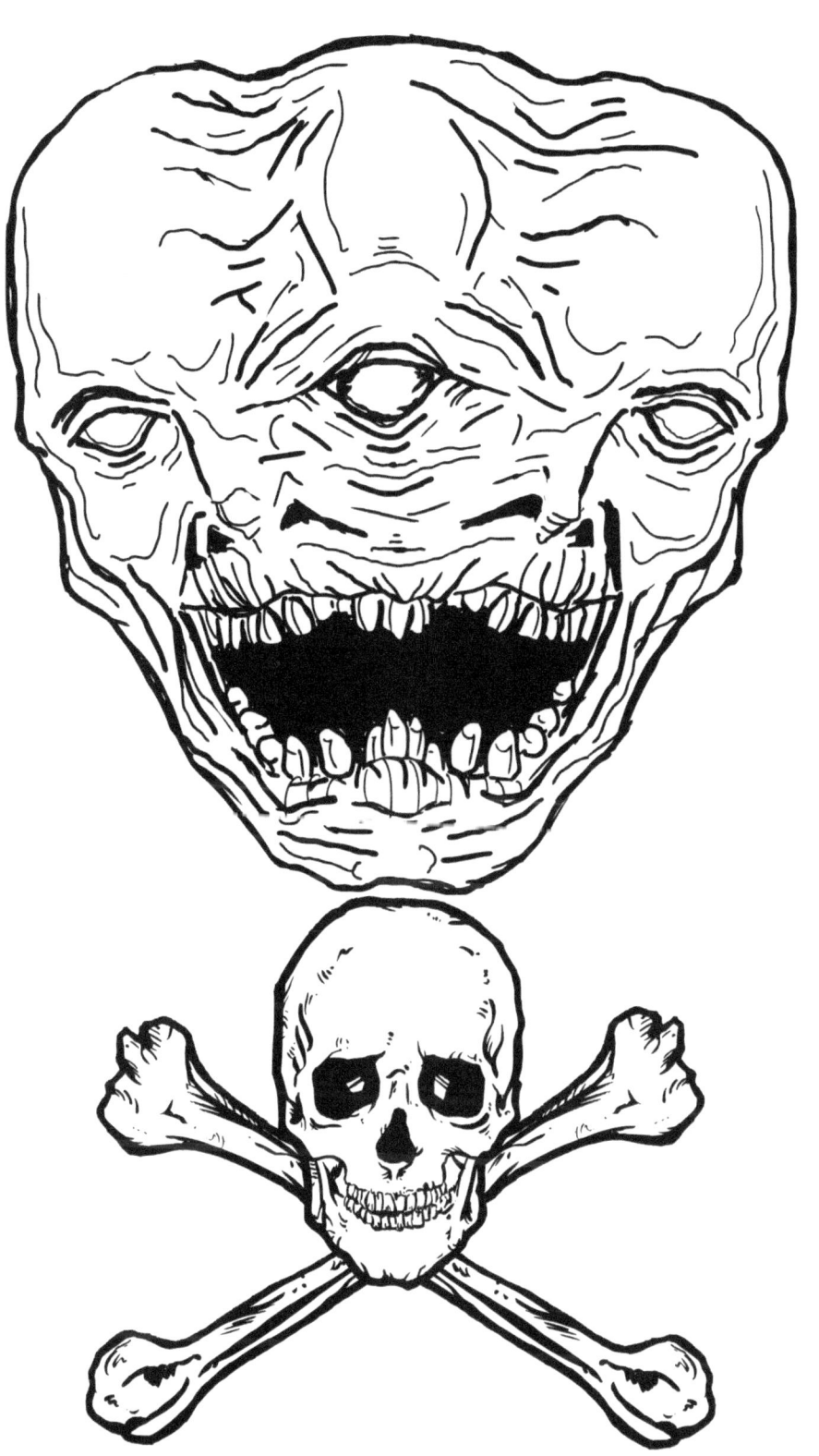

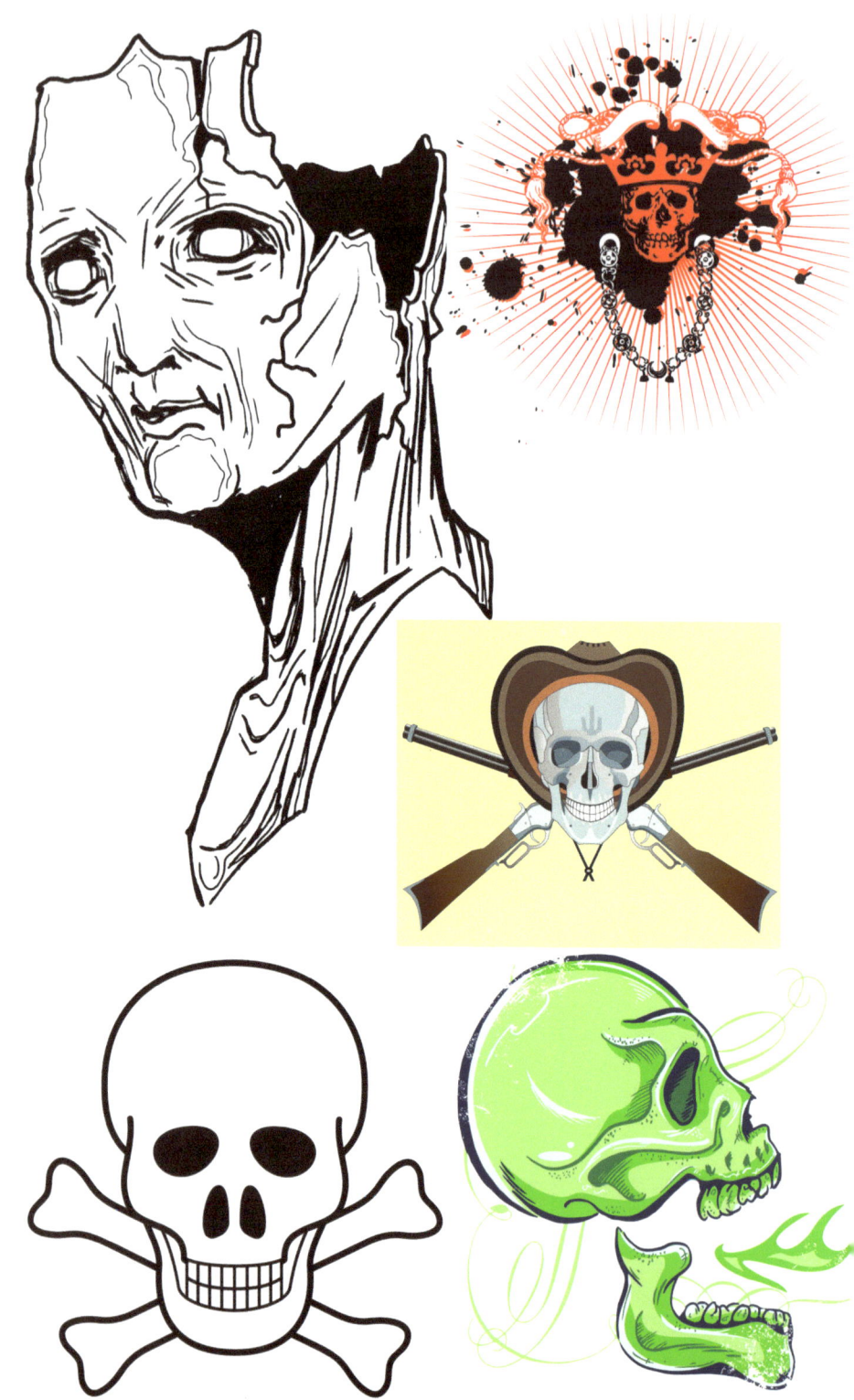

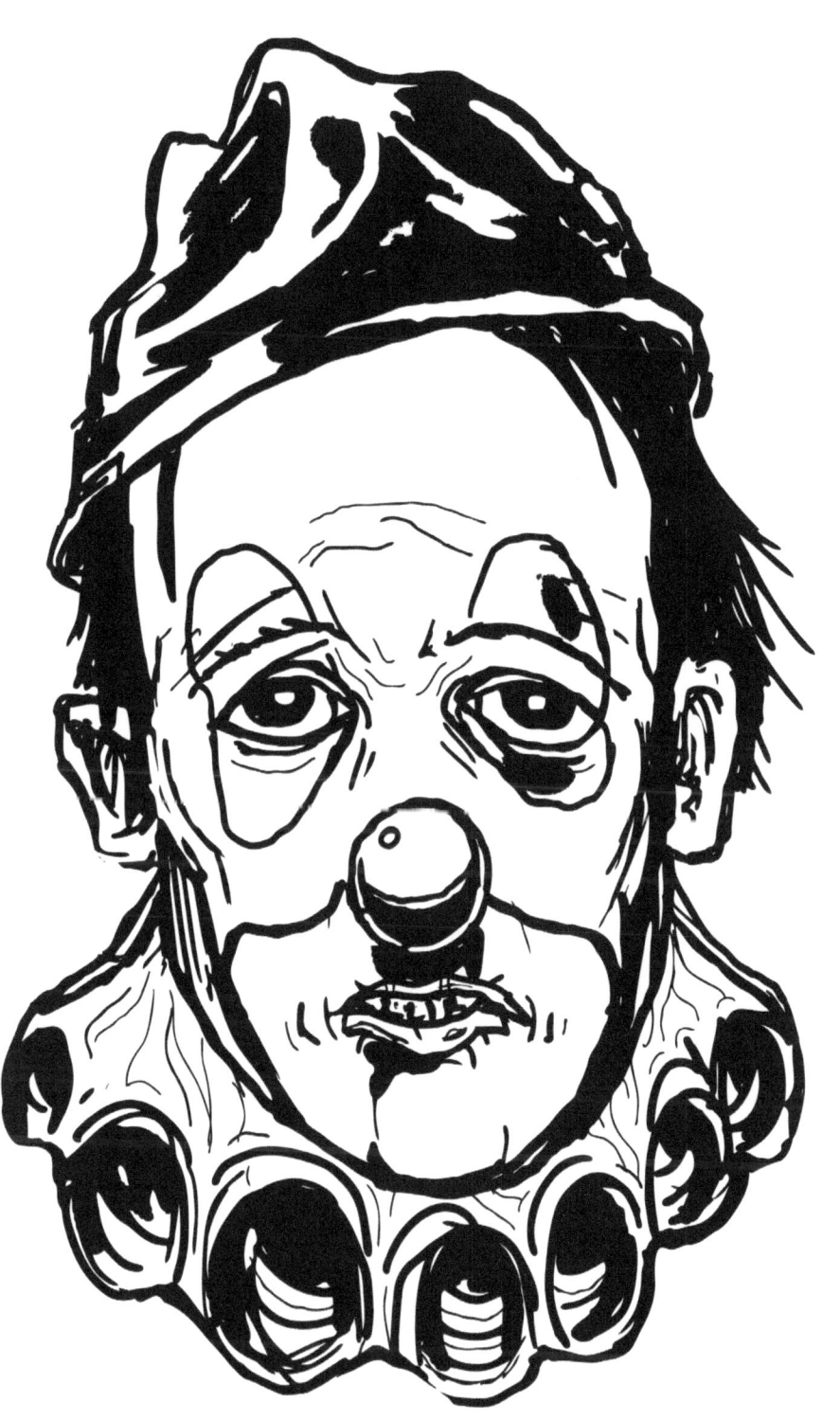

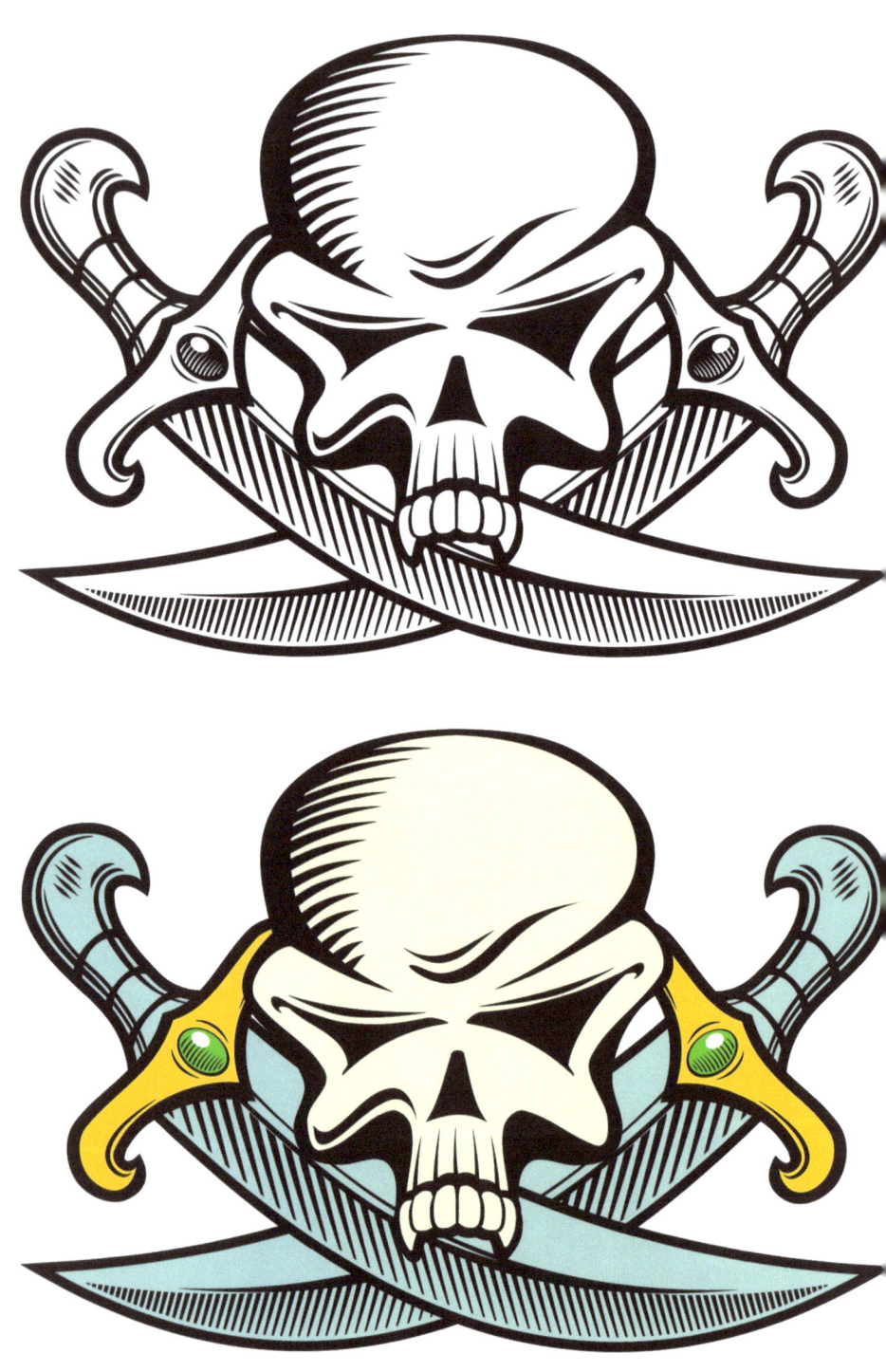

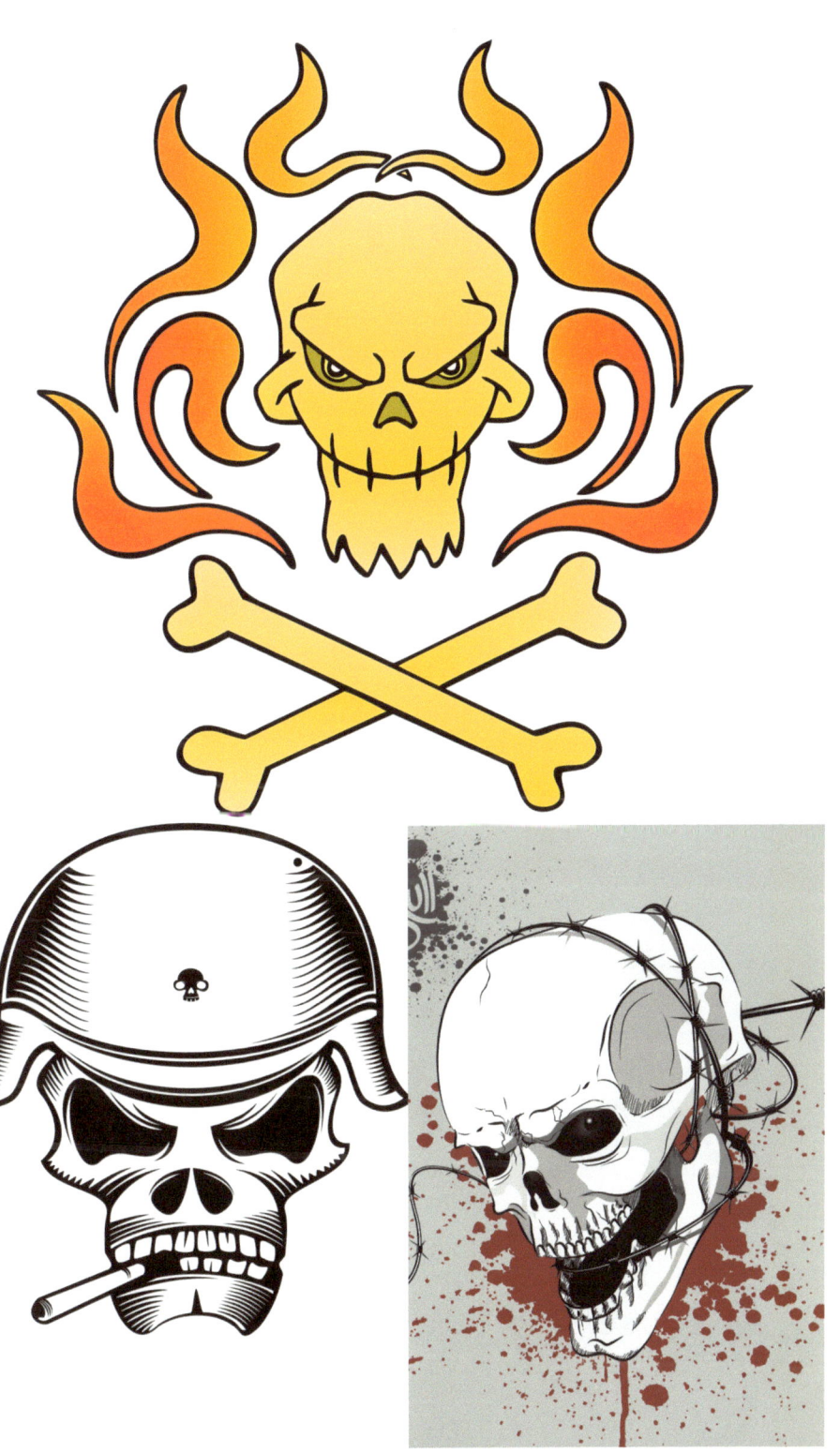

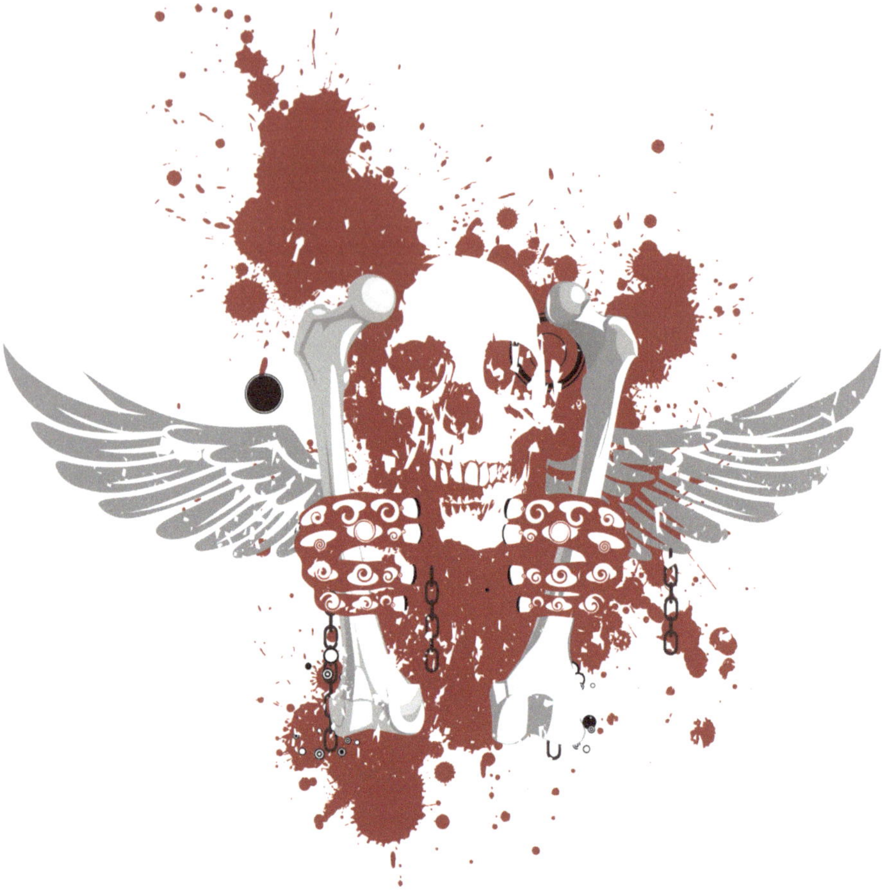

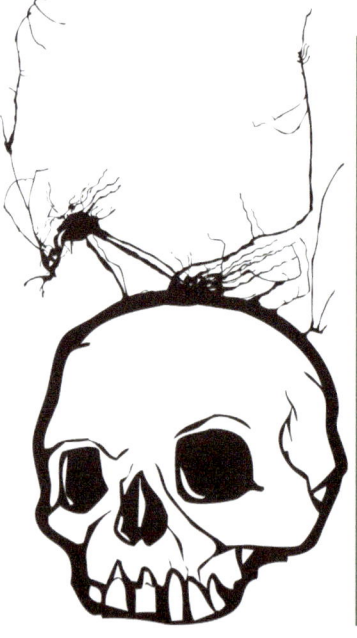
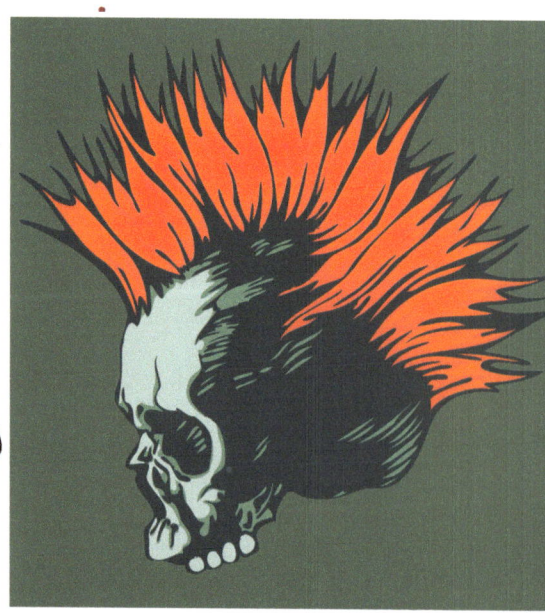

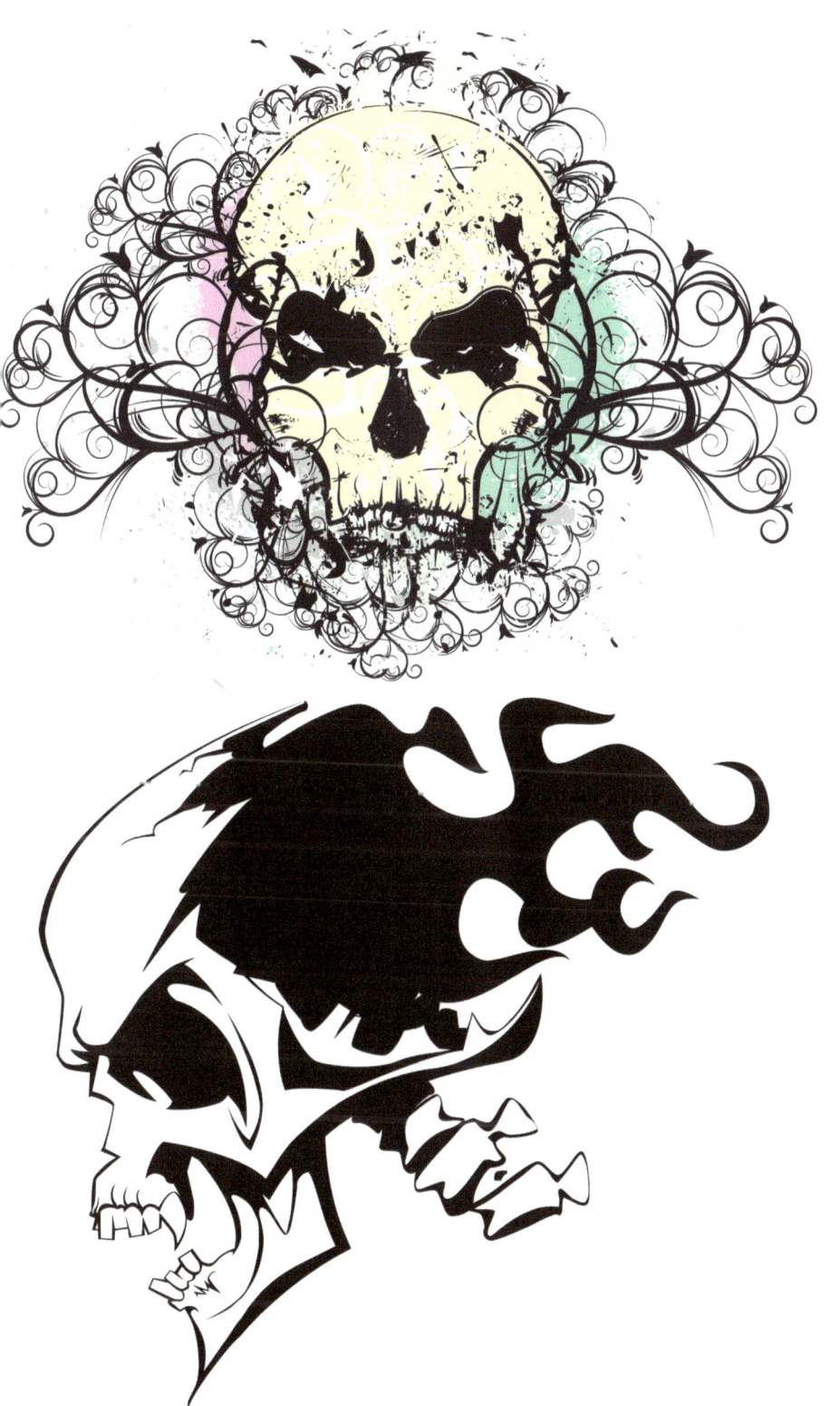

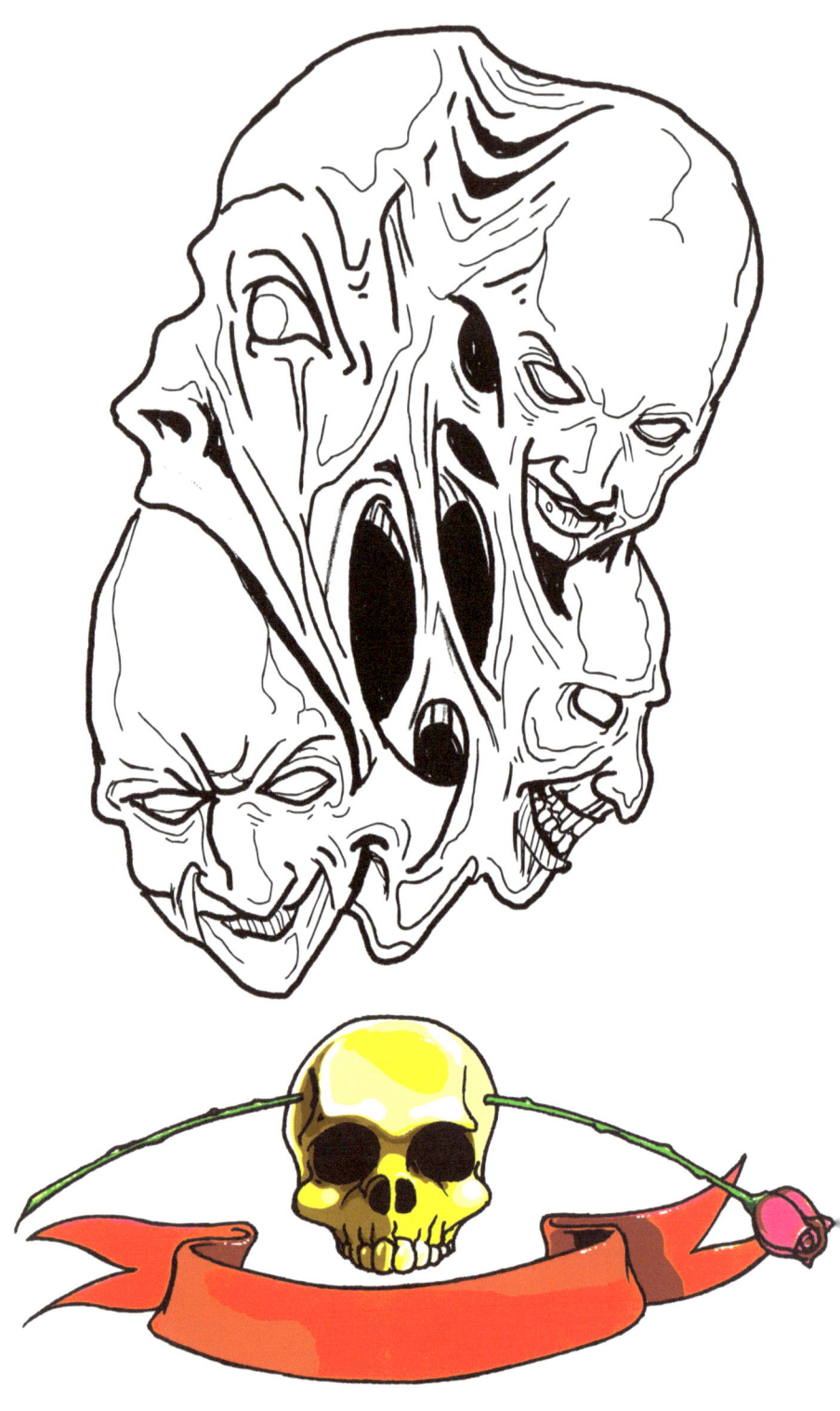

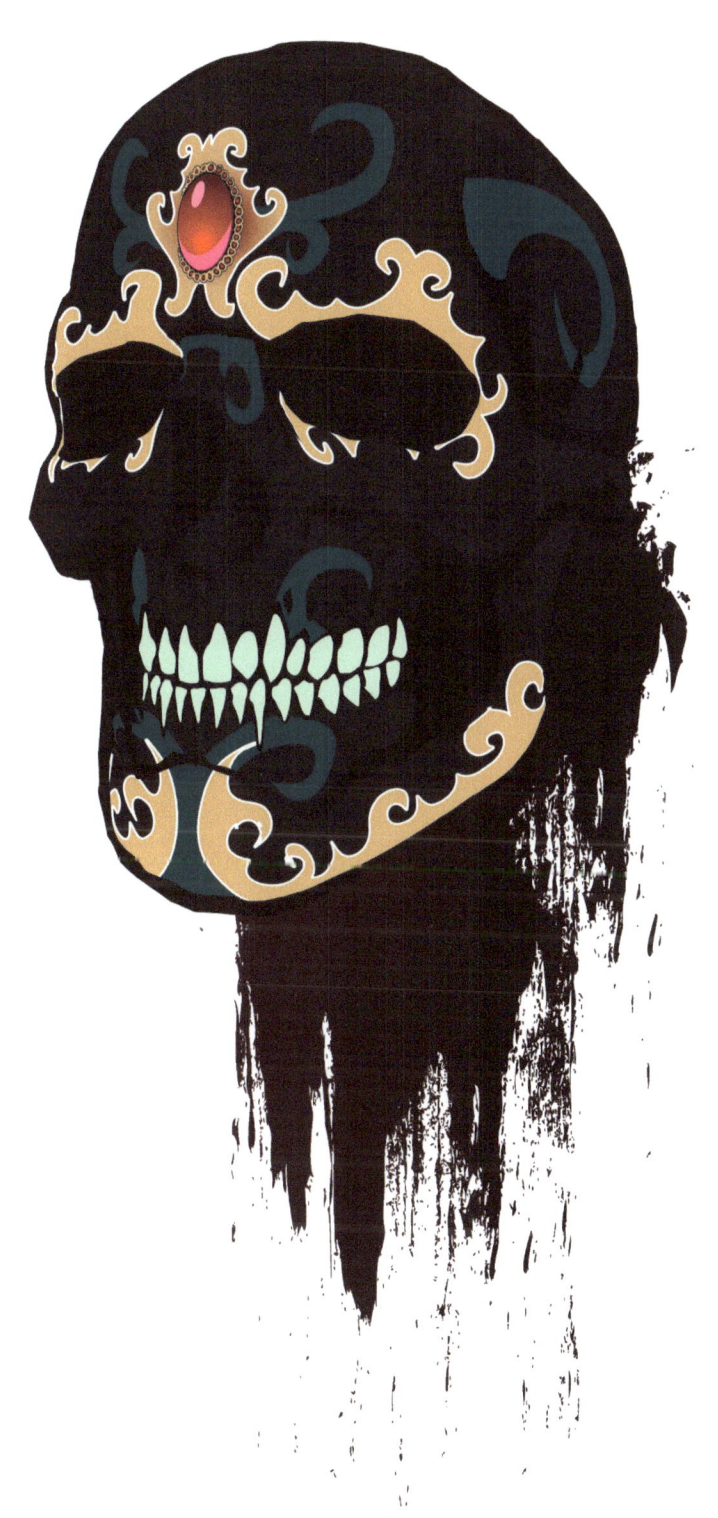

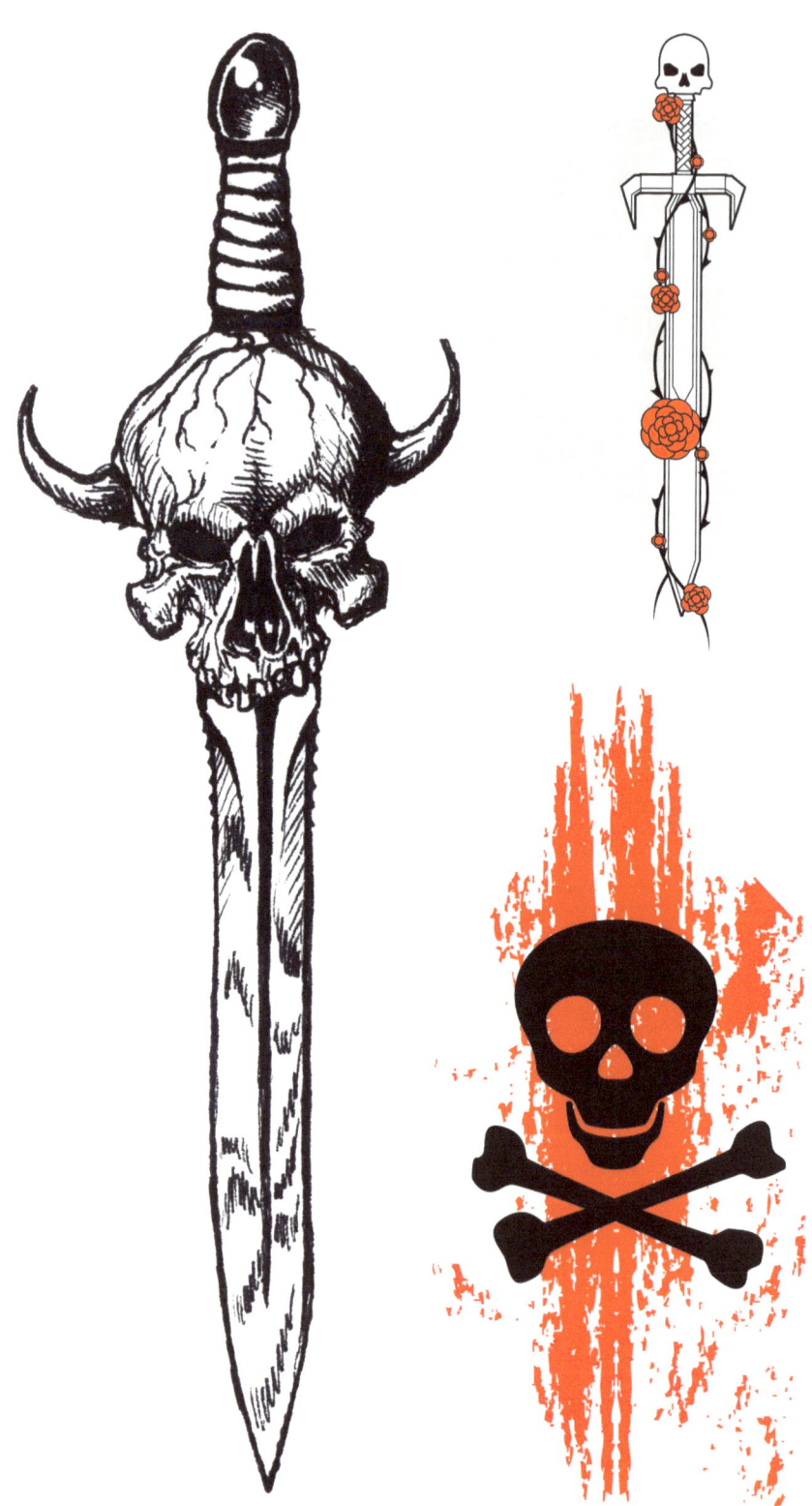

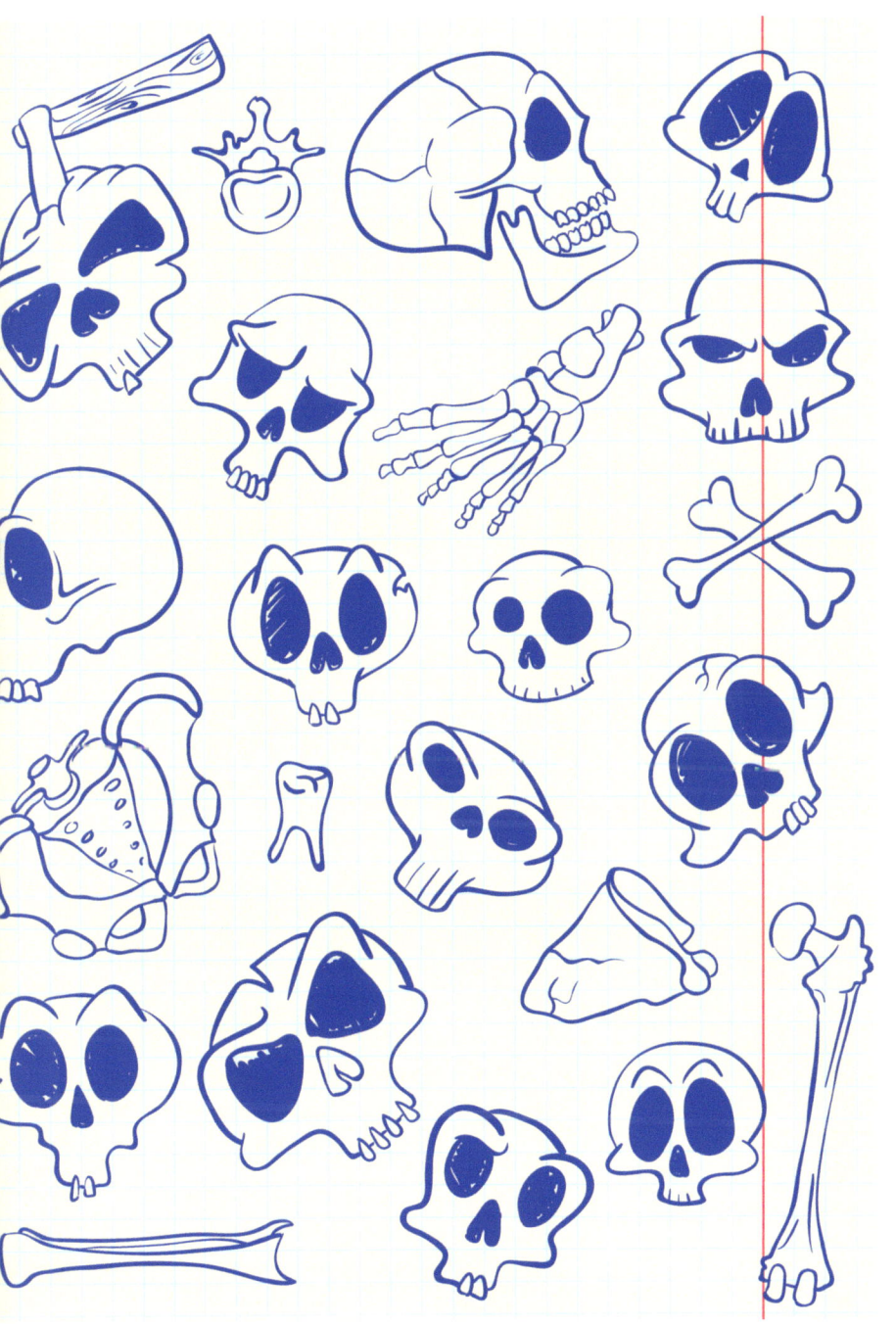

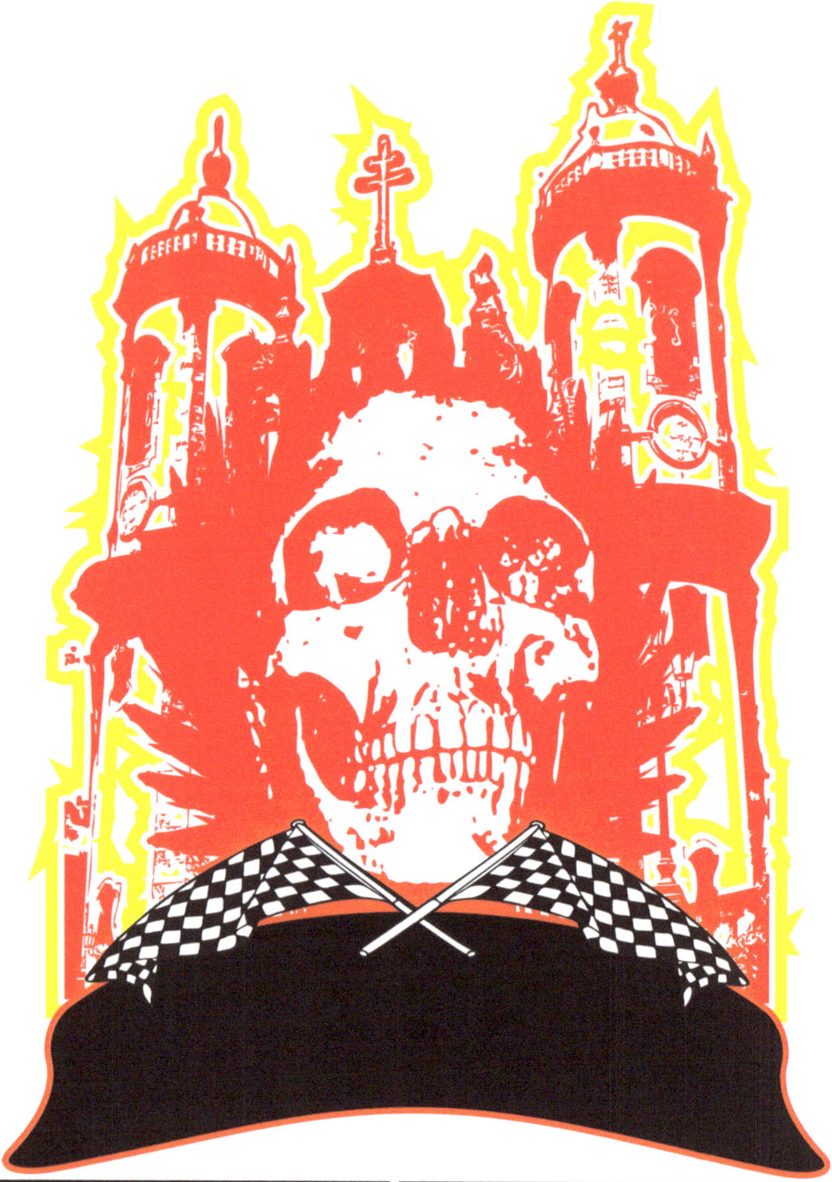

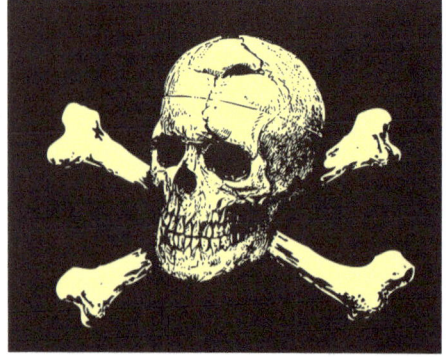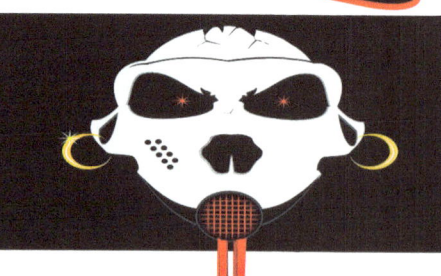

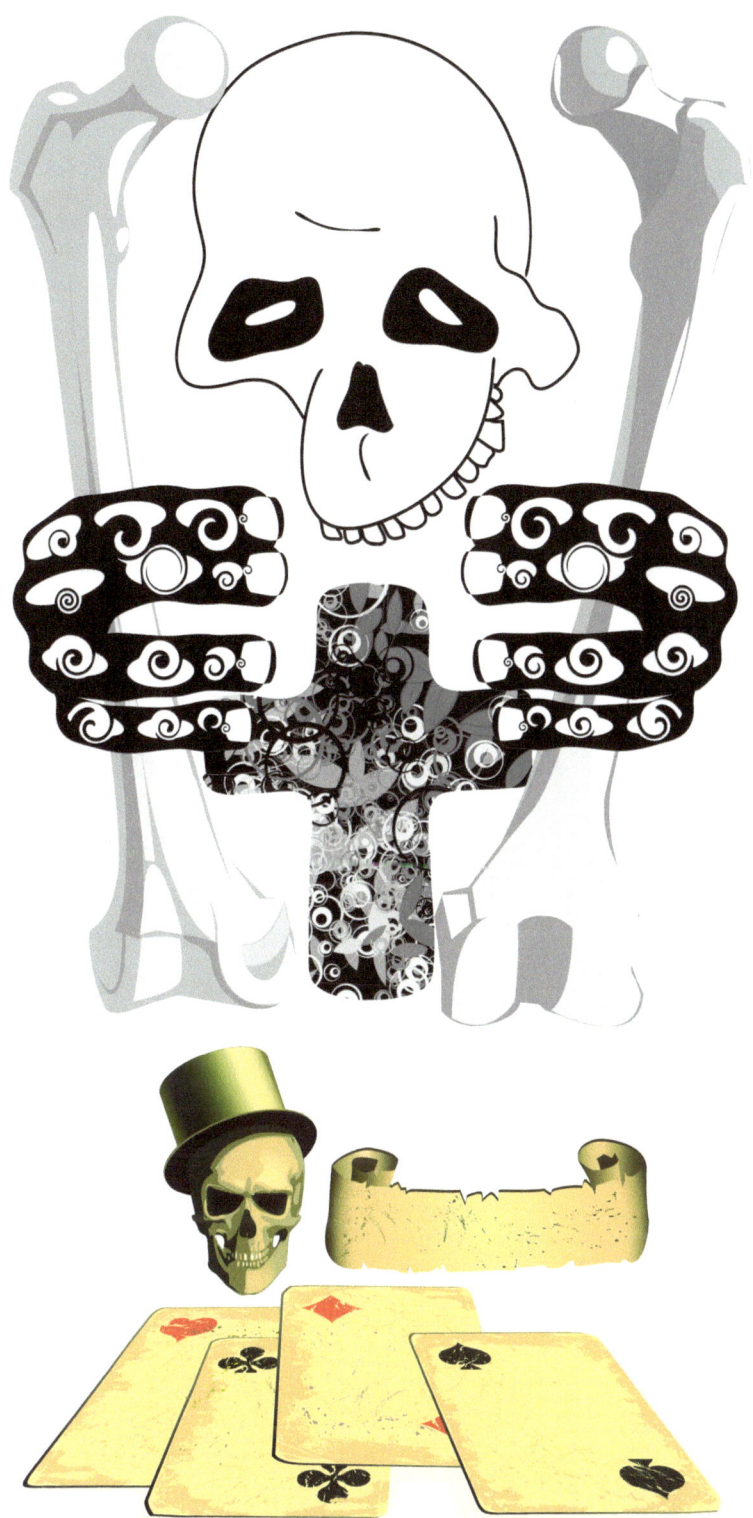

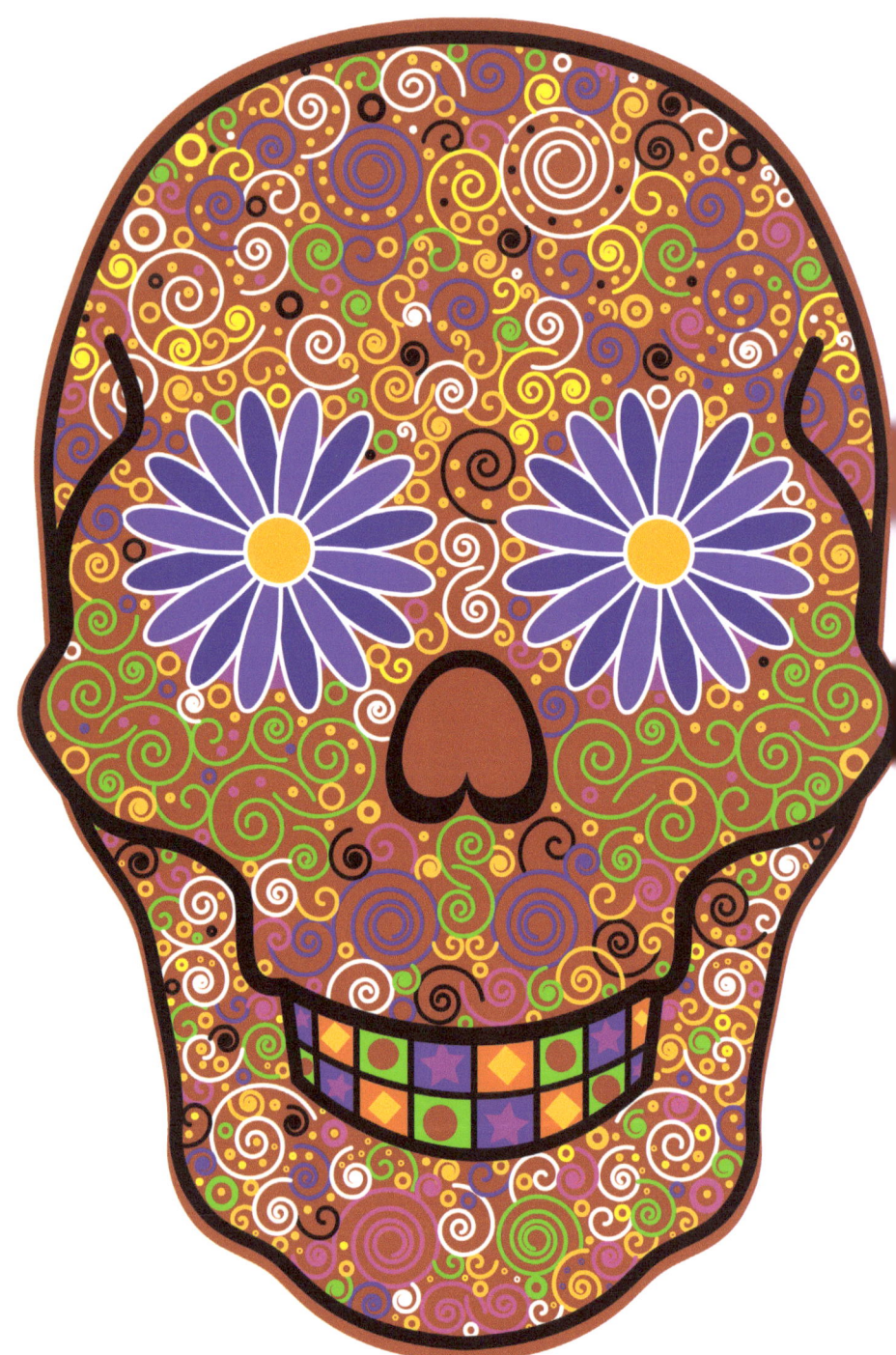

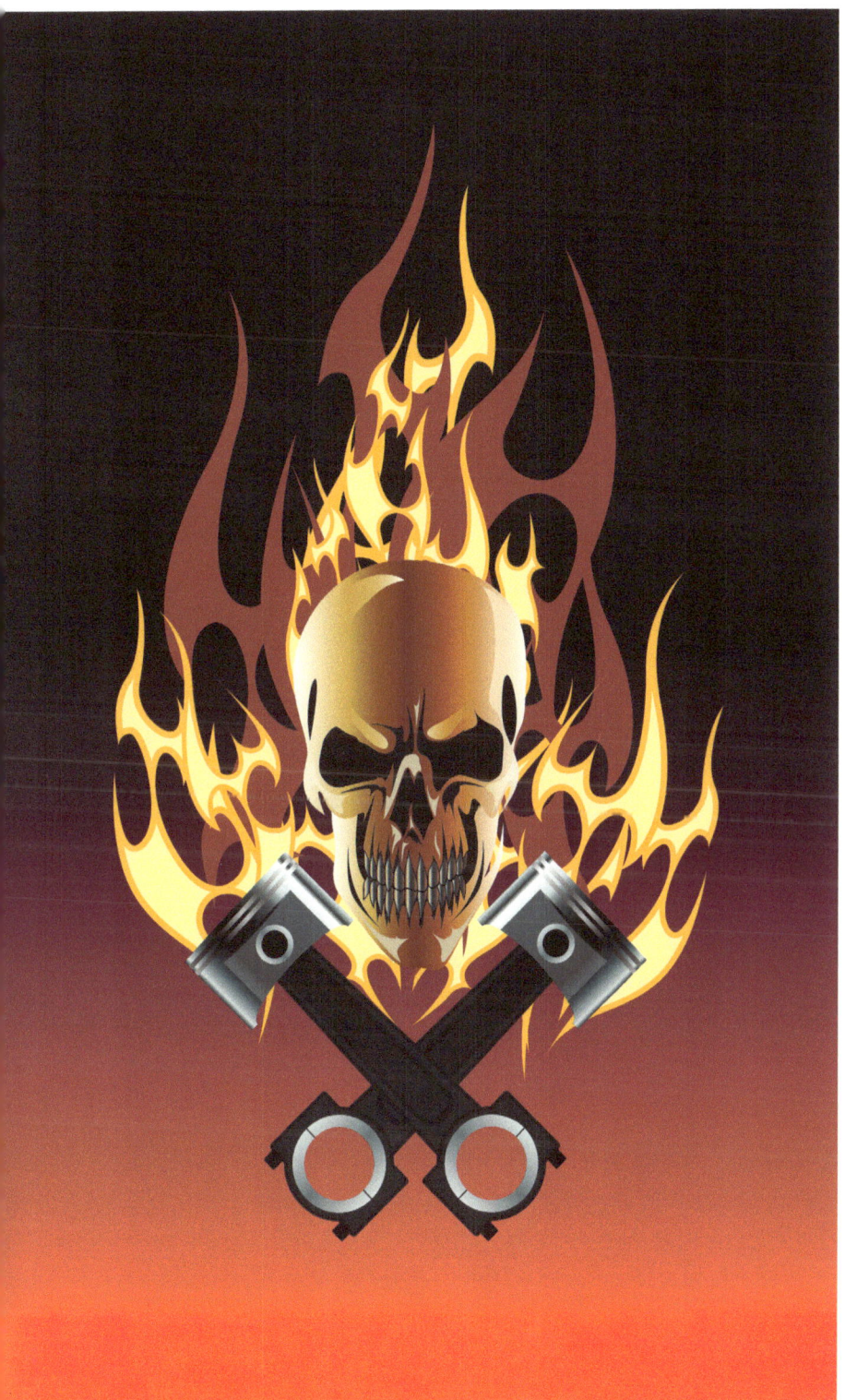

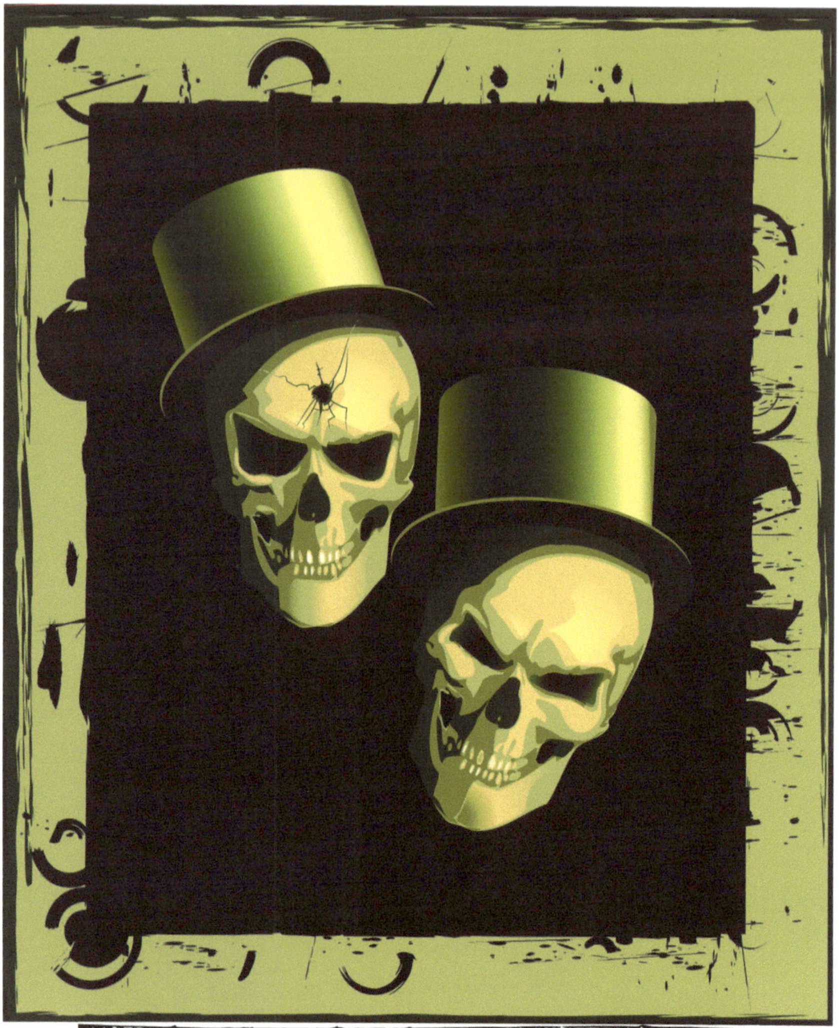

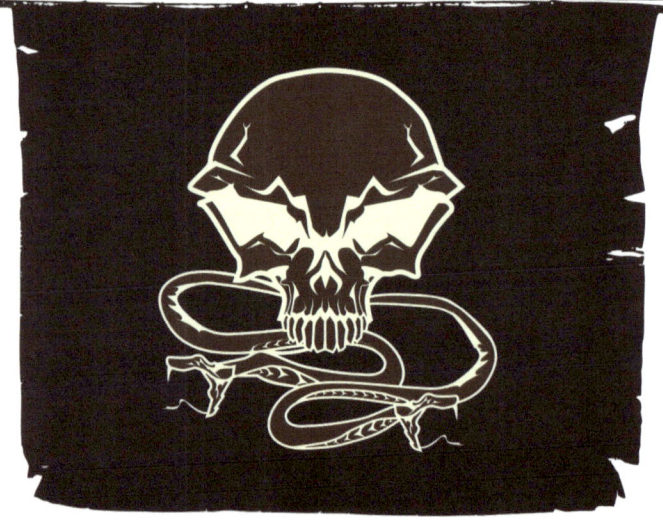

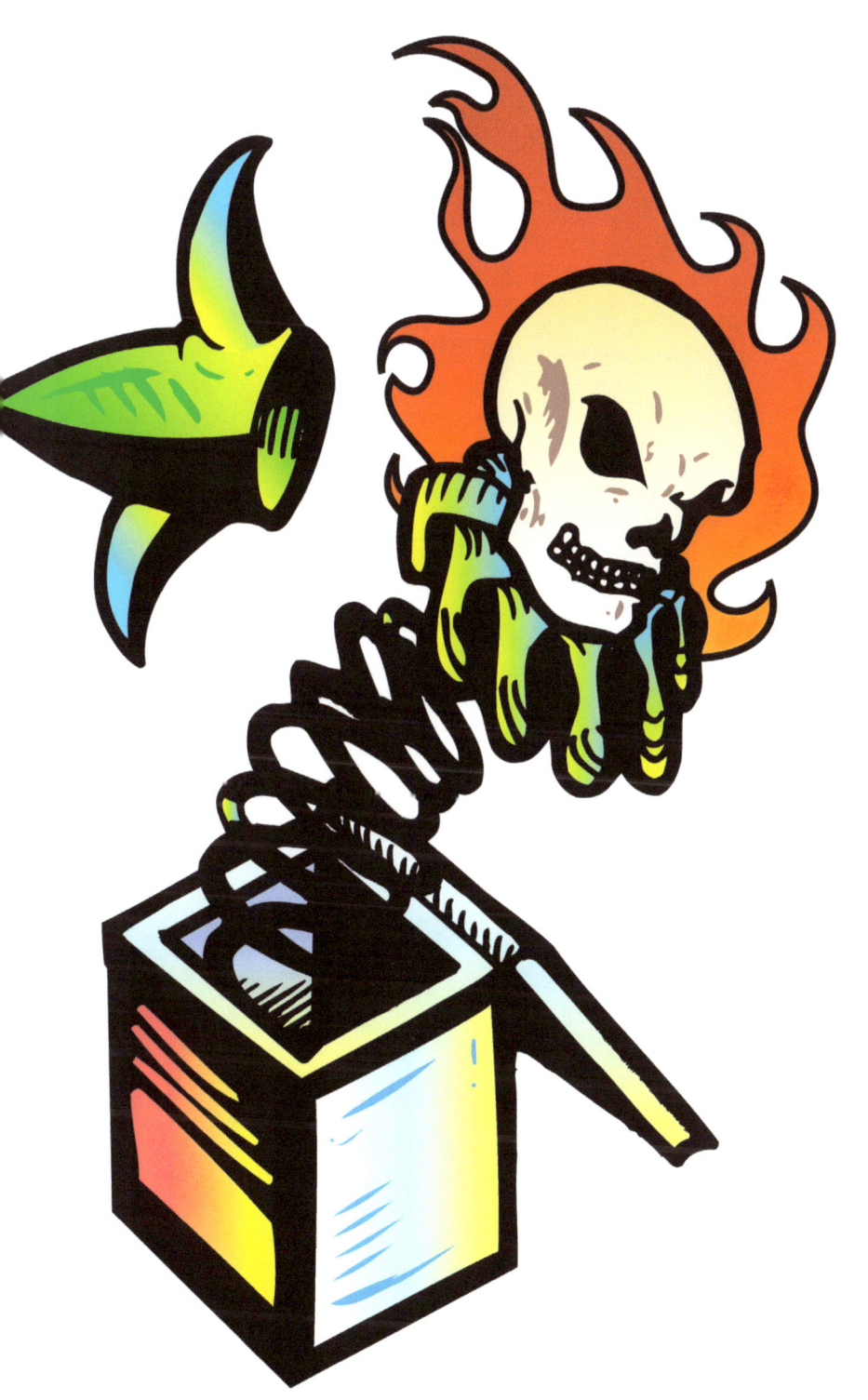

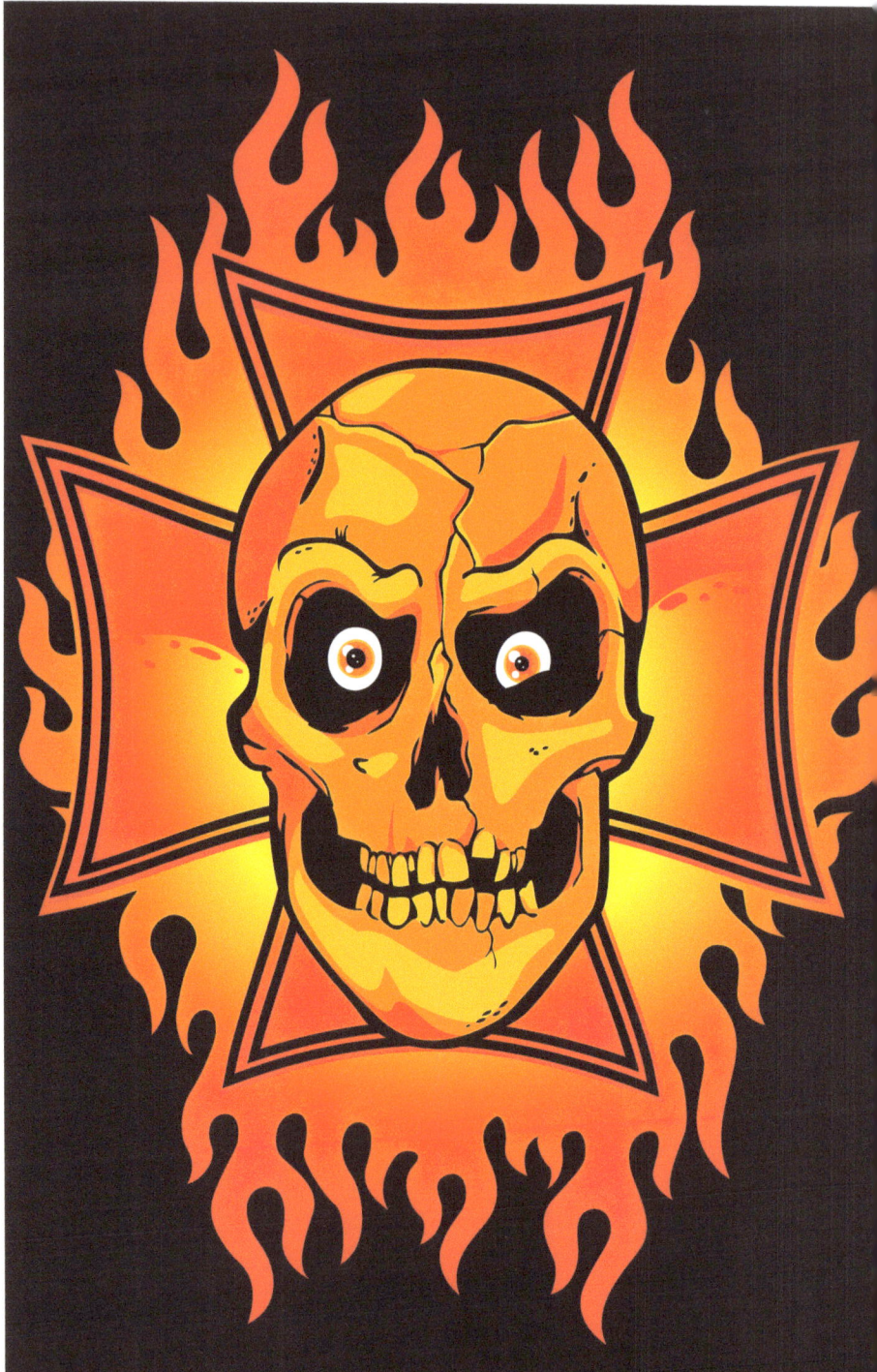

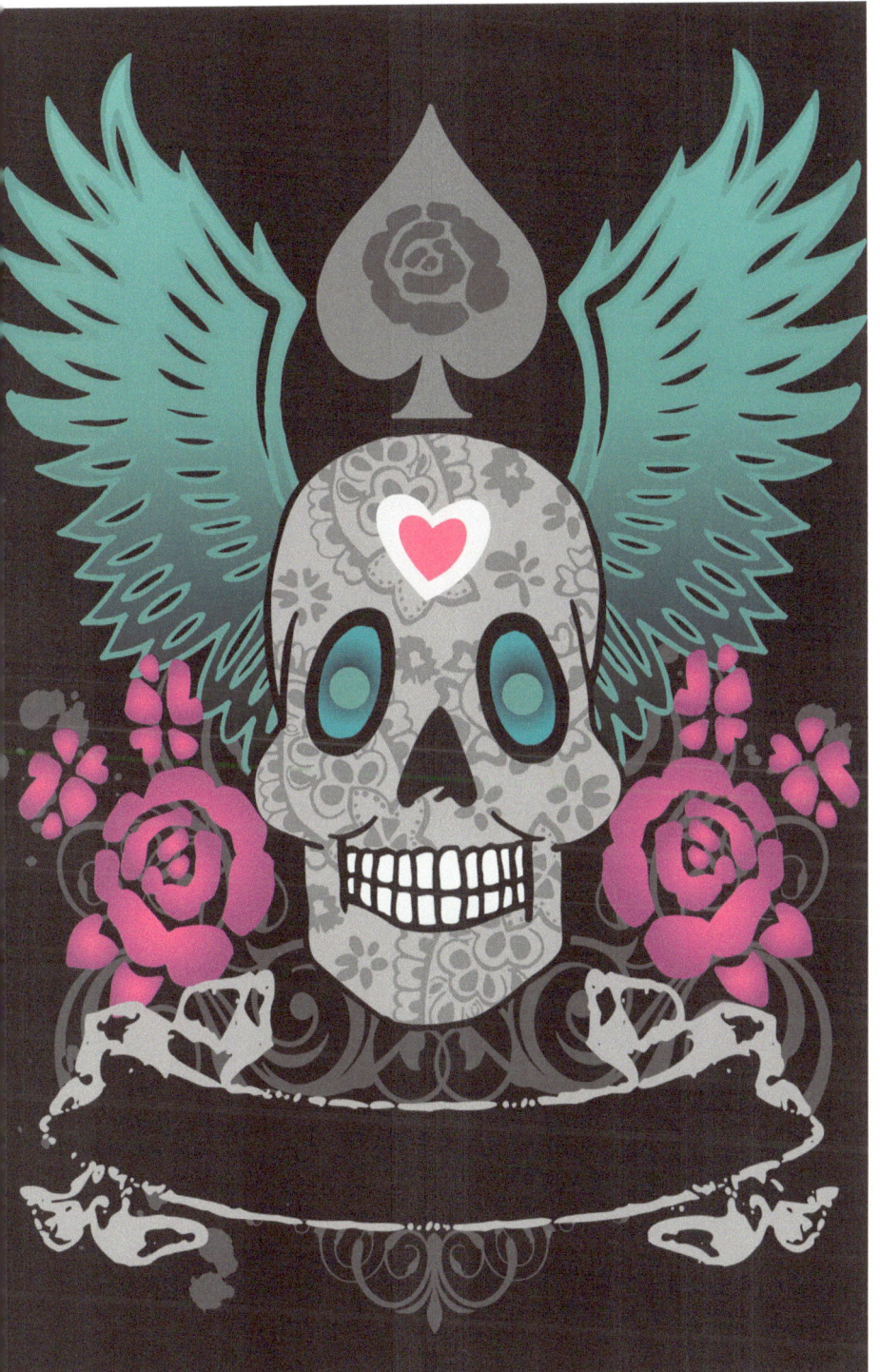

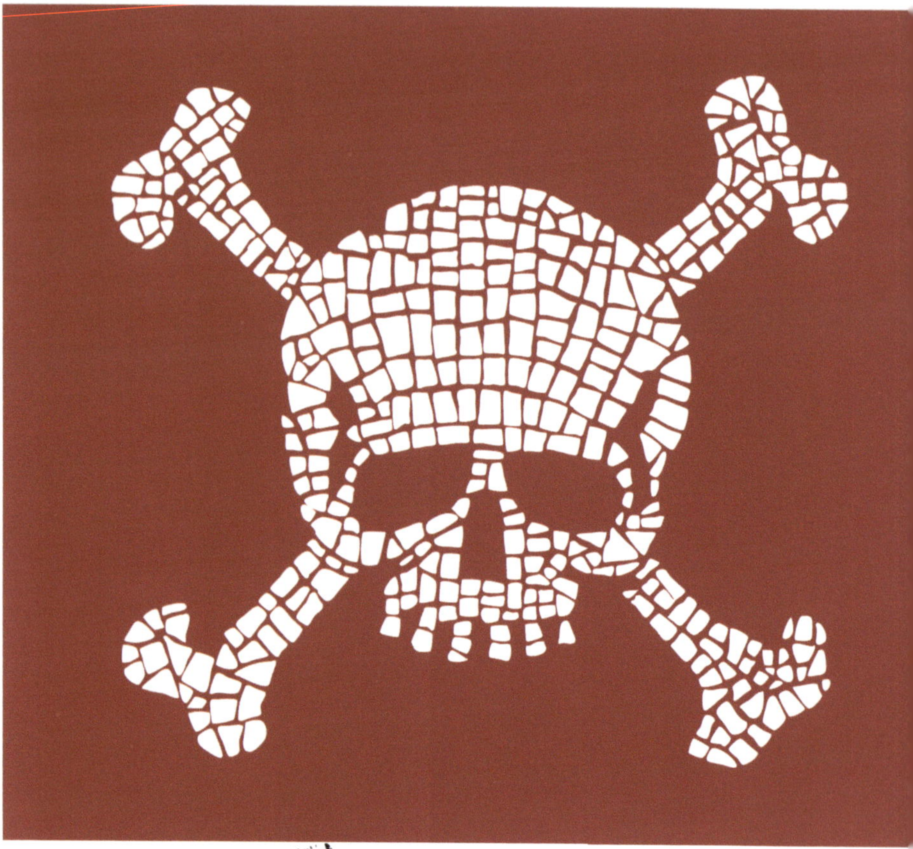

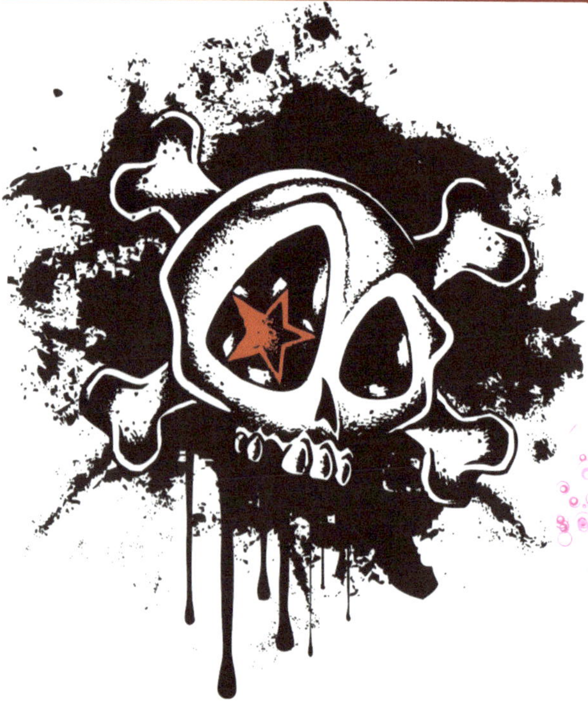

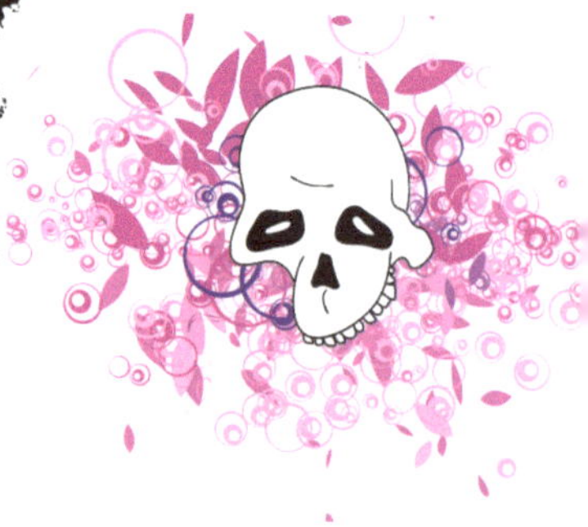

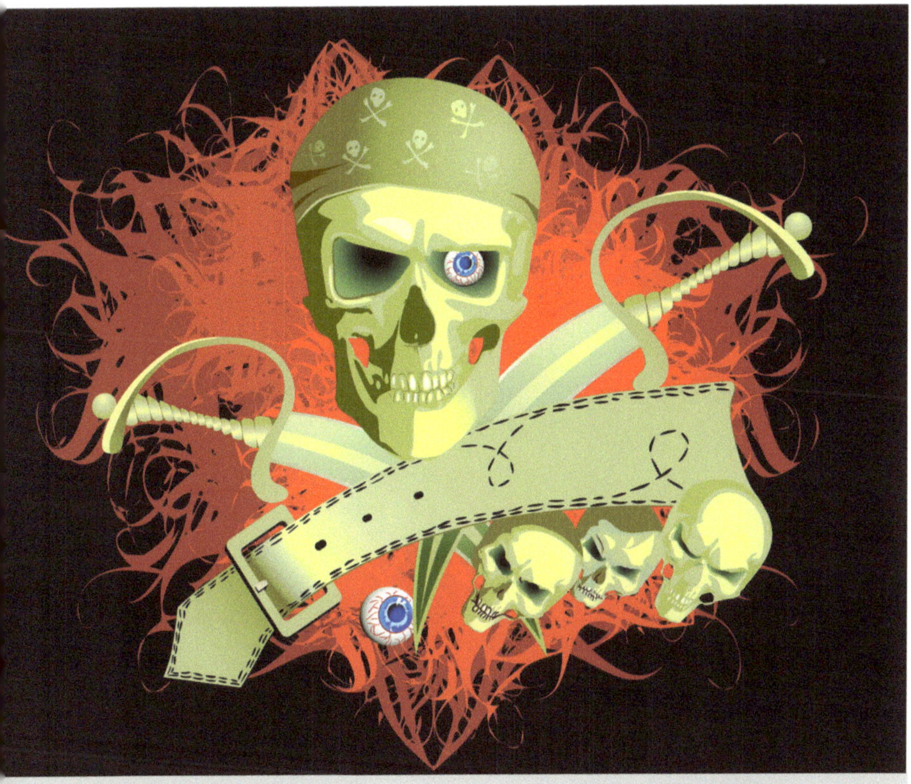

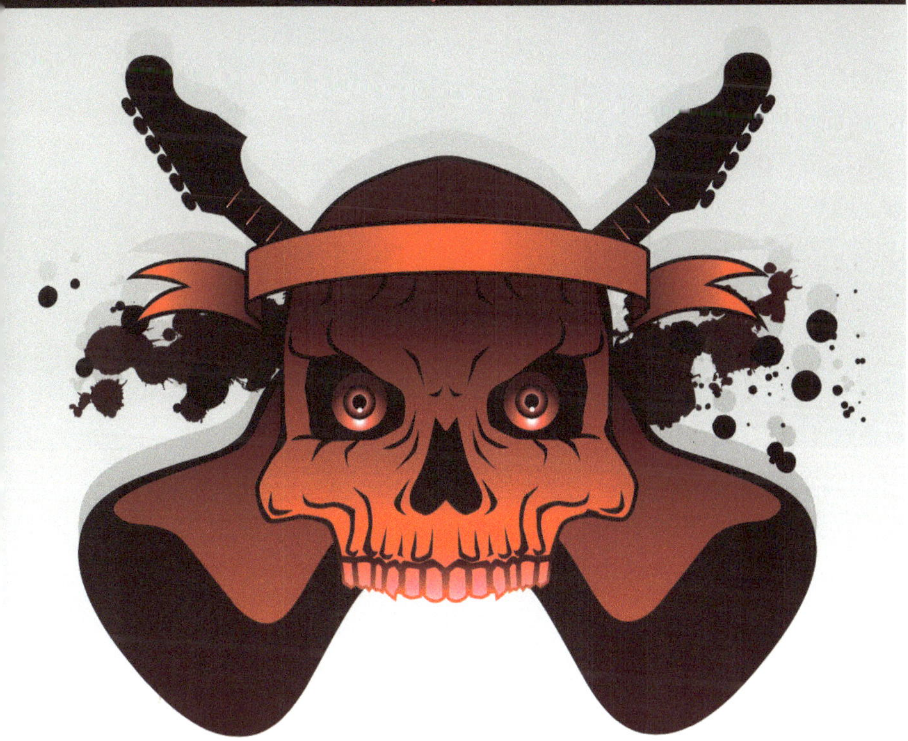

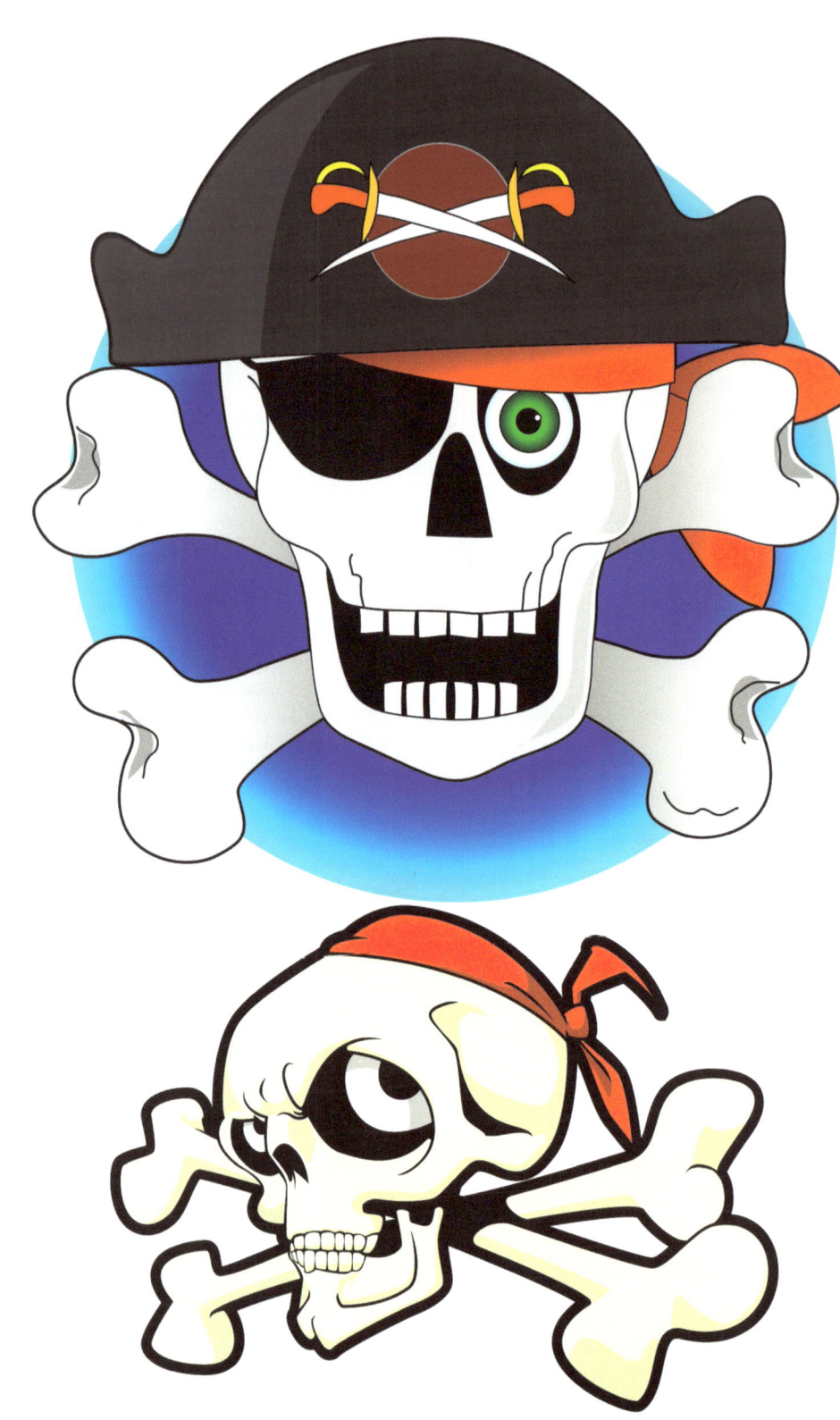

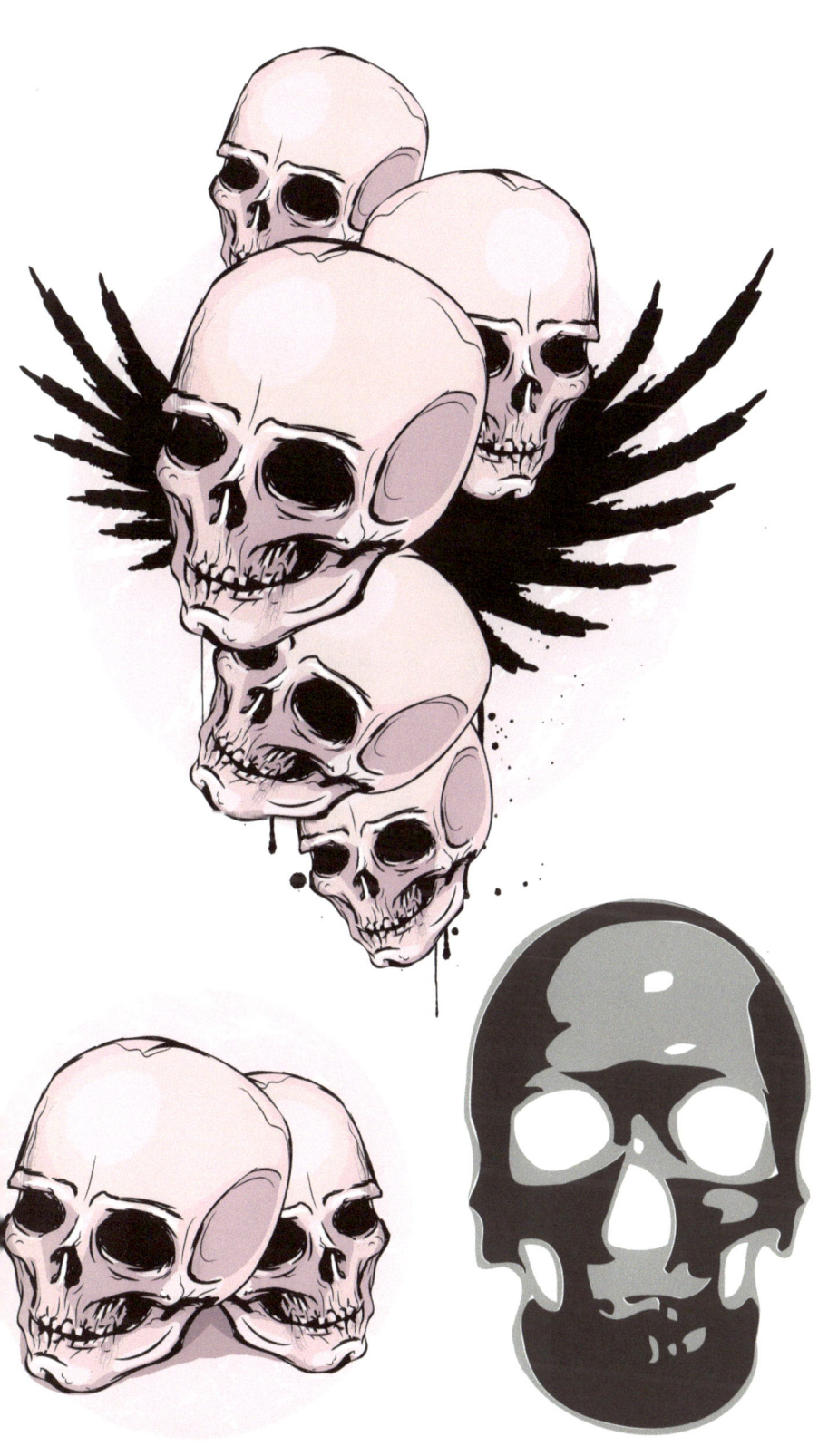

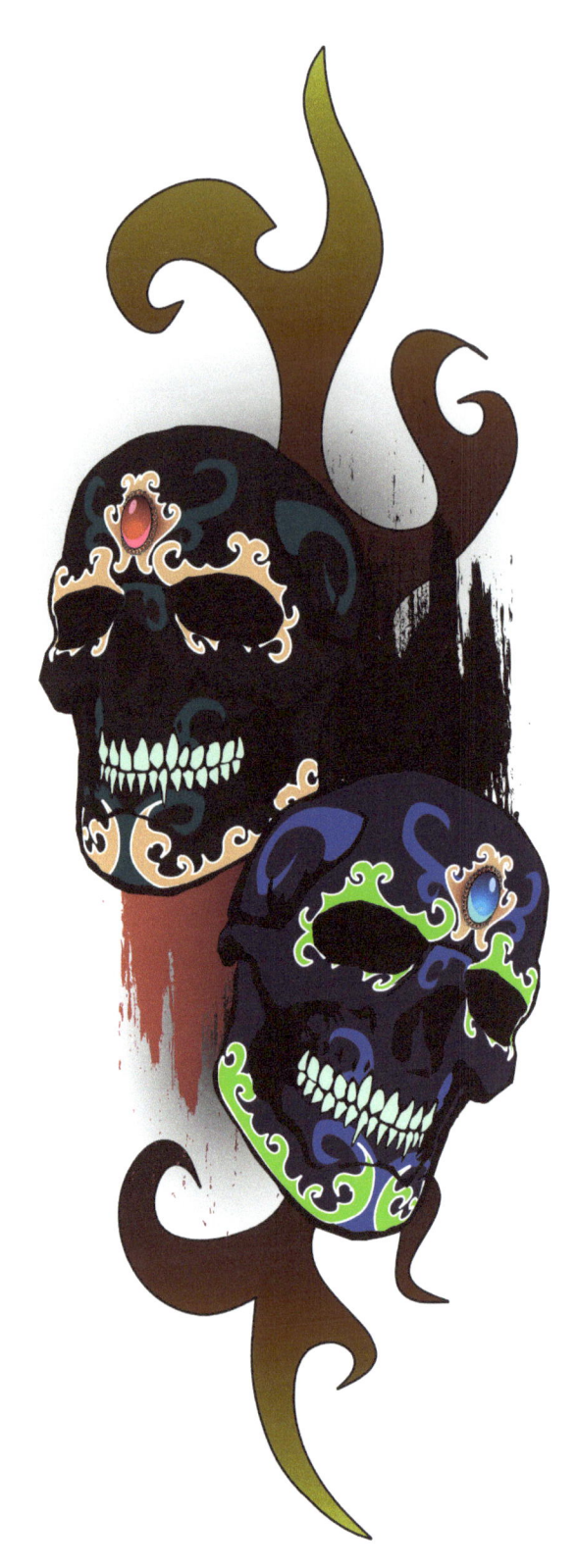

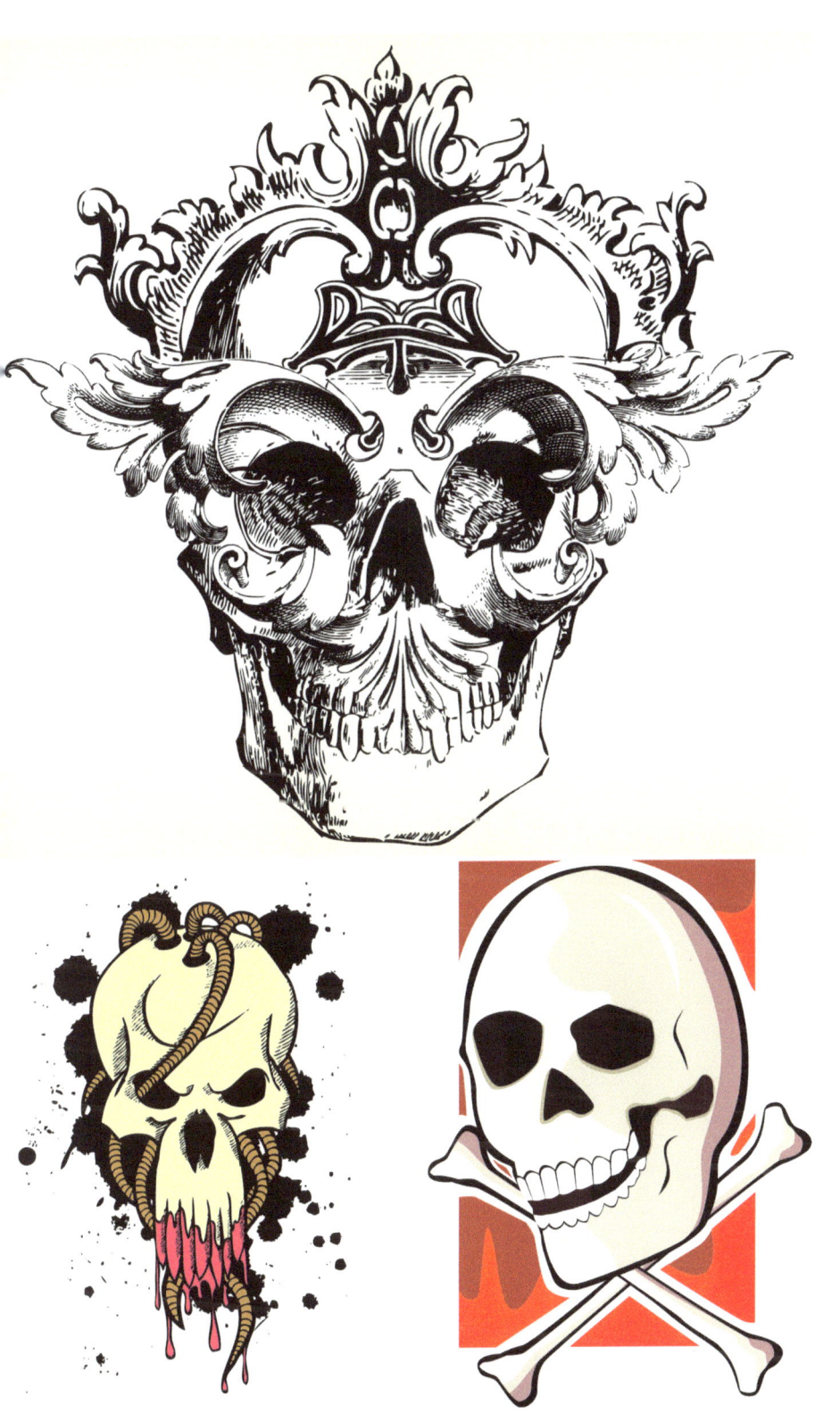

www.ingramcontent.com/pod-product-compliance
Lightning Source LLC
Chambersburg PA
CBHW040220220526
45473CB00001B/61

LETTER FROM THE EDITORS

    Climate change is real. Let's start off by thinking about that for a second. We, the human race, altered our planet to the point where, if we do nothing, we can easily kill ourselves and everything else on our planet. Easily because all it would take is for us to refuse to change any of our habits. If we do nothing, we will be the culprits for all the lives that can be lost in the future and all the beauty that will be erased because we like to drink bottled water. Lucky for us, all it takes to stop the carnage is to change the way we have decided to live and use this earth and to demand that our governments and major corporations we financially support do the same. It's a long journey, but one well worth taking, for the sake of the future and for the sake of natural beauty.
    We as creatives are inspired by the world around us. The natural wonders of this earth have been painted, written about, photographed, illustrated and so much more by immense amounts of people, all for the sake of revelling in what we find in front of us. We have been given a great gift, this planet. As creatives, what greater duty do we have than to create visual representations of this gift that others can appreciate and be inspired by. How many of you have been moved to search the night sky for visions of Van Gogh's swirls or gazed just a second longer at water lilies because of Monet? If it weren't for Ansel Adams, how much longer would it have taken for people to have fallen in love with Yosemite? It's our responsibility to drive the world froward towards greener pastures and greener times with what we can create. We can change the course of this planet, simply by making people care about the world around them. Think on this when you read the pages in this zine and think on this when you create. Save the world, one inspiration at a time.

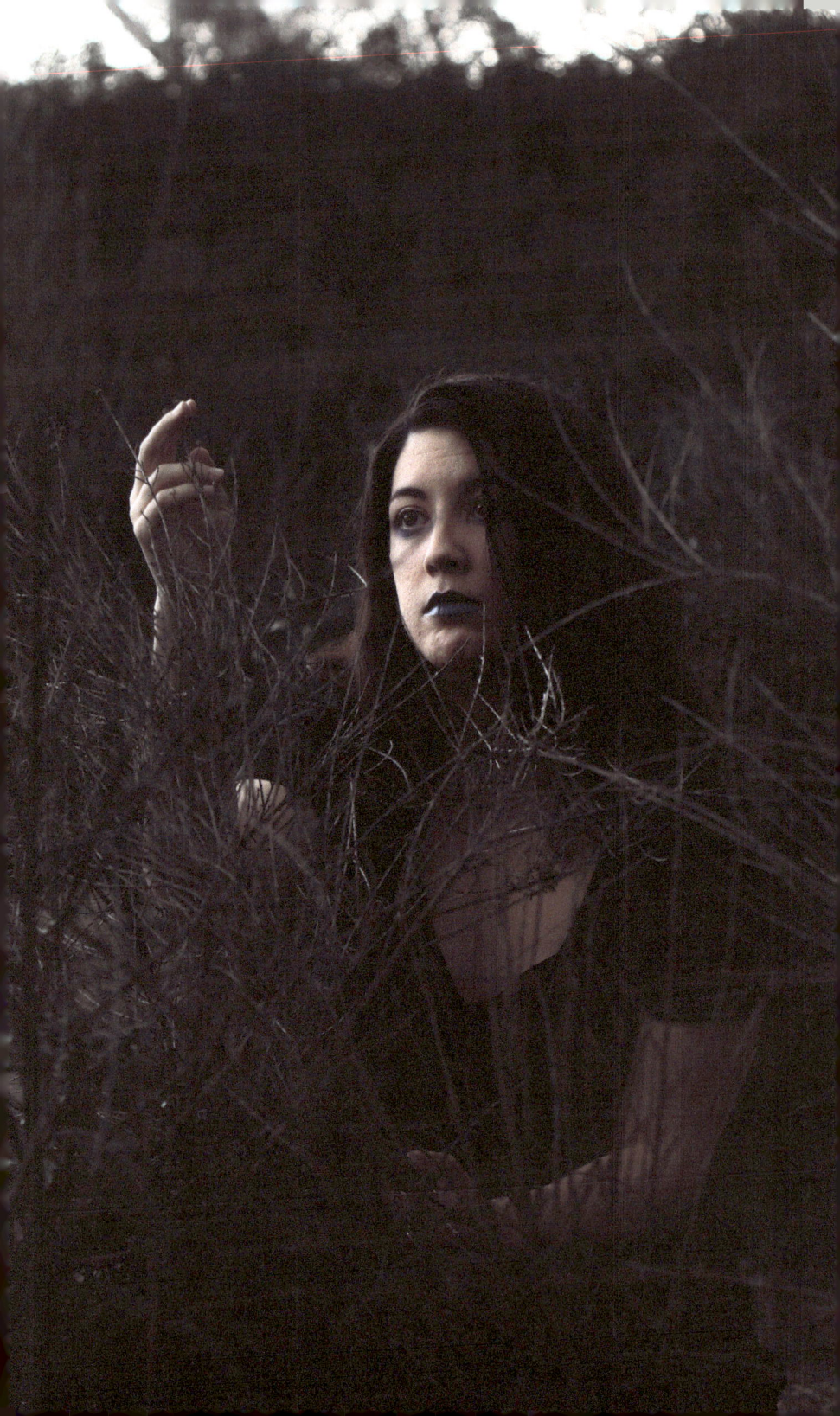